Coding Interviews
Questions, Analysis & Solutions

Harry He

Apress®

Coding Interviews: Questions, Analysis & Solutions

ISBN-13 (pbk): 978-1-4302-4761-6

ISBN-13 (electronic): 978-1-4302-4762-3

President and Publisher: Paul Manning
Lead Editor: Saswata Mishra
Technical Reviewer: Jeffrey Pepper, Robert Hutchinson
Editorial Board: Steve Anglin, Mark Beckner, Ewan Buckingham, Gary Cornell, Louise Corrigan, Morgan Ertel, Jonathan Gennick, Jonathan Hassell, Robert Hutchinson, Michelle Lowman, James Markham, Matthew Moodie, Jeff Olson, Jeffrey Pepper, Douglas Pundick, Ben Renow-Clarke, Dominic Shakeshaft, Gwenan Spearing, Matt Wade, Tom Welsh
Coordinating Editor: Jill Balzano
Copy Editor: Ann Dickson
Compositor: Apress
Indexer: SPi Global
Artist: SPi Global
Cover Designer: Anna Ishchenko

Distributed to the book trade worldwide by Springer Science+Business Media New York, 233 Spring Street, 6th Floor, New York, NY 10013. Phone 1-800-SPRINGER, fax (201) 348-4505, e-mail orders-ny@springer-sbm.com, or visit www.springeronline.com. Apress Media, LLC is a California LLC and the sole member (owner) is Springer Science + Business Media Finance Inc (SSBM Finance Inc). SSBM Finance Inc is a Delaware corporation.

For information on translations, please e-mail rights@apress.com, or visit www.apress.com.

Apress and friends of ED books may be purchased in bulk for academic, corporate, or promotional use. eBook versions and licenses are also available for most titles. For more information, reference our Special Bulk Sales–eBook Licensing web page at www.apress.com/bulk-sales.

Any source code or other supplementary materials referenced by the author in this text is available to readers at www.apress.com. For detailed information about how to locate your book's source code, go to www.apress.com/source-code/.

To my wife, Rachel, and our little boy, Lewis.

Contents at a Glance

Contents vii
About the Author xiii
Acknowledgments xv
Introduction xvii

CHAPTER 1: Interview Process 1

CHAPTER 2: Programming Languages 13

CHAPTER 3: Data Structures 33

CHAPTER 4: Algorithms 75

CHAPTER 5: High Quality Code 111

CHAPTER 6: Approaches to Solutions 143

CHAPTER 7: Optimization... 187

CHAPTER 8: Skills for Interviews...................................... 219

CHAPTER 9: Interview Cases 263

Index.. 275

Table of Contents

Contents at a Glance v
About the Author xiii
Acknowledgments xv
Introduction xvii

▨ CHAPTER 1: Interview Process 1
Types of Interviews 1
Phone Interviews.. 1
On-Site Interviews 3

Phases of Interviews 3
Behavior Interview 4
Technical Interview 7
Q/A Time 11

Summary 12

▨ CHAPTER 2: Programming Languages 13
C 13
Palindrome Numbers 16

C++ 17
C++ Concepts 18
Analyzing Execution of C++ Code.. 18
Implementing a Class or Member Function in C++ 19
Assignment Operator 19

C# 22
Singleton 23

Java 27
Java Keywords.. 27

Data Containers 29
Thread Scheduler 30

Summary... **32**

■ **CHAPTER 3: Data Structures**... **33**
Arrays **33**
Duplication in an Array..34
Search in a 2-D Matrix..37

String **42**
Strings in C/C++ 42
Strings in C# 43
Strings in Java 44
Replace Blanks in a String..45
String Matching 49

Linked Lists **53**
Print Lists from Tail to Head 54
Sort Lists...56
Loop in List..59

Trees **63**
Next Nodes in Binary Trees...64
Binary Search Tree Verification 66

Stack and Queue **70**
Build a Queue with Two Stacks 70
Build a Stack with Two Queues 72

Summary... **74**

■ **CHAPTER 4: Algorithms** **75**
Recursion and Iteration.. **75**
Fibonacci Sequence 76

Search and Sort **81**
Binary Search in Partially Sorted Arrays...84
Majorities in Arrays 87

Backtracking 90
String Path in Matrix 91
Robot Move 93

Dynamic Programming and Greedy Algorithms 94
Edit Distance 95
Minimal Number of Coins for Change 98
Minimal Times of Presses on Keyboards 99

Bit Operations 101
Number of 1s in Binary 102
Numbers Occurring Only Once 105

Summary 109

CHAPTER 5: High Quality Code 111
Clearness 111
Completeness 112
Test Cases for Completeness 112
Strategies to Handle Errors 113
Power of Integers 114
Big Numbers as Strings 117
Delete Nodes from a List 123
Partition Numbers in Arrays 127

Robustness 132
k^{th} Node from End 132
Reverse a List 135
Substructures in Trees 138

Summary 141

CHAPTER 6: Approaches to Solutions 143
Figures to Visualize Problems 143
Mirror of Binary Trees 143
Print Matrix in Spiral Order 146
Clone Complex Lists 149

Examples to Simplify Problems **152**
  Stack with Min Function 152
  Push and Pop Sequence of Stacks 157
  Print Binary Trees Level by Level 159
  Paths in Binary Trees 165

Divide and Conquer **168**
  Traversal Sequences and Binary Trees 168
  Binary Search Trees and Double-Linked Lists 174
  Permutation and Combination 179

Summary **185**

CHAPTER 7: Optimization **187**

Time Efficiency **187**
  Median in a Stream 188
  Minimum k Numbers 191
  Intersection of Sorted Arrays 194
  Greatest Sum of Sub-Arrays 196
  Digit 1 Appears in Sequence from 1 to n 198
  Concatenate an Array to Get a Minimum Number 201

Space-Time Trade-Off **203**
  Ugly Numbers 204
  Hash Tables for Characters 207
  Reversed Pairs in Array 213
  First Intersection Node in Two Lists 216

Summary **218**

CHAPTER 8: Skills for Interviews **219**

Communication and Learning Skills **219**
  Communications Skills 219
  Learning Skills 220

Knowledge Migration Skill **220**
   Time of Occurrences in a Sorted Array 221
   Application of Binary Tree Traversals 223
   Sum in Sequences 227
   Reversing Words and Rotating Strings 233
   Maximum in a Queue 236

Mathematical Modeling Skill **241**
   Probabilities of Dice Points 241
   Last Number in a Circle 243
   Minimum Number of Moves to Sort Cards 246
   Most Profit from Stock 249

Divergent Thinking Skills **251**
   Calculating $1+2+...+n$ 252
   Implementation of +, -, *, and / 255
   Final/Sealed Classes in C++ 259
   Array Construction 261

Summary **262**

CHAPTER 9: Interview Cases **263**
Integer Value from a String **263**
   The Interviewer's Comments 267

Lowest Common Parent Node in a Tree **269**
   The Interviewer's Comments 273

Index **275**

About the Author

■ **Harry He** has been a senior software engineer at Cisco since September 2010. His primary work involves development of Cesium, which is a platform for Cisco to monitor and control hardware quality of its partners (OEM/ODM). Prior to joining Cisco, Harry was associated with Autodesk and Microsoft for development of Civil 3D and Winforms respectively. Over the years, he has interviewed many candidates for different corporations where he developed his interest in coding interview questions. He has written dozens of blogs on this topic.

Harry's published works include a book on programming interview questions in Chinese, which was released in December 2011 with PHEI, China. He has exhaustive knowledge, experience, and understanding of code-related questions and interviews.

Acknowledgments

The prototype of this book is my blogs about coding interview problems. Thanks to the readers of the blogs, whose encouragement helped me make the decision to write this book.

Many friends and colleagues helped to review the first draft: Wesley Miao from Autodesk, Min Yang from Amazon, Aldrin Lee from Cisco, Jiakai Liu and Huai Wang from Facebook, Xiang Fan, Chao Tian, Pung Xu, and Bi Xue from Microsoft. They found many errors and made improvements that were invaluable additions to this text.

Thanks to the folks at Apress, who include (but are not limited to): Saswata Mishra, Jeffrey Pepper, Ann Dickson, and Jill Balzano. Their comments and revisions made this book much better.

Great thanks to my family members. My parents helped take care of the whole family. My father began to learn to cook in his 60s, and now he provides truly delicious meals. Moreover, I began to work on this book shortly after my little boy Lewis's birth. His smile and baby babble gave me great pleasure while going through the hard experience of writing a book. And, most of all, to Rachel, my wife and the love of my life. The day I finally found her was the best day in my memory and I am sure will always be so in the future.

Harry He
Shanghai, China
November 2012

Introduction

I used to be one of those who searched through the Internet to prepare for interviews of well-known companies. The information was scattered over lots of web sites, and it was not an easy task to collect coding interview problems and solutions systematically. In order to facilitate my own interview preparation, as well as others', I began to write blogs about programming problems and their solutions.

After I wrote dozens of blogs, I found that there were common strategies to solve various coding interview problems. Therefore, I gradually realized that it might be a good idea to summarize the strategies in a book. With one-year of writing and revising, as well many friends' encouragement and help, now this book is in your hands or perhaps on your screen.

Distinguishing Features

This book analyzes coding problems from interviewers' perspectives. There are many tips about the expected behaviors in this book, which are based on my own experiences as an interviewer at Autodesk, Microsoft, and Cisco. Moreover, many interview questions have different solutions. This book evaluates various solutions from an interviewer's point of view. When you read the problem analyses, you will get the idea as to why some solutions are better than others, and you will grasp the capabilities required to the assure the quality of your code through completeness, robustness, and efficiency.

This book not only solves more than 100 interview problems, but also summarizes common strategies to conquer complex problems. When I analyzed and solved dozens of coding interview problems, I found that there are many general strategies that are quite helpful to solve other similar problems during interviews. For example, if an interview problem is quite complex, we may divide it into several small subproblems, and then solve the subproblems recursively. We can also utilize hash tables implemented with arrays to solve many interview problems about strings. Similar problems are grouped in sections in this book. Pay attention to the similarities among problems in a section and the general ideas to solve them. When you meet new but similar problems at your interviews, you may reapply the strategies illustrated in this book.

Sample questions in this book are real interview problems frequently met in the famous IT companies. The coding interview is the most important phase of the whole interview process in many companies, such as Facebook, Google, and Microsoft. The sample questions collected in this book are the most typical ones adopted by interviewers in these companies. Don't be discouraged when you find that the problems in this book are not easy because interviews in big companies are not easy for most software engineers at first. You will find that there are relatively few problems that truly test the capabilities of programmers in meaningful ways. So, while you may not get a problem directly from this book, you should attain the skills required to handle whatever an interviewer can dish out. When you gradually master the strategies to solve problems summarized in this book, your capabilities to develop code and solve complex problems will be improved, and you will feel confident when interviewed by the Facebooks and Googles of the world.

Source code to solve sample interview problems along with a complete set of test cases to each problem is included. After candidates finish writing code, many interviewers will ask them to design some test cases to test their own code. Some candidates, especially fresh graduates, do not have clear ideas about how to design test cases. When you finish reading this book, you should know how to improve code quality with functional test cases, boundary test cases, performance test cases, and so on.

Summary of Chapters

The first chapter focuses on the interview process. A typical interview process can be divided into two phases: phone interviews (including phone-screen interviews) and on-site interviews. Usually there are three steps in each round of interview, which are the behavioral interview, technical interview, and general Q/A. Tips are provided for each stage of interviews.

The next three chapters cover basic programming knowledge. Technical interview questions on four popular programming languages (C, C++, C#, and Java) are discussed in Chapter 2. The most common data structures (including arrays, strings, lists, trees, stacks, and queues) and algorithms (including search, sort, backtracking, dynamic programming, greedy algorithms, and bit operations) are discussed in Chapter 3 and Chapter 4 respectively.

Chapter 5 discusses three factors of high quality code. Interviewers usually expect candidates' code to fulfill the functional requirements as well as cover corner cases and handle invalid inputs gracefully. After reading this chapter, you should get the idea so that you will write clear, complete, and robust code.

Three strategies to solve difficult coding interview problems are provided in Chapter 6. If hard problems are met during interviews, candidates should figure out solutions before they write code. After reading this chapter, you may get three strategies to solve problems: figures to visualize problems, step-by-step analysis on examples to simplify problems, and divide-and-conquer strategies to break complex problems into manageable pieces.

The topic of Chapter 7 is performance optimization. If there are multiple solutions to a problem, usually interviewers expect the most efficient one. The strategies to improve time efficiency and make trade-off decisions between time and space are discussed with several sample coding interview questions.

Chapter 8 summarizes various skills for interviews. Interviewers usually pay close attention to candidates' communication and learning skills. Additionally, many interviewers like to examine candidates' skills of reapplying knowledge, mathematical modeling, and divergent thinking.

Chapter 9 closes this book with two interview cases, which highlight good behavior expected by interviewers and the most common mistakes made by candidates.

Downloading the Code

The code for the examples shown in this book is available on the Apress web site, `www.apress.com`. A link can be found on the book's information page under the Source Code/Downloads tab. This tab is located underneath the Related Titles section of the page.

CHAPTER 1

■ ■ ■

Interview Process

Applying for a technical job is, in many ways, a unique experience. The interview process is unlike any other. Applicants who do not know what to expect are at a severe disadvantage. The purpose of this chapter is to acquaint you with the process so that, instead of being surprised, you will have an advantage over your competition. By understanding the process, you will be prepared for even the toughest interviews and have the opportunity to let your talents dictate your success.

Types of Interviews

It is often a long journey before a candidate receives an offer. Typically, a phone interview is the first step in the process. If it goes smoothly, a candidate may receive an invitation for one or more rounds of on-site interviews. A typical interview process is shown in Figure 1-1.

Figure 1-1. *The interview process*

Phone Interviews

During the phone-interview phase, interviewers examine candidates via phone calls. Many interviewers discuss time frames with candidates and schedule a specific time for the interview in advance, but others do not. In some areas of the world, such as India, it is even possible for a candidate to receive an unexpected phone call and be expected to perform an interview at that moment.

Whether the interview comes at an expected time or not, it is a good practice to find a comfortable and quiet place to take the call. The place should be free of distractions so that the candidate and interviewer can hear each other.

Compared to on-site interviews, during the phone interview the two sides on the phone can only communicate via voice. It is more difficult for candidates to describe their ideas without auxiliary tools, including body language and facial expressions, especially when describing complex data structures and algorithms. For example, it is quite easy for a candidate to describe a binary tree during an on-site interview because he or she can draw it on paper. However, interviewees on the phone can express a clear idea about a binary tree only after describing the binary tree itself in detail, including what the left child and right child of each node are. This kind of explanation can make for an awkward interview or perhaps make it bog down in unnecessary detail.

Sometimes voices are not very clear over phones. If candidates cannot hear interviewers' questions or requirements clearly, they should feel free to ask the interviewers to clarify. Providing answers irrelevant to the question should be avoided. Actually asking for more clarification is a good way for candidates to show their communication skills. In some cases, it can also buy time to think of a good response. During real software development, requirements are usually ambiguous at first, and engineers have to ask end users for clarification. Therefore, the skill of asking for clarification is an important component of the communication skills set an employer is likely to appreciate.

■ **Tip**   Candidates should communicate their thoughts in sufficient detail during phone interviews so that they are convinced interviewers understand their responses.

Phone-Screen Interviews

To facilitate phone interviews, many companies utilize online word-processing tools, such as Google Docs and Collabedit, which allow candidates to easily share and collaborate with interviewers in real time. Even though the two parties participating in the interview do not physically sit together, interviewers can examine how candidates write code on their desktop screens. An interview that occurs on the phone and uses these word-processing tools is often referred to as a phone-screen interview.

Interviewers pay a lot of attention to candidates' programming skills and habits. In most cases, they look for the following programming habits:

- *Thinking carefully before programming.* It is not usually a good idea for a candidate to begin coding hastily once he or she hears an interview question. Without reflecting on the process, a candidate will be prone to write buggy code. Remember that the interview situation puts more pressure on the candidates than they feel when they are doing their day-to-day work. Candidates usually are fearful, and sometimes panic, when their bugs are pointed out by interviewers. If they have answered in too much haste, their code might be modified to create an even bigger mess in such situations. A much better strategy for candidates is to implement code after they have clear ideas about their solutions, including data structures and algorithms to utilize, time and space efficiencies, cases requiring error handling, and so on. Generally, the interviewer will respect the thoughtfulness taken to arrive at the best result.

- *Readable naming convention and indentation.* Meaningful names of variables and functions as well as clear, logical indentation improve code readability dramatically, and they help interviewers to read and understand code. They also help if you have to debug your code as it will be read more simply.

More advanced collaboration tools are used in some interviews, such as Microsoft Lync and Cisco WebEx. Candidates share their desktops with remote interviewers to show their programming and debugging processes in an IDE, such as Visual Studio or Eclipse.

What interviewers usually require is an ability to develop a function in order to solve a certain problem. Candidates demonstrate their professional developing skills if they write unit test cases immediately after they finish implementing functions. It is a good practice for a candidate to ask his or her interviewer to review code only after all unit tests pass. It is more impressive if a candidate writes test cases before functional code since test-driven developers are somewhat rare.

It is quite common for candidates to meet difficult issues during a coding interview. Interviewers pay a lot of attention to candidates' behaviors when the candidates realize that their results are not as expected. Interviewers will believe candidates have abundant development experience if they can fix issues in a short time period by scrutinizing the code, setting break points, tracing each step, viewing memory, and analyzing call stacks. Debugging skills are accumulated by lots of practice rather than reading books, so interviewers look for them as a way of ferreting out professional developers.

On-Site Interviews

If a candidate performs well during a phone interview, it is quite possible for him or her to receive an invitation for an on-site interview.

A day or two before the on-site interview, a candidate should consider the following items:

- *Scheduling.* Candidates need to plan how they will get to the interview, estimate how much time is needed, and leave about half an hour or more for unexpected situations such as traffic jams.

- *Wearing comfortable clothes.* The dress code in most IT companies is quite casual, so usually it is not necessary for engineer candidates to be formally dressed. They can choose whatever is comfortable within reason.

- *Paying attention to the interview process.* On-site interviews often contain several rounds. For example, there are usually five rounds of on-site technical interviews for Microsoft. It is quite common to feel fatigued after long interviews. Candidates may wish to bring some vitalizing drinks or food.

- *Asking a few questions.* Interviewers generally leave a few minutes for candidates to ask some questions before a round of interview ends. Candidates would be wise to prepare some questions in advance.

On-site interviews are the most important part of the whole interview process because interviewers examine candidates' programming skills as well as their communication skills, learning skills, and so on. We will cover these skills in the following chapters.

Phases of Interviews

Each round of interview is usually split into three phases, as shown in Figure 1-2. The first phase is the behavioral interview, in which interviewers examine candidates' experience while referring to their résumés. The second phase is the technical interview when it is highly possible for a candidate to be asked to solve some coding interview problems. Finally, the candidate is given time to ask a few questions.

Figure 1-2. Three phases of a round of interview

Behavior Interview

The first five to ten minutes of a round of interview is used for becoming acquainted. Usually, this is time for the behavioral interview, and no difficult technical questions are asked. Interviewers look for someone who would be a good fit for the job in terms of technical skills as well as personality. A person who is too timid might not fit well into an environment where he or she needs to be vocal. Interviewers also look for enthusiasm and excitement. If candidates are not excited about the position, they may not be motivated to contribute, even if they are a strong technical fit.

Most interviews begin with candidates' introducing themselves. A candidate usually doesn't need to spend a lot of time introducing his or her main study and work experiences because interviewers have seen his or her résumé which contains detailed information. However, if an interviewer feels interested in a project the candidate has worked on, he or she may ask several questions on that subject in the introductory phase.

Project Experience

After a candidate has introduced him- or herself, interviewers may follow up with some questions on interesting projects listed on his or her résumé. It is recommended to use the STAR pattern to describe each project both on your résumé and during interviews (Figure 1-3).

- *Situation:* Concise information about the project background, including the size, features, and target customers of the project.

- *Task:* Concrete tasks should be listed when describing a big project. Please notice the difference between "taking part in a project" and "taking charge of a project." When candidates mentioned they have taken charge of a project, it is highly possible for them to be asked about the overall architectural design, core algorithms, and team collaboration. These questions would be very difficult to answer if the candidates only joined a team and wrote dozens of lines of code. Candidates should be honest during interviews. Reference checks will also query claims made on résumés.

- *Action:* Detailed information should be covered about how to finish tasks. If the task was architectural design, what were the requirements and how were they fulfilled? If the task was to implement a feature, what technologies were applied on which platforms? If it was to test, was it tested automatically or manually, with black boxes or white boxes?

- *Result:* Data, especially numbers, about your contribution should be listed explicitly. If the task is to implement features, how many features have been delivered in time? If the task is to maintain an existing system, how many bugs have been fixed?

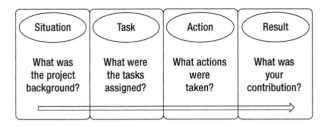

Figure 1-3. A STAR pattern describes project experiences on résumés and during interviews.

Let's look at an example of the STAR patter in use. I usually describe my experience working on the Microsoft Winforms team in the following terms:

Winforms is a mature UI platform in Microsoft .NET (*Situation*). I mainly focused on maintenance and on implementing a few new features (*Task*). For the new features, I implemented new UI styles on Winforms controls in C# in order to make them look consistent between Windows XP and Windows 7. I tried to debug most of the reproducible issues we had with Visual Studio and employed WinDbg to analyze dump files (*Action*). I fixed more than 200 bugs in those two years (*Result*).

Interviewers may follow up with a few questions if the information you supplied in these four categories has not been described clearly. Additionally, interviewers are also interested in the candidates' answers to the following questions:

- What was the most difficult issue in the project? How did you solve it?

- What did you learn from the project?

- When did you conflict with other team members (developers, testers, UI designers, or project managers)? How did you eliminate these conflicts?

It is strongly recommended that candidates prepare answers to each of the questions above when they write their résumés. The more time they spend preparing, the more confident they will be during interviews.

■ **Tip** When describing a project either on a résumé or during an interview, candidates should be concise regarding project background, but they should provide detailed information about their own tasks, actions, and contributions.

Technical Skills

Besides project experiences, technical skills are also a key element that interviewers pay close attention to on candidates' résumés. Candidates should be honest in describing the proficiency level of their skills. Only when candidates feel confident that they are capable of solving most of the problems in a certain domain, should they declare themselves experts. Interviewers have higher expectation of candidates who claim to be experts and ask them more difficult questions. It is very disappointing when you cannot meet these expectations.

For instance, I interviewed a candidate who declared himself an expert on C++, but he could not answer questions about the initialization order of parameters in constructor functions.

■ **Tip**   Candidates should be honest when they are describing their project experiences and technical skills.

"Why Do You Want to Change Your Current Job?"

If a candidate already has worked for a few years, it is highly likely for him or her to answer questions regarding his or her reasons for wanting to change jobs. Because everyone has his or her own reasons for wanting a new position, there are no standard answers. However, not all answers are appropriate for interviews.

Candidates should avoid complaining because complaining reveals passive emotions, and passive emotions are usually infectious in a team. When a candidate complains a lot, his or her interviewer worries that he or she might become the source of passive emotions and affect the morale of the team as a whole.

Complaints often arise from four categories. These complaints should be avoided during interviews:

- *My boss is rigorous with high standards and strict requirements.* If an interviewer is the manager of the hiring position and she hears such an answer, she might wonder if she would be the next rigorous boss after she hires the complaining candidate.

- *My teammates are not affable and friendly.* If a candidate believes all of his or her teammates are not easy to get along with, the candidate may be the one who is difficult to work with.

- *We work overtime too often.* All companies look for diligent workers, and it is not rare to work overtime in software and Internet companies. If the hiring position also requires overtime, this response may disqualify the candidate.

- *My salary is too low.* Having a low salary is indeed the real reason many candidates want to change jobs. However, it is not a suitable time to discuss salary requirements during the technical interviews. The only purpose for interviews is to get an offer. Candidates can discuss salary packages with the recruiters when they pass the technical interviews.

A recommended answer on job hopping is to use the job you are applying for as the model job: "My ideal job is to be working in the position you are hiring for because I am looking for a more challenging job. I do not have much passion for aspects of my current job, and I would like to take on a more fulfilling position." Some detailed reasons should be given as to why you feel unmotivated on your current job and why you are interested in the new position.

After I got on board, one of my interviewers at Microsoft told me that my answer was impressive. My previous job at Autodesk was to develop new features for Civil 3D, which is well-known software for civil engineering. I had to learn more civil engineering before I got promoted, but I was not interested in the domain knowledge such as earthwork calculation, corridor design, and so on. Therefore, I was looking for opportunities outside the company.

Technical Interview

After interviewers get candidates' background information through the behavioral interviews, they move on to the technical interview. Technical questions require about 40 to 50 minutes if the overall interview time is an hour. This is the most important phase of the whole interview process.

Interviewers are generally interested in skills in five categories:

- Basic programming knowledge, including understanding of programming languages, data structures, and algorithms

- Abilities to write clean, complete, and robust code

- Capabilities to analyze and solve complex problems

- Abilities to improve time and space efficiencies

- Skills involving communication, learning, divergent thinking, and so on.

Candidates should be well prepared before the interview and master knowledge of programming languages, common data structures, and algorithms. If the coding interview questions are simple, candidates should pay attention to details to write complete and robust code. If questions are difficult, they may try to simplify problems with figures and examples, and by dividing problems into manageable subproblems in order to get clear solutions before coding. Moreover, they should try their best to improve time and space performance. Candidates can ask interviewers to clarify their requirements in order to demonstrate communication skills. It is not difficult to get an offer if a candidate performs well on these factors.

Basic Programming Knowledge

Having abundant programming knowledge is the key to being an outstanding developer, so it is the first aptitude to be examined during the interview. It includes understanding of programming languages, data structures, and algorithms.

First, every programmer should be proficient in at least one or two programming languages. Interviewers examine the proficiency level of programming languages via coding and follow-up questions. Take C++ as an example. If there is a pointer parameter in a candidate's source code, he or she might be asked whether the parameter should be marked as const, and what the differences are if const is placed before or after an asterisk symbol (*).

Second, many interview questions focus on data structures. Lists, trees, stacks, and queues appear frequently in interviews, so candidates should be familiar with their operations. For example, candidates should write bug-free code quickly to insert and delete nodes of lists, as well as traverse binary trees iteratively and recursively with pre-order, in-order, and post-order algorithms.

Last but not least, algorithms are focal points in many interviews. Candidates should be familiar with the differences between various searching and sorting algorithms as well as scenarios suitable for each algorithm. There are many interview questions that are actually utilizations of binary search, merge sort, and quick sort algorithms. For example, interview questions "Minimum of Rotated Array" (Question 27) and "Times of Occurrences in Sorted Array" (Question 83) are about the binary search algorithm, and the problem "Reversed Pairs in an Array" (Question 81) is essentially about the merge sort algorithm. There are also many interview problems concerning dynamic programming and greedy algorithms.

Four of the most popular programming languages, C, C++, C#, and Java are covered in Chapter 2. The most common data structures are discussed in Chapter 3, and algorithms are discussed in Chapter 4.

Clean, Complete, and Robust Code

Many candidates are confused and ask themselves, "Why wasn't I hired even though the interview questions seemed simple to me?" There are many reasons why people fail, and the most common one is that there are some problems remaining in their solutions or written code. That is to say, they have to improve their code quality.

The first standard of code quality is readability. If candidates are asked to write code on paper or white boards, they must write neatly and cleanly. Additionally, readability is improved if code is written with reasonable variable names and logical indentation.

The second standard is completeness. Many interviewers examine quality through boundary checking and special inputs (such as NULL pointers and empty strings). There are lots of candidates who fail their interviews because their code only fulfills the basic functional requirement.

Let's take one of the most popular interview questions in Microsoft as an example: How would you convert a string into an integer? (See Listing 1-1.) This question seems very simple, and some candidates can finish writing code within three minutes.

Listing 1-1. *C Code to Convert a String to an Integer*

```c
int StrToInt(char* string) {
    int number = 0;
    while(*string != 0) {
        number = number * 10 + *string - '0';
        ++string;
    }

    return number;
}
```

Do you also think this problem is quite easy after reading the code above? If you think so, it is highly possible that you will be rejected by Microsoft.

The simpler the question is, the higher expectations an interviewer has. The problem above is simple, so interviewers expect candidates to solve it completely. Besides basic functional requests, boundary conditions and error handling should be considered. Converting a string into an integer is the basic functional request to be fulfilled. Additionally, candidates should pay attention to more cases, including the negative and positive symbols, the minimal and maximal integers, and overflow. The code is also expected to handle cases when the input string is not numeric, with non-digit characters. When we take all of these cases into consideration, it is not a simple problem anymore.

Besides incomplete solution and code, another intolerable mistake from an interviewer's perspective is that code is not robust enough. If we scrutinize the code above carefully, we notice that it crashes when the input string is a NULL pointer. It would be a disaster if such code were integrated into a real software system.

Not all issues related to robustness are so obvious. Let's take another popular problem as an example: how to get the kth node from the tail of a list. Many candidates read its solution with two pointers on the Internet. The first pointer moves k-1 steps, and then two pointers move together. When the first pointer reaches the tail node of the list, the second one reaches the kth node from the tail. They feel lucky and write the code in Listing 1-2 with much confidence.

Listing 1-2. C++ Code to Get the kth Node from Tail

```cpp
ListNode* FindKthToTail(ListNode* pListHead, unsigned int k) {
    if(pListHead == NULL)
        return NULL;

    ListNode *pAhead = pListHead;
    ListNode *pBehind = NULL;
    for(unsigned int i = 0; i < k - 1; ++ i) {
        pAhead = pAhead->m_pNext;
    }

    pBehind = pListHead;
    while(pAhead->m_pNext != NULL) {
        pAhead = pAhead->m_pNext;
        pBehind = pBehind->m_pNext;
    }

    return pBehind;
}
```

The candidate who writes the previous code feels more confident when he or she finds that the NULL pointer is handled and, consequently, believes he or she will definitely be hired. Unfortunately, a rejection letter might be received a few days later because there are still two serious issues left: (1) When the number of nodes in a list is less than *k*, it crashes; (2) When the input *k* is zero, it crashes.

The best approach to solving this kind of problems is to figure out some test cases before coding. Candidates may write complete code only if all possible inputs have been considered. It is not a good strategy to ask interviewers to check their code immediately after they finish writing the code. They should execute their code in their minds first and only hand the code to interviewers after they are sure it gets expected results for all test cases.

We will discuss strategies to improve code quality in more detail in Chapter 5.

■ **Tip**   Besides basic functional requirements, interviewers expect candidates to handle boundary conditions, special inputs (such as NULL pointers and empty strings), and errors.

Clear Thoughts about Solutions

Candidates cannot solve complex problems without clear thinking. Sometimes interviewers ask very difficult questions that they do not even expect candidates to solve in less than an hour. What interviewers are interested in are the candidates' thinking processes in such situations, rather than complete and correct answers. Usually, interviewers dislike candidates who write code in haste, with lots of bugs in it.

There are a few methods to help candidates to formulate clear ideas. First, candidates can employ some examples to help themselves to analyze problems. Simulating operations with one or two examples may uncover the hidden rules. Second, figures are helpful to visualize abstract data structures and algorithms. Many problems related to lists and binary trees might become easier if they are visualized with figures. Another approach is to divide a complicated problem into multiple manageable pieces and then solve them one at a time. Many recursive solutions, such as divide-and-conquer algorithms, as well as dynamic programming algorithms, are all essentially utilization of division.

For example, it is quite a complex problem to convert a binary search tree into a sorted doubly linked list. When confronted with such a problem during interviews, candidates may draw some figures about one or two sample binary search trees and their corresponding sorted doubly linked lists in order to visualize the relationship between them. They can also try to divide a binary tree into three parts: the root node, the left subtree, and the right subtree. After the left and right subtrees are converted to linked lists, they are connected with the root node to form a sorted linked list, and the problem is solved. More details about this problem are available in the section *Binary Search Trees and Double-Linked Lists*.

We will discuss how to solve difficult problems with figures, examples, and division in more detail in Chapter 6.

▨ **Tip**   Three tools are available to analyze and solve complicated problems: figures, examples, and division.

Time and Space Efficiency

Outstanding developers pay a lot of attention to time and space consumption and have the passion needed to continue improving performance of their own code. When there are multiple solutions for a problem, interviewers always expect the best one. If interviewers point out that there are better solutions, candidates should try their best to find approaches to improving time and space performance, demonstrating his or her enthusiasm to pursue excellence, which is an essential spirit to have as an outstanding developer.

The first thing candidates should understand is how to analyze time and space efficiencies. Various implementations of the same algorithm may result in dramatic performance distinctions, so it is important to analyze performance of an algorithm and its implementation. Take the calculation of the Fibonacci Sequence as an example. The classical solution is based on the recursive equation $f(n) = f(n-1) + f(n-2)$. It is not difficult to find out the time complexity increases exponentially since there are lots of duplicated calculations. However, the complexity will reduce to $O(n)$ if it is calculated iteratively. First of all, $f(1)$ and $f(2)$ are calculated, and then $f(3)$ is based on $f(1)$ and $f(2)$; $f(4)$ is get based on $f(2)$ and $f(3)$. The sequence continues until $f(n)$ is calculated in a loop. Please refer to the section *Fibonacci Sequence* for more details.

Candidates have to master pros and cons of each data structure and be able to choose the most suitable one to improve performance. For example, it seems that multiple types of data structures are available to get the median of a stream, including arrays, lists, balanced binary trees, and heaps. After analyzing the characteristics of each data type, we find that the best choice is to utilize two heaps—a maximal heap and a minimal heap (section *Median in Stream*).

Candidates should also be proficient in common algorithms. The most popular algorithms in interviews are about search and sort. It costs $O(n)$ time to scan an array sequentially. However, it is reduced to $O(\log n)$ with the binary search algorithm if an array is sorted. The problem "Maximal Number in a Unimodal Array" (Question 28) and "Times of Occurrences in a Sorted Array" (Question 83) are both solved based on the binary search algorithm. The quicksort algorithm is widely used for other problems besides sorting. The `Partition` function in quicksort can be used to get the kth maximal number out of n numbers and solve the problem "Majority in an Array" (Question 29) and "Minimal k Numbers" (Question 70).

More tips to improve time and space performance are illustrated in Chapter 7.

Soft Skills

Besides programming skills and technical capabilities, candidates should also show their soft skills, such as communication skills and learning abilities.

Since software systems have become more and more complex, it is more and more difficult for a single engineer to develop successful software. Teams, as well as communication among team members, are very important nowadays. Descriptions of project experience and algorithms with clear logical reasoning and conclusions are demonstrations of communication skills. Moreover, candidates reveal their consciousness about team cooperation through their tone and facial expressions. In general, interviewers dislike arrogant candidates who despise their teammates.

Developers should have strong learning spirits and capabilities because knowledge and technologies in the IT industry are replaced by more advanced ones at a frequent pace. Therefore, learning ability is also an important factor during interviews. There are two strategies for interviewers to examine learning ability. The first strategy is to ask candidates what books they have read recently and what new knowledge and skills they have learned. The other one is to raise some new concepts and observe how much time candidates need to understand them. For example, an interviewer asks to get the 1500th ugly number, which is a new concept for many candidates. A candidate with strong learning ability usually follows the process of asking questions to the interviewer, thinking to him- or herself based on the interviewer's clarification, asking questions again, and so on, until he or she finally finds the rules of ugly numbers and solves the problem.

The knowledge migration skill is a special capacity to learn new things. It is easier to learn new technologies and solve new problems if we can apply our own knowledge to new domains. Interviewers often ask a simple question at first and then follow up with a difficult one. In such situations, they expect candidates to get some hint from the solution of the simple question. For example, an interviewer asks how to calculate the Fibonacci Sequence and then asks a question about jumping frogs: There is a stair with n levels. A frog can jump up one level or two levels at each step on the stair. How many possible ways are available for this frog to jump from the bottom of the stair to the top? If candidates have strong skills to borrow ideas from experiences, they may find out that it is actually a utilization of the Fibonacci Sequence.

Some interview problems also require mathematical modeling skills. These kinds of questions are abstracted from our daily life. In order to solve them, candidates have to discover the hidden rules and choose appropriate data structures and algorithms. For instance, the problem "Minimal Number of Moves to Sort Cards" (Question 97) is closely related to the classical problem "Longest Increasing Sequence in an Array," which can be solved with dynamic programming algorithms.

Many interviewers are interested in a candidate's divergent thinking and innovation capabilities. They disallow candidates to use common solutions and expect candidates to explore creative approaches to analyzing and solving problems. For example, it needs divergent thinking skills to implement addition, subtraction, multiplication, and division without +, -, * and / operators.

Each of these soft skills is discussed in detail in Chapter 8 with several sample interview problems.

Q/A Time

Five to ten minutes before the end of an interview, a candidate is invited to ask a few questions. The quality of the candidate's questions also impacts the interview result because it reflects the candidate's communication skills. Usually, a person who is good at asking questions has strong communication skills.

Candidates should ask at least one or two questions to show their interest in the hiring company and position. Sometimes candidates become exhausted due to many hard interview problems, so it is difficult for them to think of some interesting questions right away. Therefore, it is suggested to prepare some questions in advance.

Not all questions are suitable to ask during technical interviews. One type of inappropriate questions is irrelevant to the hiring position. For example, the question about the company strategy in the following five years is appropriate only for a CTO candidate when the interviewer is a CEO. It is too far away from interests of a junior developer. Moreover, it is also very difficult for the interviewer to answer if he or she is an ordinary engineer.

It is not recommended that you ask about salary during technical interviews. It is not going to impress interviewers if they notice the most important issue in a candidate's mind is salary. Please leave this kind of question to recruiters afterward.

It is not suggested that you ask for the interview result immediately either: "Do you thing I am qualified enough?" A single interviewer cannot give an answer because the final result is the comprehensive consideration of all interviewers. In some companies, such as Google, all hiring decisions are made by a specific committee. Moreover, such a question is evidence that the candidate who asks it lacks self-evaluation abilities.

Recommended questions are about hiring positions and projects. It is not easy to ask this type of question, so candidates should be prepared in order to collect the related background information. There are two methods available: The first one is to collect information on the Internet. Candidates should be familiar with the history of the company, its business domain, position requirements, and so on. The other method is to pay attention to interviewers' words. Most interviewers describe the hiring position and project progress before asking questions. Candidates may come up with some questions accordingly.

When I was interviewed at Cisco, the manager of the hiring position was the last on-site interviewer. She told me that her team was tasked with the responsibility to develop a platform to test network equipment for Cisco. I asked several questions based on this information: Is it necessary for her team members to take part in network equipment tests? What knowledge is required about hardware tests as well as network equipment?

Summary

The interview process is the focus of this chapter. The interview process usually starts with a phone interview. Some companies use collaboration tools during phone calls to interview candidates remotely. If the phone interview goes smoothly, a candidate may receive an invitation e-mail for an on-site interview.

Each round of interview generally has three phases. The first phase is the behavioral interview, when interviewers inquire about candidates' project experience. It moves on to a technical interview, which is the most important phase. Programming capabilities and soft skills, including communication and learning skills, are examined. Candidates are allowed to ask a few questions in the Q/A phase before the end of an interview.

The section *Technical Interview* was an overview of the content of the whole book. It covers five key factors for interviews: basic programming skills, code quality, clear thinking through solutions, performance optimization, and soft skills. These factors are discussed in more detail in later chapters.

CHAPTER 2

■ ■ ■

Programming Languages

There are a number of popular programming languages these days. Different companies, even different departments within the same company, prefer to use different languages. Driver developers get used to writing code in C. Many programmers who work on Linux develop applications in C++, while other programmers working on Windows prefer C#. Many cross-platform systems are developed in Java. Objective C becomes more and more popular due to sales of iPads and iPhones. Additionally, scripting languages, such as Perl and Python, are very suitable to toolkit development.

Massive books have been written about each language. It is not a goal to cover all languages in detail in this book because of the space limitation, so Coding Interviews only discusses interview questions for the four most popular programming languages: C, C++, C#, and Java[1].

C

One of the reasons why the C programming language is so popular is the flexibility of its use for memory management. Programmers have opportunities to control how, when, and where to allocate and deallocate memory. Memory is allocated statically, automatically, or dynamically in the C programming language.

Static variables and global variables are static-duration variables, which are allocated along with the executable code of the program and persist during the execution of the application. When a local variable is declared as static inside a function, it is initialized only once. Whatever values the function puts into its static local variables during one call will be present when the function is called again. The following is a typical interview question about static local variables: What is the output when the function test executes? (See Listing 2-1.)

Listing 2-1. C Code with Static Variables

```c
int hasStatic(int n) {
    static int x = 0;
    x += n;
    return x;
```

---

[1] The TIOBE company publishes the monthly *TIOBE Programming Community Index*, which is an authoritative indicator of the popularity of programming languages. Please refer to the web site www.tiobe.com/index.php/content/paperinfo/tpci/index.html for the latest ranking.

```
}

void test() {
    int sum = 0;
    for(int i = 1; i <= 4; ++i)
        sum += hasStatic(i);

    printf("Result of sum is %d.\n", sum);
}
```

The variable x in the function hasStatic is declared as static. When the function is called the first time with a parameter 1, the static variable x is initialized as 0, and then set to 1. When the function is called the second time with a parameter 2, it is not initialized again and its value 1 persists. It becomes 3 after execution. Similarly, its value becomes 6 and 10 after execution with parameters 3 and 4. Therefore, the result is the sum 1+2+6+10=19.

Automatic-duration variables, also called local variables, are allocated on the stack. They are allocated and deallocated automatically when the program execution flow enters and leaves their scopes. In the sample code in Listing 2-2, there is a local array str in the function allocateMemory. What is the problem with it?

Listing 2-2. *C Code to Allocate Memory*

```
char* allocateMemory() {
    char str[20] = "Hello world.";
    return str;
}

void test() {
    char* pString = allocateMemory();
    printf("pString is %s.\n", pString);
}
```

Because the array str is a local variable, it is deallocated automatically when the execution flow leaves the function allocateMemory. Therefore, the returned memory to pString in the function test is actually invalid, and its content is somewhat random.

One limitation of static-duration and automatic-duration variables is that their size of allocation is required to be compile-time constant. This limitation can be avoided by dynamic memory allocation in which memory is more explicitly, as well as more flexibly, managed. In the C programming language, the library function malloc is used to allocate a block of memory dynamically on the heap, where size is specified at runtime. This block of memory is accessible via a pointer that malloc returns. When the memory is no longer needed, the pointer should be passed to another library function, free, which deallocates the memory in order to avoid memory leaks.

The function allocateMemory in Listing 2-3 utilizes the function malloc to allocate memory dynamically. What is the problem in it?

Listing 2-3. *C Code to Allocate Memory*

```c
void allocateMemory(char* pString, int length) {
    pString = (char*)malloc(length);
}

void test() {
    char* pString = NULL;
    allocateMemory(pString, 20);
    strcpy(pString, "Hello world.");
}
```

The parameter pString in the function allocateMemory is a pointer, and the string content it points to can be modified. However, the memory address it owns cannot be changed when the function allocateMemory returns. Since the input parameter pString of allocateMemory in the function test is NULL, it remains NULL after the execution of allocateMemory, and it causes the program to crash when the NULL address is accessed in test. In order to fix this problem, the first parameter of allocateMemory should be modified as char** pString.

Macros are commonly used in the C programming language and also commonly asked about in technical interviews. Since it is tricky and error-prone to use macros, unexpected results are gotten when they are misused. For example, what is the output when the function test in Listing 2-4 gets executed?

Listing 2-4. *C Code with Macros*

```c
#define SQUARE(x) (x*x)

void test() {
    printf("Square of (3+4) is %d.\n", SQUARE(3+4));
}
```

The result of 3+4 is 7, and the square of 7 is 49. However, 49 is not the result of SQUARE(3+4). Macros are substituted by the preprocessor, so SQUARE(3+4) becomes 3+4*3+4, which is actually 19. In order to make the result as expected, the macro should be modified to #define SQUARE(x) ((x)*(x)).

Even in the revised version of macro SQUARE, its result might look surprising if it is not analyzed carefully in some cases. For instance, what are the results of x and y after the code in Listing 2-5 is executed?

Listing 2-5. *C Code with Macros*

```c
#define SQUARE(x) ((x)*(x))

void test() {
    int x = 5;
    int y = SQUARE(x++);
    printf("Result of x is %d, y is %d.\n", x, y);
}
```

It looks like that the variable x increases only once in the code above. However, when the macro is substituted, the variable y is assigned as ((x++)*(x++)). The result of y is 25, and x becomes 7 because it increases twice.

Many coding interview questions can be solved in the C programming language. A question in the following subsection is an example, and more questions are discussed in later chapters.

Palindrome Numbers

■ **Question 1**   Please implement a function that checks whether a positive number is a palindrome or not. For example, 121 is a palindrome, but 123 is not.

Converting a Number into a String

It is easy to check whether a string is a palindrome or not: We can check whether the first character and the last one are identical, and then compare the second character and the second one from the end, and so on. If the converted string is a palindrome, the original should also be a palindrome.

This solution can be implemented with the code in Listing 2-6, which converts a number into a string with the library function sprintf.

Listing 2-6. C Code to Verfiy Palindrome Numbers (Version 1)

```c
/* It returns 1 when number is palindrome, otherwise returns 0. */
#define NUMBER_LENGTH 20
int IsPalindrome_solution1(unsigned int number) {
    char string[NUMBER_LENGTH];
    sprintf(string, "%d", number);

    return IsPalindrome(string);
}

int IsPalindrome(const char* const string) {
    int palindrome = 1;
    if(string != NULL) {
        int length = strlen(string);
        int half = length >> 1;

        int i;
        for(i = 0; i < half; ++ i) {
            if(string[i] != string[length - 1 - i]) {
                palindrome = 0;
                break;
            }
        }
    }
```

```
    }

    return palindrome;
}
```

Usually, this solution is not the one expected by interviewers. One reason is that while it is intuitive, interviewers expect something innovative, and another reason is that it requires auxiliary memory to store the converted string.

Composing a Reversed Number

As we know, it is easy to get digits from right to left via the / and % operators. For example, digits in the number 123 from right to left are 3, 2, and 1. A reversed number 321 is constructed with these three digits. Let's check whether the reversed number is identical to the original one. If it is, the original number is a palindrome.

The implementation is shown in Listing 2-7.

Listing 2-7. C Code to Verfiy Palindrome Numbers (Version 2)

```
/* It returns 1 when number is palindrome, otherwise returns 0. */
int IsPalindrome_solution2(unsigned int number) {
    int reversed = 0;
    int copy = number;

    while(number != 0) {
        reversed = reversed * 10 + number % 10;
        number /= 10;
    }

    return (reversed == copy) ? 1 : 0;
}
```

Source Code:

    001_PalindromeNumber.c

Test Cases:

- Palindrome numbers with odd length
- Palindrome numbers with even length
- Non-palindrome numbers

C++

C++ might be the most difficult programming language in many software engineers' judgment. Many interviewers believe a candidate who is proficient on C++ has the abilities needed to master other technical skills, so questions about C++ are quite popular during interviews.

Interview questions about the C++ programming language can be divided into three categories: C++ concepts, tricky C++ coding problems, and implementing a class or member function.

C++ Concepts

Questions in the first category are about C++ concepts, especially about C++ keywords. For example, what are the four keywords for type casting, and under what are scenarios would you use each of them?

The most popular questions in this category concern the keyword `sizeof`.

For instance, the following dialog is repeated again and again in many interviews:

Interviewer: There is an empty class, without any member fields and functions inside its definition. What is the result of `sizeof` for this class?

Candidate: It is 1.

Interviewer: Why not 0?

Candidate: The size seems to be 0 since the class is empty without any data. However, it should occupy some memory; otherwise, it cannot be accessed. The size of memory is decided by compilers. It occupies 1 byte in Visual Studio.

Interviewer: What is the result of `sizeof` if we add the constructor and destructor functions in the class?

Candidate: It is also 1. The addresses for functions are irrelevant to instances, and compilers do not add any data in instances of this class.

Interviewer: How about declaring the destructor function as a virtual function?

Candidate: When a C++ compiler sees a virtual function inside a class, it creates a virtual function table for the class and adds a pointer to the table in each instance. A pointer in a 32-bit machine occupies 4 bytes, so the result of `sizeof` is 4. The result on a 64-bit machine is 8 because a pointer occupies 8 bytes there.

Analyzing Execution of C++ Code

The second type of interview questions in C++ concerns analyzing execution results of some sample code. Candidates without deep understanding of C++ are prone to make mistakes because the code to be analyzed is usually quite tricky.

For example, an interviewer hands a piece of paper printed with the code in Listing 2-8 to a candidate and asks the candidate what the result is if we try to compile and execute the code: (A) Compiling error; (B) It compiles well, but crashes in execution; or (C) It compiles well, and executes smoothly with an output of 10.

Listing 2-8. *C++ Code about Copy Constructor*

```
class A {
private:
    int value;
```

```
public:
    A(int n) {
        value = n;
    }
    A(A other) {
        value = other.value;
    }
    void Print() {
        std::cout << value << std::endl;
    }
};

int main(int argc, _TCHAR* argv[]) {
    A a = 10;
    A b = a;
    b.Print();

    return 0;
}
```

The parameter in the copy constructor A(A other) is an instance of type A. When the copy constructor is executed, it calls the copy constructor itself because of the pass-by-value parameter. Since endless recursive calls cause call stack overflow, a pass-by-value parameter is not allowed in the C++ standard, and both Visual Studio and GCC report an error during compiling time. We have to modify the constructor as A(const A& other) to fix this problem. That is to say, the parameter in a copy constructor should be passed by a reference.

Implementing a Class or Member Function in C++

The third type of C++ interview questions is based on implementing a class or some member functions. Usually it is more difficult to write code than to read and analyze sample code. Many C++ coding interview questions focus on constructor or destructor functions as well as overloading operators. For instance, the following problem about an assignment operator is such an example.

Assignment Operator

■ **Question 2**   The declaration of class CMyString is found in Listing 2-9. Please add an assignment operator to it.

Listing 2-9. C++ Code for Declaration of CMyString

```
class CMyString {
```

```
public:
    CMyString(char* pData = NULL);
    CMyString(const CMyString& str);
    ~CMyString(void);

private:
    char* m_pData;
};
```

Classic, but Only Suitable for Newbie Developers

When an interviewer asks a candidate to overload the assignment operator, he or she asks the following questions to check the candidate's code:

- Does it return a reference? Before the assignment operator function ends, it should return the instance itself (*this) as a reference. If an assignment operator is overloaded as a void function, it has no chance to chain multiple assignments together. Suppose that there are three instances of the CMyString type: str1, str2, and str3. They cause a compiling error at str1=str2=str3 if the assignment operator is overloaded as a void function.

- Is the argument passed by a constant reference? If the argument is passed by value, a copy constructor is called, and it is a waste of time. The call of the copy constructor is avoided if the argument is passed by reference. Additionally, it should not modify the status of the input instance during assignment, so the reference should be declared as const.

- Is the existing memory freed? If the old memory for m_pData is not deallocated before it allocates new memory, memory leaks occur.

- Does it protect against self-assignment? It returns directly and does nothing if the assignment source (input instance) is identical to the assignment target (*this). Otherwise if *this is the same as the input instance, its memory will be freed and its content cannot be gotten back anymore.

Listing 2-10 is a piece of C++ code, covering all four items.

Listing 2-10. *C++ Code for Assignment Operator (Version 1)*

```
CMyString& CMyString::operator =(const CMyString &str) {
    if(this == &str)
        return *this;

    delete []m_pData;
    m_pData = NULL;

    m_pData = new char[strlen(str.m_pData) + 1];
    strcpy(m_pData, str.m_pData);

    return *this;
}
```

This is a classic solution in textbooks. A junior candidate can pass this round of interview with the code above. However, it is far from perfection. An interviewer will have more stringent requirements if the candidate is a senior C++ programmer.

Exception Safety

In the previous code, the old m_pData is deleted before it is renewed. If an exception is thrown while reallocating memory due to insufficient memory, m_pData is a NULL pointer and it is prone to crash the whole application. In other words, when an exception is thrown in the assignment operator function, the status of a CMyString instance is invalid. It breaks the requirement of exception safety: If an exception is thrown, everything in the program must remain in a valid state.

Two approaches are available to achieve the goal of exception safety. The first one is to allocate memory with the new operator before deleting. It makes sure the old memory is deleted only after it allocates memory successfully, and the status of CMyString instances is valid if it fails to allocate memory.

A better choice is to create a temporary instance to copy the input data and then to swap it with the target. The code in Listing 2-11 is based on the copy-and-swap solution.

Listing 2-11. C++ Code for Assignment Operator (Version 2)

```
CMyString& CMyString::operator =(const CMyString &str) {
    if(this != &str) {
        CMyString strTemp(str);

        char* pTemp = strTemp.m_pData;
        strTemp.m_pData = m_pData;
        m_pData = pTemp;
    }

    return *this;
}
```

In this code, a temporary instance strTemp is constructed first, copying data from the input str. Next, it swaps strTemp.m_pData with this->m_pData. Because strTemp is a local variable, its destructor will be called automatically when the execution flow exits this function. The memory pointed to by strTemp.m_pData is what was pointed to by this->m_pData before, so the memory of the old instance is deleted when the destructor of strTemp is invoked.

It allocates memory with the new operator in the constructor of CMyString. Supposing that a bad_alloc exception is thrown due to insufficient memory, the old instance has not been modified, and its status is still valid. Therefore, it is an exception-safe solution.

Source Code:

   002_AssignmentOperator.cpp

Test Cases:

- Assign an instance to another

- Assign an instance to itself

- Chain multiple assignments together

- Stress tests to check whether the code contains memory leaks

C#

The C# programming language is based on Microsoft .NET, the popular platform in the Windows ecosystem. Many companies focusing on Windows development include requirements on C# skills in their job descriptions.

C# can be viewed as a managed programming language based on C++, so there are many similarities between them. It does not take much time for a C++ programmer to learn C#. It is easy to learn the similarities, but it is difficult to distinguish differences. Many interviewers like to ask questions about the confusing differences. For example, the following is a piece of dialog from an interview:

Interviewer: Types in C++ can be defined as **struct** and **class**. What are the differences between these two types?

Candidate: The default access level in a **struct** is public, while in a **class** is private.

Interviewer: How about in C#?

Candidate: It is different in C#. The default access level for both **struct** and **class** is private in C#. However, their memory allocation models are different. A **struct** is a value type, and its instances are created on the stack. A type declared as a **class** is a reference type, and its instances are created on the heap.

Similar to C++, every type in C# has a constructor at least. Additionally, there might be two different methods (finalizer and **Dispose**) used to release resources in C#. The finalizer method looks similar to the destructor in C++, which is the type name followed by a complement symbol (~). However, the time to invoke them is different. The time to invoke a destructor in C++ is fixed, but the time to invoke the finalizer in C# is determined by the runtime. The finalizer is invoked by the garbage collector, and the time is unknown to programmers.

Additionally, there is a special constructor in C#, named static constructor. It is invoked automatically when its type is executed by the runtime at the first time, and it is invoked only once. There are many interesting interview questions about the static constructor. For example: What is the output of the C# code in Listing 2-12?

Listing 2-12. *C# Code about Static Constructors*

```
class A {
    public A(string text) {
        Console.WriteLine(text);
    }
}

class B{
    static A a1 = new A("a1");
    A a2 = new A("a2");
```

```
    static B() {
        a1 = new A("a3");
    }

    public B() {
        a2 = new A("a4");
    }
}

class Program {
    static void Main(string[] args) {
        B b = new B();
    }
}
```

Before any code of the type **B** gets executed, its static constructor will be invoked first. It initializes static data fields and then executes statements inside the static constructor. Therefore, it prints a line of "a1", and then another line of "a3".

When the execution flow reaches the statement **B b = new B()**, the ordinary constructor is invoked. It initializes its data fields first and then the statements in its constructor method, so it prints a line of "a2", and then another line of "a4".

Singleton

▪ **Question 3**   Please design and implement a class of which we can only create a single instance.

A class follows the singleton pattern if it can have one instance at most. Design patterns are very important in object-oriented design and development, so many interviewers like questions related to patterns. Singleton is the only pattern that can be implemented in dozens of lines of code, so it is quite suitable for interviews.

Workable Only in Single-Threading Applications

When the constructor is defined as a private method, none of the code outside the class can create its instances. A static method inside the class is defined to create an instance on demand. The class Singleton1 is implemented based on the solution in Listing 2-13.

Listing 2-13. C# Code for Singleton (Version 1)

```
public class Singleton1 {
    private Singleton1() {
    }
```

```
    private static Singleton1 instance = null;
    public static Singleton1 Instance {
        get {
            if (instance == null)
                instance = new Singleton1();
            return instance;
        }
    }
}
```

In this class, an instance is created only when static field `Singleton1.instance` is null, so it does not have the opportunity to get multiple instances.

Works with Multiple Threads but Is Inefficient

`Singleton1` works when there is only one thread, but it has problems when there are multiple threads in an application. Supposing that there are two threads concurrently reaching the `if` statement to check whether `instance` is null. If `instance` is not created yet, each thread will create one separately. It violates the definition of the singleton pattern when two instances are created. In order to make it work in multithreading applications, a lock is introduced as shown in the `Singleton2` in Listing 2-14.

Listing 2-14. C# Code for Singleton (Version 2)

```
public class Singleton2 {
    private Singleton2() {
    }

    private static readonly object syncObj = new object();

    private static Singleton2 instance = null;
    public static Singleton2 Instance {
        get {
            lock (syncObj) {
                if (instance == null)
                    instance = new Singleton2();
            }

            return instance;
        }
    }
}
```

Suppose there are two threads that are both going to create their own instances. As we know, only one thread can get the lock at a time. When one thread gets it, the other one has to wait. The first thread that gets the lock finds that `instance` is null, so it creates an instance. After the first thread releases the lock, the second thread gets it. Since the `instance` was already created by the first thread, the `if` statement is `false`.

An instance will not be recreated again. Therefore, it guarantees that there is one instance at most when there are multiple threads executing concurrently.

The class `Singleton2` is far from perfect. Every time `Singleton2.Instance.get` executes, it has to get and release a lock. Operations to get and release a lock are time-consuming, so they should be avoided as much as possible.

Double-Check around Locking

Actually a lock is needed only before the only instance is created in order to make sure that only one thread get the chance to create an instance. After the instance is created, no lock is necessary. We can improve performance with an additional `if` check before the lock as shown in Listing 2-15.

Listing 2-15. C# Code for Singleton (Version 3)

```
public class Singleton3 {
    private Singleton3() {
    }

    private static object syncObj = new object();

    private static Singleton3 instance = null;
    public static Singleton3 Instance {
        get {
            if (instance == null) {
                lock (syncObj) {
                    if (instance == null)
                        instance = new Singleton3();
                }
            }

            return instance;
        }
    }
}
```

In the class `Singleton3`, it locks only when `instance` is `null`. When the instance has been created, it is returned directly without any locking operations. Therefore, the time efficiency of `Singleton3` is better than `Singleton2`.

`Singleton3` employs two `if` statements to improve time efficiency. It is a workable solution, but its logic looks a bit complex, and it is error-prone for many candidates during interviews. Let us explore simpler, and also better, solutions.

Utilization of Static Constructors

It is guaranteed that a static constructor in a C# class is called only once at most. If it only creates an instance in the static constructor, there is one instance at most. A concise solution for the singleton pattern with a static constructor is shown in Listing 2-16.

Listing 2-16. *C# Code for Singleton (Version 4)*

```
public class Singleton4 {
    private Singleton4() {
    }

    private static Singleton4 instance = new Singleton4();
    public static Singleton4 Instance {
        get {
            return instance;
        }
    }
}
```

In the class Singleton4 above, an instance is created when the static field instance gets initialized. Static fields in C# are initialized when the static constructor is called. Since the static constructor is called only once by the .NET runtime, it is guaranteed that only one instance is created even in a multithreading application.

The time to execute the static constructor is out of the programmers' control. When the .NET runtime reaches any code of a class the first time, it invokes the static constructor automatically. Therefore, the time to initialize instance is not the first time to invoke Singleton4.Instance. If a static method is added into Singleton4, it is not necessary to create an instance to invoke such a static method. However, the .NET runtime invokes the static constructors automatically to create an instance when it reaches any code for Singleton4. Therefore, it is possible to create an instance too early, and it impairs the space efficiency.

Creating an Instance When Necessary

In the last implementation of the singleton pattern in Listing 2-17, Singleton5, it creates the only instance on demand.

Listing 2-17. *C# Code for Singleton (Version 5)*

```
public class Singleton5 {
    Singleton5() {
    }

    public static Singleton5 Instance {
        get {
            return Nested.instance;
        }
```

```
    }

    class Nested {
        static Nested() {
        }

        internal static readonly Singleton5 instance = new Singleton5();
    }
}
```

There is a nested private class `Nested` in the code for `Singleton5`. When the .NET runtime reaches the code of the class `Nested`, its static constructor is invoked automatically, which creates an instance of type `Singleton5`. The class `Nested` is used only in the property `Singleton5.Instance`. Since the nested class is defined as private, it is inaccessible outside of the class `Singleton5`.

When the `get` method of `Singleton5.Instance` is invoked the first time, it triggers execution of the static constructor of the class `Nested` to create an instance of `Singleton5`. The instance is created only when it is necessary, so it avoids the waste associated with creating the instance too early.

Solution Comparison

Five solutions are introduced in this section. The first solution is workable only in a single-threading application. The second one works in a multiple-threading application, but it is inefficient because of unnecessary locking operations. The first two solutions are not acceptable from an interviewer's perspective. In the third solution, it employs two `if` statements and one lock to make sure it works in a multiple-threading application efficiently. The fourth one utilizes the static constructor to guarantee only an instance is created. The last solution improves space efficiency with a nested class to create the instance only when it is necessary. The last two solutions are recommended for interviews.

Source Code:

003_Singleton.cs

Java

The Java programming language is a common choice for developing cross-platform applications and systems. Additionally, it has attracted more attention because of the popularity of Android mobile phones in recent years. Therefore, many companies have requirements on their candidates' Java proficiency level.

Java Keywords

Similar to C++ and C#, there are many interview questions on Java keywords or concepts. One of the most frequently met questions is: What are the uses of `finalize`, `finally`, and `final` in Java? The `finalize` method is related to the garbage collector in Java. Java is a managed programming language, and its runtime periodically reclaims memory occupied by objects that are not referenced by others. If an object is holding some resources besides memory, such as files and network connections, we might want to make sure these resources are released before the object is destroyed. Java provides a mechanism called finalization to handle such situations. We define specific actions in the method of `finalize` that will occur when an object is about to be reclaimed by the garbage collector.

The keyword `finally` is related to the exception handling mechanism. The `finally` block always executes when the corresponding `try` block exists. This ensures that the `finally` block is executed even if an unexpected exception occurs. Usually, the `finally` block contains code to clean up resources.

The keyword `final` in the Java programming language is used in several different contexts to define an entity that cannot be modified later:

- No classes can derive from `final` classes.

- A `final` method cannot be overridden by subclasses.

- A `final` variable can only be initialized once, either via an assignment statement at the point of declaration or a constructor. Some `final` variables, named blank `final` variables, are not initialized at the point of declaration. A blank `final` variable of a class must be definitely assigned in every constructor of the class in which it is declared. Additionally, `final` arguments, which are declared in argument lists of methods, are similar to `final` variables.

The use for `final` variables gets more complex when they are references. If a `final` variable is a reference, it cannot be rebound to reference another object. However, the object it references is still mutable.

The piece of code in Listing 2-18 uses `final` variables. Which methods will cause compile-time errors?

Listing 2-18. *Java Code to Modify Final Fields*

```java
public class WithFinal {
    public final int number = 0;
    public final int[] array;

    public WithFinal() {
        array = new int[10];
        for(int i = 0; i < array.length; ++i)
            array[i] = i;
    }

    public void ModifyFinal1() {
        ++number;
    }

    public void ModifyFinal2() {
        for(int i = 0; i < array.length; ++i)
            array[i] += i;
    }

    public void ModifyFinal3() {
        array = new int[10];
```

```
        for(int i = 0; i < array.length; ++i)
            array[i] = i;
    }
}
```

In the class WithFinal, there are two data fields. The field number is a primitive while the field array is a reference and it is also a blank final variable.

Blank final variables can be initialized in constructors, so the constructor method in the class WithFinal has no problems. It tries to modify the constant primitive number inside the method ModifyFinal1, which is not allowed by the Java compiler. The method ModifyFinal2 modifies the object referenced by array, but it does not modify the reference itself. It is allowed to do so. Inside the method ModifyFinal3, a new array is created and it is rebound to the constant reference array, so it raises compiling errors.

Data Containers

The Java programming language provides many useful data containers. Data containers can be divided into two categories: one is collection, such as LinkedList and Stack; and the other is map, such as the type HashMap. Both are commonly used in practical development and also frequently met in interviews. For example, the following is an interview question about HashMap: What is the output of the piece of code in Listing 2-19?

Listing 2-19. Java Code with HashMap

```java
public class MyString {
    public MyString(String data) {
        this.data = data;
    }

    private String data;
}

public static void main(String args[]) {
    Map<String, Integer> map1 = new HashMap<String, Integer>();
    String str1 = new String("Hello World.");
    String str2 = new String("Hello World.");
    map1.put(str1, new Integer(10));
    map1.put(str2, new Integer(20));

    Map<MyString, Integer> map2 = new HashMap<MyString, Integer>();
    MyString str3 = new MyString(str1);
    MyString str4 = new MyString(str2);
    map2.put(str3, new Integer(10));
    map2.put(str4, new Integer(20));

    System.out.println(map1.get(str1));
    System.out.println(map2.get(str3));
}
```

Java checks the existence of a key in a HashMap via its hash code, which is returned by the method hashCode. The method hashCode is defined in the class Object, and it can be overridden by subclasses. When two keys have the same hash code, it calls the method equals to check their equality. Similar to hashCode, equals is also defined in the class Object and can be overridden by subclasses.

The type of key in the map1 is String, which overrides the method hashCode and equals. The method String.hashCode returns the same hash code when two instances have the same string content. Because the contents in str1 and str2 are the same, they share the same hash code. When it tries to put the record with key str2 to map1, a key str1 exists already with the same hash code. The method equals also shows that these two keys are equal to each other because their contents are the same. Therefore, it just updates the corresponding value of the key str1 to 20, instead of inserting a new record.

The type of key in map2 is MyString, which does not override the methods hashCode and equals. It has to call the method Object.hashCode to compare hash codes of keys, which returns the object addresses. The keys str3 and str4 have different hash codes because they are two different objects and have different addresses. A new record with key str4 is inserted into the map2, and the value responding to the key str3 remains 10.

Therefore, the output of the code above contains two lines: The first line is a number 20, and the second one is a number 10.

Java has good support for threads and synchronization. There are many interesting interview problems related to multithreading programming, and the following one is an example.

Thread Scheduler

Question 4   There are three threads in a process. The first thread prints 1 1 1 …, the second one prints 2 2 2 …, and the third one prints 3 3 3 … endlessly. How do you schedule these three threads in order to print 1 2 3 1 2 3 …?

Java defines methods wait, notify, and notifyAll in the base class Object. The method wait is used when a thread is waiting for some condition that is typically controlled by another thread. It allows us to put a thread to sleep while waiting for the condition to change, and the thread will be wakened up when a notify or notifyAll occurs. Therefore, wait provides a method to synchronize activities between threads, and it is applicable to solve this problem.

A solution based on methods wait and notify is found in Listing 2-19.

Listing 2-19. Java code to schedule threads

```
public class SimpleThread extends Thread {
    private int value;
    public SimpleThread(int num) {
        this.value = num;
```

```
            start();
        }

    public void run() {
        while(true) {
            synchronized(this) {
                try {
                    wait();
                } catch (InterruptedException e) {
                    throw new RuntimeException(e);
                }

                System.out.print(value + " ");
            }
        }
    }
}
public class Scheduler {
    static final int COUNT = 3;
    static final int SLEEP = 37;

    public static void main(String args[]) {
        SimpleThread threads[] = new SimpleThread[COUNT];
        for(int i = 0; i < COUNT; ++i)
            threads[i] = new SimpleThread(i + 1);

        int index = 0;
        while(true){
            synchronized(threads[index]) {
                threads[index].notify();
            }

            try {
                Thread.sleep(SLEEP);
            } catch (InterruptedException e) {
                throw new RuntimeException(e);
            }

            index = (++index) % COUNT;
        }
    }
}
```

There are four threads in the code above. The first is the main thread in the Java application, which acts as the scheduler, and it creates three printing threads and stores them into an array. The main thread awakens threads one by one according to their index in the array via the method notify. Once a thread wakes up, it prints a number and then sleeps again to wait for another notification.

Source Code:

    004_Scheduler.java

Summary

Programming languages are basic tools for software engineers. Many interviewers like to check candidates' proficiency level on one or more programming languages.

This chapter discusses interview questions of the four most popular languages: C, C++, C#, and Java. Usually interview questions of programming languages can be divided into three categories: understanding of keywords and concepts, analyzing execution of a given piece of code, and writing code. Sample interview questions are discussed in each category. More coding interview questions solved in these four languages are available in the next chapters.

CHAPTER 3

■ ■ ■

Data Structures

The primary purpose of most computer programs is to store, retrieve, and process information. Consequently, data structures and algorithms that manipulate information are at the heart of computer science. For this reason, many interviewers often focus a number of their questions on these aspects. This chapter will cover typical interview questions about the most common data structures, including arrays, strings, lists, trees, stacks, and queues.

Arrays

Arrays might be the most simple data structure. Elements are sequentially stored in continuous memory in arrays. When an array is created, its size should be specified. Even though it may only store one element at first, the size is required because we have to allocate memory for all of the elements. Since there may be vacancies in arrays, they are not efficient in memory utilization.

In order to improve space efficiency, dynamic arrays were developed. The class **vector** in the standard template library (STL) of C++ is one such example. Memory is allocated for a few elements in dynamic arrays at first. When the number of elements is greater than the capacity of a dynamic array, more memory is allocated (the capacity doubles when it has to enlarge the capacity of a **vector** in C++), existing elements are copied to the newly allocated space, and the previous memory is released. It reduces waste in memory, but many extra operations are required to enlarge capacity, so it has negative impact on time efficiency. Therefore, it is better to reduce the times needed to enlarge the capacity of dynamic arrays. The type **ArrayList** in both C# and Java is similar to **vector** in C++.

Because memory allocation for arrays is sequential, it only costs O(1) time to access to an element based on its index, and it is very efficient. A simple hash table can be implemented with an array to utilize its advantage of time efficiency. Each index is treated as a key and every element in an array is treated as a value, so an index and its corresponding element form a pair of key and value. Many problems can be solved with such a hash table, and examples are illustrated in the section *Hash Tables for Characters*. It is a practical solution especially when built-in hash tables are not available in some programming languages such as C/C++.

Arrays and pointers are closely related to each other in C/C++ and also different from each other. The C code in Listing 3-1 shows the relationship between them. What is the output of this code?

Listing 3-1. C Code about Arrays and Pointers

```
int GetSize(int data[]) {
    return sizeof(data);
}

int _tmain(int argc, _TCHAR* argv[]) {
```

```
    int data1[] = {1, 2, 3, 4, 5};
    int size1 = sizeof(data1);

    int* data2 = data1;
    int size2 = sizeof(data2);

    int size3 = GetSize(data1);

    printf("%d, %d, %d", size1, size2, size3);
}
```

The output should be "20, 4, 4" in a 32-bit system. data1 is an array, and sizeof(data1) gets its size. There are five integers in the array, and each integer occupies four bytes, so the total size of array is 20 bytes.

The name of an array is the address of the first element in the array, so data2 points to the first element of an array with the statement data2 = data1. data2 is declared as a pointer, and the sizeof operator returns 4 for any pointers in a 32-bit system.

When an array is passed as a parameter in C/C++, the compiler treats it as a pointer. What gets passed is the address of the first element in an array, rather than the whole array. Therefore, the result of sizeof(data) is also 4 in the function GetSize even though data is declared as an array in the parameter list.

Duplication in an Array

■ **Question 5**   An array contains n numbers ranging from 0 to n-2. There is exactly one number duplicated in the array. How do you find the duplicated number? For example, if an array with length 5 contains numbers {0, 2, 1, 3, 2}, the duplicated number is 2.

Suppose that the duplicated number in the array is m. The sum of all numbers in the array, denoted as *sum1*, should be the result of 0+1+...+(n-2)+m. It is not difficult to get the sum result of 0+1+...+(n-2), which is denoted as *sum2*. The duplicated number m is the difference between *sum1* and *sum2*. The corresponding code in Java is shown in Listing 3-2.

Listing 3-2. Java Code to Get a Duplicated Number in an Array

```
int duplicate(int numbers[]) {
    int length = numbers.length;

    int sum1 = 0;
    for(int i = 0; i < length; ++i) {
        if(numbers[i] < 0 || numbers[i] > length - 2)
            throw new IllegalArgumentException("Invalid numbers.");

        sum1 += numbers[i];
```

```
    }

    int sum2 = ((length - 1) * (length - 2)) >> 1;

    return sum1 - sum2;
}
```

Source Code:

005_Duplication.java

Test Cases:

- Normal case: an array with size *n* has a duplication

- Boundary case: an array {0, 0} with size 2

- Some numbers are out of the range of 0 to *n*-2 in an array of size *n*

■ **Question 6**   An array contains *n* numbers ranging from 0 to *n*-1. There are some numbers duplicated in the array. It is not clear how many numbers are duplicated or how many times a number gets duplicated. How do you find a duplicated number in the array? For example, if an array of length 7 contains the numbers {2, 3, 1, 0, 2, 5, 3}, the implemented function (or method) should return either 2 or 3.

A naive solution for this problem is to sort the input array because it is easy to find duplication in a sorted array. As we know, it costs $O(n\log n)$ time to sort an array with *n* elements.

Another solution is the utilization of a hash set. All numbers in the input array are scanned sequentially. When a number is scanned, we check whether it is already in the hash set. If it is, it is a duplicated number. Otherwise, it is inserted into the set. The data structure HashSet in Java is quite helpful in solving this problem. Even though this solution is simple and intuitive, it has costs: $O(n)$ auxiliary memory to accommodate a hash set. Let's explore a better solution that only needs $O(1)$ memory.

Indexes in an array with length *n* are in the range 0 to *n*-1. If there were no duplication in the *n* numbers ranging from 0 to *n*-1, we could rearrange them in sorted order, locating the number *i* as the ith number. Since there are duplicate numbers in the array, some locations are occupied by multiple numbers, but some locations are vacant.

Now let's rearrange the input array. All numbers are scanned one by one. When the ith number is visited, first it checks whether the value (denoted as *m*) is equal to *i*. If it is, we continue to scan the next number. Otherwise, we compare it with the mth number. If the ith number equals the mth number, duplication has been found. If not, we locate the number *m* in its correct place, swapping it with the mth number. We continue to scan, compare, and swap until a duplicated number is found.

Take the array {2, 3, 1, 0, 2, 5, 3} as an example. The first number 2 does not equal its index 0, so it is swapped with the number with index 2. The array becomes {1, 3, 2, 0, 2, 5, 3}. The first number after swapping is 1, which does not equal its index 0, so two elements in the array are swapped again and the array becomes {3, 1, 2, 0, 2, 5, 3}. It continues to swap since the first number is still not 0. The array is {0, 1, 2, 3, 2, 5, 3} after swapping the first number and the number with index 3. Finally, the first number becomes 0.

Let's move on to scan the next numbers. Because the following three numbers, 1, 2 and 3, are all equal to their indexes, no swaps are necessary for them. The following number, 2, is not the same as its index, so we check whether it is the same as the number with index 2. Duplication is found since the number with index 2 is also 2.

With an understanding of the detailed step-by-step analysis, it is time to implement code. Sample code in Java is shown in Listing 3-3.

Listing 3-3. *Java Code to Get a Duplicated Number in an Array*

```java
int duplicate(int numbers[]) {
    int length = numbers.length;
    for(int i = 0; i < length; ++i) {
        if(numbers[i] < 0 || numbers[i] > length - 1)
            throw new IllegalArgumentException("Invalid numbers.");
    }

    for(int i = 0; i < length; ++i) {
        while(numbers[i] != i) {
            if(numbers[i] == numbers[numbers[i]]) {
                return numbers[i];
            }

            // swap numbers[i] and numbers[numbers[i]]
            int temp = numbers[i];
            numbers[i] = numbers[temp];
            numbers[temp] = temp;
        }
    }

    throw new IllegalArgumentException("No duplications.");
}
```

It throws two exceptions in the code to make the code complete and robust. If there are any numbers out of the range between 0 and *n*-1, the first exception is thrown. If there is no duplication in the array, the second exception is thrown. It is important for candidates to write complete and robust code during interviews.

Source Code:

006_Duplication.java

Test Cases:

- Normal cases: an array with size *n* has one or more duplicated numbers
- Boundary cases: the array {0, 0} with size 2
- Some numbers are out of the range from 0 to *n*-1 in an array of size *n*
- No duplication in the array

Search in a 2-D Matrix

■ **Question 7**   In a 2-D matrix, every row is increasingly sorted from left to right, and the last number in each row is not greater than the first number of the next row. A sample matrix follows. Please implement a function to check whether a number is in such a matrix or not. It returns `true` if it tries to find the number 7 in the sample matrix, but it returns `false` if it tries to find the number 12.

1 3 5

7 9 11

13 15 17

There are many solutions for this problem. The naive solution with brute force is to scan all numbers in the input matrix. Obviously, it costs O(mn) time if the size of the matrix is $m \times n$.

Since each row in the matrix is sorted and the first number of a row is guaranteed to be greater than or equal to the last number of the preceding row, the matrix can be viewed as a 1-D sorted array. If all rows in the sample matrix are concatenated in top down order, it forms a sorted array {1, 3, 5, 7, 9, 11, 13, 15, 17}. The binary search algorithm is suitable for such a scenario, as shown in Listing 3-4.

Listing 3-4. Java Code to Search in a Sorted Matrix

```java
boolean find(int matrix[][], int value) {
    int rows = matrix.length;
    int cols = matrix[0].length;
    int start = 0;
    int end = rows * cols - 1;

    while (start <= end) {
        int mid = start + (end - start) / 2;
        int row = mid / cols;
        int col = mid % cols;
        int v = matrix[row][col];

        if (v == value)
            return true;

        if (v > value)
            end = mid - 1;
        else
            start = mid + 1;
    }

    return false;
}
```

If there are *m* rows and *n* columns in a matrix, the time efficiency for the binary search algorithm is O(log*mn*).

Source Code:

`007_FindInSortedMatrix.Java`

Test Cases:

- The matrix contains the target value (including cases where the target value is the maximum or minimum in the matrix)

- The matrix does not contain the target value (including cases where the target is larger than the maximum or less than the minimum)

- Special matrices, including matrices with only one row, only one column, or with only one element

---

■ **Question 8**   In a 2-D matrix, every row is increasingly sorted from left to right, and every column is increasingly sorted from top to bottom. Please implement a function to check whether a number is in such a matrix or not. For example, all rows and columns are increasingly sorted in the following matrix. It returns `true` if it tries to find number 7, but it returns `false` if it tries to find number 5.

```
1  2  8  9
2  4  9  12
4  7  10  13
6  8  11  15
```

Different from the previous problem, the first number in a row may be less than the last number of the preceding row. For instance, the first number in the second row (the number 2) is less than the last number of the first row (the number 9). Therefore, we cannot utilize the binary search algorithm on the 2-D matrix as a whole.

Since each row is sorted, it improves efficiency if a binary search is utilized. It costs O(log*n*) time for a binary search on *n* numbers, so the overall time efficiency is O(*m*log*n*) for an *m*×*n* matrix. This solution does not fully take advantage of characteristics of an input matrix: all rows are sorted, and all columns are also sorted. More efficient solutions can be found if we fully utilize these characteristics.

Binary Search on a Diagonal

Because all rows and all columns in an input matrix are sorted, numbers on the diagonal from the top left corner to the bottom right corner are also sorted. Therefore, the binary search algorithm can be applied on numbers on the diagonal. If the target value is on the diagonal, it is done. Otherwise, it gets the greatest number on the diagonal that is less than the target value.

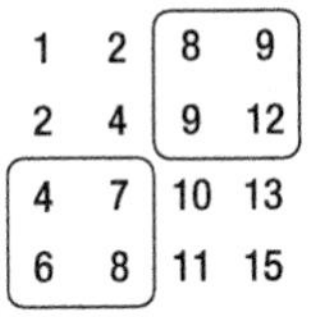

```
1   2 ⎡ 8   9 ⎤
2   4 ⎣ 9  12 ⎦
⎡ 4   7 ⎤ 10  13
⎣ 6   8 ⎦ 11  15
```

Figure 3-1. Find 7 in a 2-D Matrix. The number 4 on the diagonal is located first, which is the greatest number less than the target 7. The whole matrix is split into four sub-matrices by the number 4, and it continues to search in two of them in the rounded rectangles.

The greatest number that is less than the target value on the diagonal splits the whole matrix into four sub-matrices, and it continues to search in two of them. Searching in a sub-matrix is similar to searching in a matrix, so it can be solved recursively.

As shown in Figure 3-1, the target value 7 is not on the diagonal from the top left corner to the bottom right corner. The greatest number less than 7 on the diagonal (the number 4) is found first. Since the target number is greater than 4, it may appear in the northeast area or southwest area (numbers in rounded rectangle). All numbers in the northwest area should be less than 7, and numbers in the southeast area should be greater than 7.

Listing 3-5 provides sample code in Java based on the solution just discussed.

Listing 3-5. Java Code to Search in a Partially Sorted Matrix (Version 1)

```java
boolean find_solution1(int matrix[][], int value) {
    int rows = matrix.length;
    int cols = matrix[0].length;
    return findCore(matrix, value, 0, 0, rows - 1, cols - 1);
}

boolean findCore(int matrix[][], int value, int row1, int col1, int row2, int col2) {
    if(value < matrix[row1][col1] || value > matrix[row2][col2])
        return false;

    if(value == matrix[row1][col1] || value == matrix[row2][col2])
        return true;

    int copyRow1 = row1, copyRow2 = row2;
    int copyCol1 = col1, copyCol2 = col2;

    int midRow = (row1 + row2) / 2;
    int midCol = (col1 + col2) / 2;

    // find the last element less than value on diagonal
    while((midRow != row1 || midCol != col1)
            && (midRow != row2 || midCol != col2)) {
        if(value == matrix[midRow][midCol])
            return true;

        if(value < matrix[midRow][midCol]) {
            row2 = midRow;
            col2 = midCol;
```

```
    }
    else {
        row1 = midRow;
        col1 = midCol;
    }

    midRow = (row1 + row2) / 2;
    midCol = (col1 + col2) / 2;
}

// find value in two sub-matrices
boolean found = false;
if(midRow < matrix.length - 1)
    found = findCore(matrix, value, midRow + 1, copyCol1, copyRow2, midCol);
if(!found && midCol < matrix[0].length - 1)
    found = findCore(matrix, value, copyRow1, midCol + 1, midRow, copyCol2);

return found;
}
```

If the diagonal length of the input matrix is l, the time efficiency of the solution can be calculated with the equation $T(l)=2T(l/2)+\log l$. According to the master theory, $T(l)=O(l)$. Additionally, the length l in a $m \times n$ matrix is $l=O(m+n)$. Therefore, the time efficiency of the solution above is $O(m+n)$.

Removing a Row or a Column at Each Step

When complicated problems are encountered during interviews, an effective method is to use examples to simplify complexity. We can also start from some examples to solve this problem. Let's analyze the step-by-step process to find the number 7 out of the sample matrix in the problem description.

First, we choose the number 9 at the top right corner of the matrix. Since 9 is greater than 7, and 9 is the first number, also the least one, in the fourth column, all numbers in the fourth column should be greater than 7. Therefore, it is not necessary to search in the last column any more, and it is safe to just focus on the other three columns, as shown in Figure 3-2(a).

The number at the top right corner of the remaining matrix is 8, which is also greater than 7, so the third column can also be removed. Let's just focus on the remaining two columns, as shown in Figure 3-2(b).

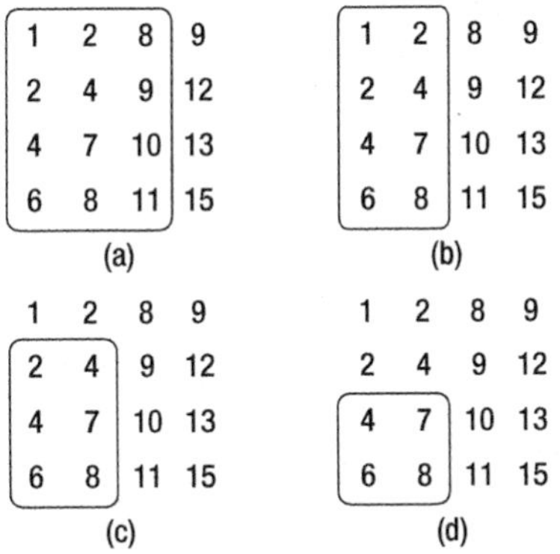

Figure 3-2. *Find 7 in a 2-D Matrix. Numbers in the rounded rectangle are the focus of the next round of searching. (a) The number 9 at the top right corner is greater than the target value 7, so the column containing 9 is removed. (b) 8 is also greater than 7, so we remove the column containing 8. (c) The number 2 at the top right corner is less than 7, so the row containing 2 is removed. (d) 4 is less than 7 too, so the row containing 4 is removed.*

The number 2 is at the top right corner of the remaining matrix with only two columns. Since 2 is less than 7, the target number 7 may be at the right side of 2 or below 2 according to the sorting rules. All columns at the right side of the number 2 have been removed, so it is safe to ignore them. Therefore, the target number 7 should be below the number 2, and the row containing 2 can also be removed. It is only necessary to search in a 3×2 sub-matrix (Figure 3-2(c)).

Similarly to the previous step, the row containing the number 4 can be removed as well because 4 is less than 7. The sub-matrix left with two rows and two columns is shown in Figure 3-2(d).

The number 7 at the top right corner of the remaining 2×2 sub-matrix equals the target number, so the target has been found and we stop searching here.

The following rules can be summarized based on the detailed analysis step-by-step. The number at the top right corner is selected in each round of searching, and it is compared with the target value. When it is the same as the target value, it stops to search. If it is greater than the target value, the last column in the remaining sub-matrix is removed. If it is less than the target value, the first row in the remaining sub-matrix is removed. Therefore, it reduces the sub-matrix by a row or a column if the target value is not at the top right corner.

It is not difficult to develop code after clearly understanding the searching process. Some sample code in Java is found in Listing 3-6.

Listing 3-6. *Java Code to Search in a Partially Sorted Matrix (Version 2)*

```java
boolean find_solution2(int matrix[][], int value) {
    boolean found = false;
    int row = 0;
    int col = matrix[0].length - 1;

    while(row < matrix.length && col >= 0) {
        if(matrix[row][col] == value) {
            found = true;
            break;
        }
```

```
            if(matrix[row][col] > value)
                --col;
            else
                ++row;
    }

    return found;
}
```

Since a row or a column is removed in each round of searching, it costs O($m+n$) time for a matrix with m rows and n columns.

In the previous analysis, the number at the top right corner is selected in each round of searching. Similarly, we can also select the number at the bottom left corner. Please try using the numbers at the bottom left corner if you are interested. However, numbers at the top left corner or bottom right corner are not appropriate choices. Let's take numbers at the top left corner as a quick example. The number 1 is at the top left corner of the original matrix. Since the target value 7 is greater than 1, it may be at the right side of 1 or be in rows below 1. Neither a row nor a column can be removed based on this comparison.

Source Code:

008_FindInPatiallySortedMatrix.Java

Test Cases:

- The matrix contains the target value (including cases where the target value is the maximum or minimum in the matrix)

- The matrix does not contain the target value (including cases where the target is larger than the maximum or less than the minimum)

- Special matrices, including matrices with only one row, only one column, or with only one element

String

A string, which is composed of a sequence of characters, is quite an important data structure. Many programming languages have special rules for strings for the optimization purpose, some of which are highlighted in C/C++, C#, and Java.

Strings in C/C++

All literal strings in C/C++ end with a special character '\0', so it is easy to find the end of a string. However, there is an extra cost for the special character, and it is easy to make mistakes. This is easy to see in Listing 3-7.

Listing 3-7. C/C++ Code for End of a String

```
char str[10];
strcpy(str, "0123456789");
```

A character array with length 10 is declared first, and the content of a string "0123456789" is copied into it. It seems that the string "0123456789" only has 10 characters, but its actual length is 11 because there is an extra character '\0' at its end. The length should be at least 11 for a character array to accommodate the string.

Strings in C#

Strings are encapsulated in a class `System.String` in C#, whose contents are immutable. When we try to modify the content of a string, a new instance will be created. There are many interview questions about immutable strings. For example, what is the final content of `str` in the C# code in Listing 3-8?

Listing 3-8. C# Code for Immutable Strings

```
String str = "hello";
str.ToUpper();
str.Insert(0, " WORLD");
```

Although there are two operations, `ToUpper` and `Insert`, on `str`, it keeps the original content "hello" unchanged. When we try to modify the content of a string, the modified result is in return value.

If there are multiple editing operations on a string, multiple temporary instances will be created, and it has a negative impact on both time and space efficiencies. A new class related to string, `StringBuilder`, is defined to accommodate the modified result. Usually, `StringBuilder` is a better choice if we continue modifying strings many times.

Similar to editing strings, a new instance will be created when we try to assign a literal string to another string. An example is shown in Listing 3-9.

Listing 3-9. C# Code to Assign Strings

```
void ValueOrReference(Type type) {
    String result = "The type " + type.Name;

    if (type.IsValueType)
        Console.WriteLine(result + " is a value type.");
    else
        Console.WriteLine(result + " is a reference type.");
}

void ModifyString(String text) {
    text = "world";
}

void Main(string[] args) {
    String text = "hello";
```

```
        ValueOrReference(text.GetType());
        ModifyString(text);

        Console.WriteLine(text);
}
```

This example checks whether the class `String` is a value type and reference type first. Since it is defined as `public sealed class String {...}`, it is a reference type.

It assigns a new string "world" to `text` in the method `ModifyString`. A new string instance with content "world" is created here, and it is referenced by `text`. The variable `text` references the original string outside the method `ModifyString` because `text` is not marked as `ref` or `out` in the argument list. Therefore, the output for `text` is still "hello". If the expected output is "world", we have to mark the parameter `text` with `ref` or `out`.

Strings in Java

A section of memory is allocated for literal strings in Java. When a string is created once, it can be referenced by other instances. This optimization mechanism avoids recreation, but it makes identity and equality tests more complicated and confusing. Please read the code in Listing 3-10. What is the result?

Listing 3-10. *Java Code for Equality and Identity of Strings*

```
void testEquality() {
    String str1 = "Hello world.";
    String str2 = "Hello world.";

    if (str1 == str2)
        System.out.print("str1 == str2\n");
    else
        System.out.print("str1 != str2\n");

    if(str1.equals(str2))
        System.out.print("str1 equals to str2\n");
    else
        System.out.print("str1 doesn't equal to str2\n");

    String str3 = new String("Hello world.");
    String str4 = new String("Hello world.");

    if (str3 == str4)
        System.out.print("str3 == str4\n");
    else
        System.out.print("str3 != str4\n");

    if(str3.equals(str4))
        System.out.print("str3 equals to str4\n");
    else
        System.out.print("str3 doesn't equal to str4\n");
}
```

When the first line of code `String str1 = "Hello world."` executes, a string "Hello world." is created, and the variable `str1` references to it. Another string "Hello world." will not be created again when the next line of code executes because of optimization. The variable `str2` also references the existing "Hello world.".

The operator `==` checks the identity of the two objects (whether two variables reference the same object). Since `str1` and `str2` reference the same string in memory, they are identical to each other. The method `equals` checks equality of two objects (whether two objects have the same content). Of course, the contents of `str1` and `str2` are the same.

When code `String str3 = new String("Hello world.")` executes, a new instance of `String` with content "Hello world." is created and it is referenced by the variable `str3`. Then another instance of `String` with content "Hello world." is created again, and referenced by `str4`. Since `str3` and `str4` reference two different instances, they are not identical, but their contents are the same.

Therefore, the output contains four lines:

```
str1 == str2
str1 equals to str2
str3 != str4
str3 equals to str4
```

Replace Blanks in a String

ease implement a function to replace each blank in a string with "%20". For instance, it
%20happy." if the input is "We are happy.".

r contains some special characters in web programming, such as blanks and '#'s, it
from retrieving correct parameter information. Therefore, it is necessary to convert
nto strings understandable by servers. The conversion rule is to append the ASCII
character to a '%'. For example, the ASCII value for a blank is 32, 0x20 in hexadecimal, so a blank is converted to "%20". Take '#' as another example: its ASCII value is 35, 0x23 in hexadecimal, so it is replaced with "%23".

There are library methods to replace a piece of string with another, such as `String.Replace` in C# and `String.replaceAll` in Java. However, usually it is not the interviewers' intention to ask candidates to just call existing methods in libraries. They are more interested to know whether candidates have the ability to implement the replacement functionality.

A string with blanks will become longer if each blank is replaced with three characters: '%', '2', and '0'. If the replacement is on the original string, the longer converted string may overlap with memory behind the string. If it is allowed to create a new string and replace blanks on the new string, we can allocate enough memory to accommodate the longer converted string. Since there are two options, candidates should ask interviewers to clarify their requirements. Let's suppose the requirement is to replace blanks on the original string, and there is enough vacant memory behind it.

Replace from Left to Right in $O(n^2)$ Time

An intuitive solution is to scan a string from beginning to end and replace each blank when it is met. Because a character is replaced with three, we must move characters behind blanks; otherwise, two characters will be overlapped.

Let's take a string "We are happy." as an example. We employ grids to visualize characters in a string, as shown in Figure 3-3(a).

When the first blank is replaced, the string becomes the content of Figure 3-3(b). We have to move the characters in the area in the light gray background. When the second blank is replaced, it becomes the content in Figure 3-3(c). Note that characters in "happy." are moved twice.

(a)	W	e		a	r	e		h	a	p	p	y	.	\0				

(b)	W	e	%	2	0	a	r	e		h	a	p	p	y	.	\0		

(c)	W	e	%	2	0	a	r	e	%	2	0	h	a	p	p	y	.	\0

Figure 3-3. *Replace every blank in "We are happy." with "%20" from left to right. (a) This is the original string, "We are happy.". (b) Replace the first blank with "%20". It requires you to move characters with the light gray background. (c) Replace the second blank with "%20". It requires you to move characters with the dark gray background again.*

Supposing the length of the string is n. $O(n)$ characters are moved for each blank, so the total time efficiency is $O(n^2)$ to replace $O(n)$ blanks.

Interviewers may not be satisfied when they are told of this solution. What they expect is a more efficient solution. In the previous analysis, there are many characters moved multiple times. Is it possible to reduce the number of movements? Fortunately, the answer is yes. Let's have a try by replacing blanks from the end to the beginning.

Replace from Right to Left in O(*n*) Time

The number of blanks in the original string is gotten when it is scanned, and then the length of the converted string can also be gotten. The length increases by two when a blank is replaced, so the length after conversion is obtained by adding the original length to double the number of blanks. Take the string "We are happy." as an example again. Its length is 14 (including '\0'), and the length of the replaced string is 18 since there are two blanks in the original string.

Characters are copied or replaced from right to left at this time. Two pointers, P_1 and P_2, are declared. P_1 is initialized to the end of original string, and P_2 is initialized to the end of replaced string, as shown in Figure 3-4(a). The character pointed to by P_1 is copied to where P_2 points, and both pointers are moved backward until P_1 points to a blank (Figure 3-4(b)). Characters with the light gray background are copied. When a blank is met, P_1 moves backward one cell. Three characters "%20" are inserted to where P_2 points, and then P_2 moves backward three cells, as shown in Figure 3-4(c).

This process continues until it meets a blank again (Figure 3-4(d)). Similarly, P_1 moves backward one cell. Three characters "%20" are inserted to where P_2 points, and then P_2 moves backward three cells (Figure 3-4(e)). All blanks have been replaced because P_1 and P_2 overlap with each other.

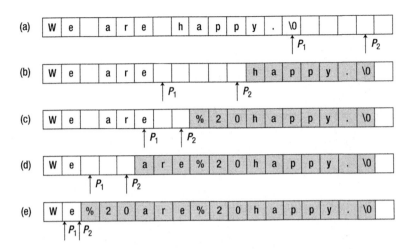

Figure 3-4. *Replace every blank in "We are happy." with "%20" backward. (a)* P_1 *is initialized to the end of the original string, and* P_2 *is initialized to the end of the replaced string. (b) Copy the character pointed to by* P_1 *to where* P_2 *points until the first blank is met. (c) "%20" is inserted where* P_2 *points.* P_1 *moves one cell, and* P_2 *moves three cells backward. (d) Copy the character pointed to by* P_1 *to where* P_2 *points until the second blank is met. (e) "%20" is inserted to where* P_2 *points.* P_1 *moves one cell, and* P_2 *moves three cells backward. All blanks have been replaced because* P_1 *overlaps with* P_2.

Note that all characters are copied (moved) once at most, so its time efficiency is O(n) and it is faster than the first solution.

It is time to implement code when your solution is accepted by interviewers. Some sample code is shown in Listing 3-11.

Listing 3-11. *C Code to Replace Blanks with "%20"*

```c
/*capacity is total capacity of a string, which is longer than its actual length*/
void ReplaceBlank(char string[], int capacity) {
    int originalLength, numberOfBlank, newLength;
    int i, indexOfOriginal, indexOfNew;

    if(string == NULL || capacity <= 0)
        return;

    /*originalLength is the actual length of string*/
    originalLength = numberOfBlank = i = 0;
    while(string[i] != '\0') {
        ++ originalLength;

        if(string[i] == ' ')
            ++ numberOfBlank;

        ++ i;
    }
```

```
    /*newLength is the length of the replaced string*/
    newLength = originalLength + numberOfBlank * 2;
    if(newLength > capacity)
        return;

    indexOfOriginal = originalLength;
    indexOfNew = newLength;
    while(indexOfOriginal >= 0 && indexOfNew > indexOfOriginal) {
        if(string[indexOfOriginal] == ' ') {
            string[indexOfNew --] = '0';
            string[indexOfNew --] = '2';
            string[indexOfNew --] = '%';
        }
        else {
            string[indexOfNew --] = string[indexOfOriginal];
        }

        -- indexOfOriginal;
    }
}
```

Source Code:

    009_ReplaceBlanks.c

Test Cases:

- A string contains some blanks (including cases where some blanks are at the beginning or end of a string, or inside a string; some blanks are continuous)

- A string does not contain any blanks

- Special strings (such as empty strings, a string with only a blank, a string with only some continuous blanks, the input string pointer is NULL)

■ **Question 10**   Given two sorted arrays, denoted as *array1* and *array2*, please merge them into *array1* and keep the merged array sorted. Suppose there is sufficient vacant memory at the end of *array1* to accommodate elements of *array2*.

All elements in an array are sequential, so some elements will be shifted when a new element is inserted. Supposing *array1* has m elements and *array2* has n elements. Since $O(m)$ elements will be shifted when an element of *array2* is inserted to *array1*, it costs $O(mn)$ time to merge two arrays via insertions.

Inspired by the solution of the previous problem, it is better to copy and move elements from right to left. The last two elements of these two arrays are compared, and the greater one is copied to the location with index $(m+n-1)$. It continues to compare and copy until no numbers in *array2* are left. Sample code in C is shown in Listing 3-12.

Listing 3-12. C Code to Merge Sorted Arrays

```c
// Supposing there is enough memory at the end of array1,
// in order to accommodate numbers in array2
void merge(int* array1, int length1, int* array2, int length2) {
    int index1, index2, indexMerged;

    if(array1 == NULL || array2 == NULL)
        return;

    index1 = length1 - 1;
    index2 = length2 - 1;
    indexMerged = length1 + length2 - 1;

    while(index1 >= 0 && index2 >= 0) {
        if(array1[index1] >= array2[index2])
            array1[indexMerged--] = array1[index1--];
        else
            array1[indexMerged--] = array2[index2--];
    }

    while(index2 >= 0)
        array1[indexMerged--] = array2[index2--];
}
```

Since only one element in *array1* or *array2* is copied and moved once in each step, the overall time complexity is $O(m+n)$.

Source Code:

010_MergeSortedArrays.c

Test Cases:

- Merge two sorted arrays (including cases where there are duplicated numbers in two arrays)
- Special arrays (including cases where one or two pointers to arrays are NULL)

■ **Tip**   If each element is shifted multiple times while merging two arrays (strings) from left to right, it may improve performance if elements are copied and moved from right to left.

String Matching

Regular expressions are an important topic in text processing, and many programming languages provide libraries to support them. For example, Java has a package java.util.regex and C# has a namespace System.Text.RegularExpressions for regular expressions. However, interviewers usually disallow candidates to employ library utilities to solve problems related to regular expressions, and candidates have to implement matching mechanisms to demonstrate their coding capabilities.

■ **Question 11**   How do you implement a function to match regular expressions with '.' and '*' in patterns? The character '.' in a pattern matches a single character, and '*' matches zero or any number of characters preceding it. Matching means that a string fully matches the pattern where all characters in a string match the whole pattern. For example, the string "aaa" matches the pattern "a.a" and the pattern "ab*ac*a". However, it does not match the pattern "aa.a" nor "ab*a".

Our solution matches a character after another from a string and a pattern. Let's first analyze how to match a character. When the character *ch* in the pattern is a '.', it matches whatever character is in the string. If the character *ch* is not a '.' and the character in the string is *ch*, they match each other. When the first characters in a string and a pattern are matched, we continue to match the remaining string and pattern.

It is easy to match when the second character in the remaining pattern is not a '*'. If the first character in the remaining string matches the first character in the remaining pattern, it advances the string and pattern and continues to match next characters; otherwise, it returns `false` directly.

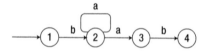

Figure 3-5. *The nondeterministic finite automaton for the pattern ba*ab. There are two choices when it enters the state 2 with an input 'a': it advances to the state 3 or returns back to the state 2.*

It is more complex when the second character in the remaining pattern is a '*' because there might be multiple matching choices. One choice is to advance the pattern by two characters because a '*' may match zero characters in a string. In such a case, a '*' and its preceding character are ignored. If the first character in the remaining string matches the character before the '*' in the pattern, it may advance forward in the string and it has two choices in the pattern: it may advance the pattern by two characters or keep the pattern unchanged.

As shown in the nondeterministic finite automaton of Figure 3-5, it has two choices in the state 2 with an input 'a': it may advance to the state 3 (advance on the pattern by two characters) or return back to state 2 (keeping the pattern unchanged for the next round of matching).

The solution can be implemented based on recursion, as shown in Listing 3-13.

Listing 3-13. C++ Code for Simple Regular Expression Matching

```cpp
bool match(char* string, char* pattern) {
    if(string == NULL || pattern == NULL)
        return false;

    return matchCore(string, pattern);
}
```

```cpp
bool matchCore(char* string, char* pattern) {
    if(*string == '\0' && *pattern == '\0')
        return true;

    if(*string != '\0' && *pattern == '\0')
        return false;

    if(*(pattern + 1) == '*') {
        if(*pattern == *string || (*pattern == '.' && *string != '\0'))
                    // move on the next state
            return matchCore(string + 1, pattern + 2)
                    // stay on the current state
                || matchCore(string + 1, pattern)
                    // ignore a '*'
                || matchCore(string, pattern + 2);
        else
                    // ignore a '*'
            return matchCore(string, pattern + 2);
    }

    if(*string == *pattern || (*pattern == '.' && *string != '\0'))
        return matchCore(string + 1, pattern + 1);

    return false;
}
```

Source Code:

011_SimpleRegularExpression.cpp

Test Cases:

- A string matches or does not match a pattern (including cases where there are '.' and/or '*' in the pattern)

- Special inputs (including cases where a string or pattern is empty, pointers to a sting or pattern are NULL, or an invalid pattern with '*' is at the beginning)

■ **Question 12**   How do you check whether a string stands for a number or not? Numbers include positive and negative integers and floats.

For example, strings "+100.", "5e2", "-.123", "3.1416", and "-1E-16" stand for numbers, but "12e", "1a3.14", "1.2.3", "+-5", and "12e+5.4" do not.

A numeric string follows this format:

[sign]integral-digits[.[fractional-digits]][e|E[sign]exponential-digits].

Elements in square brackets '[' and ']' are optional. The *sign* element is a negative sign symbol ('-') or a positive sign symbol ('+'). There is only one leading sign at most. The *integral-digits* element is a series of digits ranging from 0 to 9 that specify the integral part of the number. It can be absent if the string contains the *fractional-digits* element, which is also a series of digits ranging from 0 to 9 that specify the fractional part of a number. The 'e' or 'E' character indicates that the value is represented in exponential (scientific) notation, which is another series of digits ranging from 0 to 9 specified in *exponential-digits.*

First, it checks whether the leading character is the positive or negative sign symbol, and then it moves on to check the following substring. If the number in the string is a float value, there is a floating point ('.'). Additionally, there might be an exponential notation at the end of an integer or a float number if there is an 'e' or `E' in the string. The overall process to verify a numeric string is shown in Listing 3-14.

Listing 3-14. *C++ Code to Verify Numeric Strings*

```cpp
bool isNumeric(char* string) {
    if(string == NULL)
        return false;

    if(*string == '+' || *string == '-')
        ++string;
    if(*string == '\0')
        return false;

    bool numeric = true;

    scanDigits(&string);
    if(*string != '\0') {
        // for floats
        if(*string == '.') {
            ++string;
            scanDigital(&string);

            if(*string == 'e' || *string == 'E')
                numeric = isExponential(&string);
        }
        // for integers
        else if(*string == 'e' || *string == 'E')
            numeric = isExponential(&string);
        else
            numeric = false;
    }

    return numeric && *string == '\0';
}
```

The function scanDigits scans a segment of a string that only contains digital characters ranging from `0' to `9', as implemented in Listing 3-15.

Listing 3-15. *C++ Code to Scan Digits*

```cpp
void scanDigits(char** string) {
    while(**string != '\0' && **string >= '0' && **string <= '9')
        ++(*string);
}
```

The function `isExponential` is to verify exponential notation at the end of a string. Exponential notation begins with an `e` or `E` and may have a sign symbol following it. Therefore, the function `isExponential` can be implemented, as shown in Listing 3-16.

Listing 3-16. C++ Code to Verify an Exponential Notation

```cpp
bool isExponential(char** string) {
    if(**string != 'e' && **string != 'E')
        return false;

    ++(*string);
    if(**string == '+' || **string == '-')
        ++(*string);

    if(**string == '\0')
        return false;

    scanDigits(string);
    return (**string == '\0') ? true : false;
}
```

Source Code:

   012_NumericStrings.cpp

Test Cases:

- Numeric/Non-numeric strings with/without a sign symbol

- Numeric/Non-numeric strings with/without some fractional digits

- Numeric/Non-numeric strings with/without exponential notation

- Special inputs (including cases where a string is empty, the input pointer to a sting is NULL)

Linked Lists

Arrays are quite useful in all programming languages. However, they also have some limitations. They require creating a new array with bigger size and copying the existing elements from the old array to the new one when the capacity of an array is overrun. Additionally, they have to shift some elements in an array when a new element is inserted because memory of an array is sequentially allocated. Such limitations can be overcome by dynamic structures, such as linked lists.

It is not necessary to know the size of a list when it is created, so it is treated as a dynamic data structure. Rather than allocate memory for all elements when a list is initialized, memory is allocated for each node on demand when it is inserted. The space efficiency of lists is better than arrays because there is no vacant memory in lists.

Memory allocation of a list is not continuous because nodes are inserted dynamically and their memory is not allocated at the same time. It costs $O(n)$ time to get the ith node in a list since it has to traverse nodes one by one starting from the head node. It only takes $O(1)$ time to get the ith element in an array. Therefore, time efficiency to search lists is not as good as for arrays.

Linked lists are the most frequently met data structures during interviews. It only takes about 20 lines of code to create a list, insert a node into a list, or delete a node from a list. Compared to other complex data structures, such as hash tables and graphs, lists are more suitable for interviews due to their moderate code size. Additionally, lots of pointer operations are required to handle a list. Candidates without qualified programming abilities cannot implement complete and robust code related to lists. Moreover, lists are also flexible and challenging interview questions can be constructed with them. Therefore, many interviewers like questions related to lists.

Most lists met during interviews are single-linked lists, where each node has a link to its successor. For example, "Print a List from Tail to Head" (Question 13), "Delete a Node from a List in O(1) Time" (Question 43) , "k^{th} Node from the End" (Question 47), "Reverse Lists" (Question 48), and "First Intersection Node of Two Lists" (Question 82) are all about single-linked lists.

Not only are single-linked lists popular for interviews, but other types of lists are also frequently met:

- Usually the tail node in a single-linked list does not have a successor. If every node in a finite list has a successor, a loop is formed. The section *Loop in List* discusses lists with loops.

- If there is also a link to a predecessor besides a link to a successor in each node of a list, it is a double-linked list. The interview question "Binary Search Trees and Double-Linked Lists" (Question 64) is in this category.

- A complex list is composed if each node has a link to any other node (including the node itself). Please refer to the interview question "Clone Complex Lists" (Question 54) for more details on the complex list.

Print Lists from Tail to Head

■ **Question 13**   Please implement a function to print a list from its tail to head.

When meeting this question, many candidates' intuition is to reverse links between all nodes and to reverse the direction of a list. It fulfills the requirement if all nodes in the reversed list are printed from head to tail. However, it has to modify the structure of the input list. Is it OK to do so? It depends on the requirement in an interviewers' minds. You should ask your interviewers to clarify their requirement before you describe your solution.

■ **Tip**   If you are going to modify the input data, you should ask interviewers whether it is allowed to do so.

Usually, printing is a read-only operation, and it is not allowed to modify the content to be printed. Supposing interviewers disallow to reverse the direction of lists here.

Nodes in a list are linked from the head to the tail, but the printing order is from the tail to the head. That is to say, the first node in the list is the last one to be printed, and the last node is the first one to be printed. It is typical "Last In, First Out," so a stack can help to solve this problem. Every node is pushed into a stack when it is visited. After all nodes are visited and pushed into the stack, they are printed from the top of the stack and popped one by one. The printing order is opposite to the order in the list.

The sample code in Listing 3-17 is based on stack in the C++ standard template library.

Listing 3-17. *C++ Code to Print a List Reversely (Iterative Version)*

```cpp
void PrintListReversingly_Iteratively(ListNode* pHead) {
    std::stack<ListNode*> nodes;
    ListNode* pNode = pHead;
    while(pNode != NULL) {
        nodes.push(pNode);
        pNode = pNode->m_pNext;
    }
    while(!nodes.empty()) {
        pNode = nodes.top();
        printf("%d\t", pNode->m_nValue);
        nodes.pop();
    }
}
```

It can be solved with a stack and since recursion is essentially equivalent to stacks, so it can also be solved recursively. To print a list in reverse, the next nodes are printed first when a node is visited, and then the currently visited node is printed. The recursive code is shown in Listing 3-18.

Listing 3-18. *C++ Code to Print a List Reversely (Recursive Version)*

```cpp
void PrintListReversingly_Recursively(ListNode* pHead) {
    if(pHead != NULL) {
        if (pHead->m_pNext != NULL) {
            PrintListReversingly_Recursively(pHead->m_pNext);
        }
        printf("%d\t", pHead->m_nValue);
    }
}
```

The previous recursive code looks more concise, but it has a limitation: the recursive calls may have too many levels to cause call stack overflow errors when the list is very long. The iterative solution with an explicit stack is more robust. More discussion about recursion and iteration are available in the section *Recursion and Iteration*.

Source Code:

013_PrintListsReversely.cpp

Test Cases:

- Lists with multiple nodes or only one node
- The head node of a list is NULL

Sort Lists

■ **Question 14**   Please implement a function to sort a given list.

The most efficient sorting algorithm in general, quicksort, is applicable to arrays because elements in arrays can be accessed in O(1) time based on indexes. It takes more time to locate a node in a list, so we have to utilize other algorithms to sort lists.

Let's take a list with four nodes as an example to analyze the process of the insert sort algorithm (Figure 3-6(a)). A list is split into two parts. The first part contains nodes already sorted, and the second part is not sorted yet. The node pointed by P_1 is the last sorted node, which is initialized to the first node, and the node pointed to by P_2 is the next one to be sorted.

When node 1 is the next node to be sorted, there is only one node (node 2) in the sorted list. Because the value 1 is less than the value in the list head, node 1 becomes the new head of the sorted list, and node 2 is linked to the next node of the previous node 1, which is node 4 (Figure 3-6(b)). Node 2 is still the last node in the sorted list, so it does not move P_1, and only moves P_2 to the next node of node 2.

The next node to be sorted is node 4. It traverses from the head node in order to find an appropriate location in the sorted list. Since the value 4 is greater than the value 2 in the last node of the sorted list, it is not necessary to relink nodes. Node 4 becomes the new last node of the sorted list, so it is pointed to by P_1 (Figure 3-6(c)).

Now the next node to be sorted is node 3. It traverses from the head node again in order to find an appropriate location in the sorted list. Node 3 is linked between node 2 and node 4. Node 4 is still the last node in the sorted list. Since there are no nodes left after node 4, the whole list is sorted (Figure 3-6(d)).

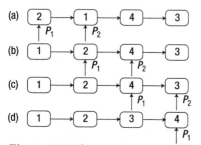

Figure 3-6. *The process to sort a list with four nodes.* P_1 *points to the last node in the sorted list, and* P_2 *points to the next node to be inserted into the sorted list, which always follows* P_1. *(a)* P_1 *is initialized to the first node, and* P_2 *is initialized to the second one. (b) The node with value 2 is inserted into the sorted list. (c) The node with value 4 is inserted into the sorted list. (d) The node with value 3 is inserted into the sorted list.*

The insert sort algorithm for lists can be implemented in C++, as shown in Listing 3-19.

Listing 3-19. C++ Code to Sort a List

```
void Sort(ListNode** pHead) {
    if(pHead == NULL || *pHead == NULL)
        return;
```

```
    ListNode* pLastSorted = *pHead;
    ListNode* pToBeSorted = pLastSorted->m_pNext;
    while(pToBeSorted != NULL) {
        if(pToBeSorted->m_nValue < (*pHead)->m_nValue) {
            pLastSorted->m_pNext = pToBeSorted->m_pNext;
            pToBeSorted->m_pNext = *pHead;
            *pHead = pToBeSorted;
        }
        else {
            ListNode* pNode = *pHead;
            while(pNode != pLastSorted
                && pNode->m_pNext->m_nValue < pToBeSorted->m_nValue) {
                pNode = pNode->m_pNext;
            }

            if(pNode != pLastSorted) {
                pLastSorted->m_pNext = pToBeSorted->m_pNext;
                pToBeSorted->m_pNext = pNode->m_pNext;
                pNode->m_pNext = pToBeSorted;
            }
            else
                pLastSorted = pLastSorted->m_pNext;
        }

        pToBeSorted = pLastSorted->m_pNext;
    }
}
```

Because it has to scan $O(n)$ nodes on the sorted list in order to find an appropriate location to insert a new node, it costs $O(n^2)$ time to sort a list with n nodes.

Source Code:

014_SortLists.cpp

Test Cases:

- Sort a list with multiple nodes, with/without duplicated values

- The input list has only one node

- The input head node of a list is NULL

■ **Question 15**   Please implement a function to merge two sorted lists into a single sorted list. For example, the merged list of two sorted lists, L_1 and L_2 in Figure 3-7, is L_3.

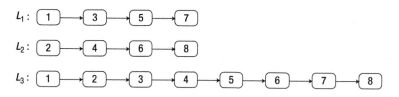

Figure 3-7. *The lists* L_1 *and* L_2 *are two sorted lists. They compose the list* L_3 *when* L_1 *and* L_2 *are merged.*

The process begins to merge lists from head nodes because traversal on lists begins from head nodes. The head node of L_1 with value 1 is the head node of the merged list because its value is less than the value in the head of node of L_2, as shown in Figure 3-8(a).

It continues to merge the nodes remaining in L_1 and L_2 (the nodes in the rectangles with dashed edges in Figure 3-8). The steps to merge are similar to the ones before because nodes remaining in the two lists are still sorted. It continues to compare values in the head nodes of the two lists. Because the value in the head node of L_2 is less than the value of head node in the remaining L_1, it links the head node of L_2 to the tail of the merged list, as shown in Figure 3-8(b).

When the head node of one list with a lower value than the other is linked to the tail of the merged list, the nodes remaining in two lists are still increasingly sorted, so the steps to merge are the same as before. It is a typical recursive process, so let's implement it based on recursion.

It is important to know when to stop in recursion. It exits recursion when one of these two lists is empty. When L_1 is an empty list, the merged list is L_2. Similarly, the merged list is L_1 if L_2 is empty. If both lists are empty, the merged list is obviously empty.

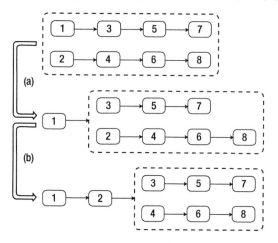

Figure 3-8. *The process to merge two sorted lists. (a) The head of* L_1 *becomes the head of the merged list because the value in the head node of* L_1 *is less than the value in the head node of* L_2*. (b) The value in the head node of* L_2 *is less than the value in the head node of the remaining* L_1*, so the head node of* L_2 *is connected to the tail of the merged list.*

It is time to write code with careful analysis. A piece of sample code is shown in Listing 3-20.

Listing 3-20. C++ Code to Merge Sorted List

```cpp
ListNode* Merge(ListNode* pHead1, ListNode* pHead2) {
    if(pHead1 == NULL)
        return pHead2;
    else if(pHead2 == NULL)
        return pHead1;

    ListNode* pMergedHead = NULL;

    if(pHead1->m_nValue < pHead2->m_nValue) {
        pMergedHead = pHead1;
        pMergedHead->m_pNext = Merge(pHead1->m_pNext, pHead2);
    }
    else {
        pMergedHead = pHead2;
        pMergedHead->m_pNext = Merge(pHead1, pHead2->m_pNext);
    }

    return pMergedHead;
}
```

Sorted lists can also be merged iteratively. Actually, the iterative solution is more robust with long lists. If you feel interested, please try to implement your own iterative version.

Source Code:

015_MergeSortedLists.cpp

Test Cases:

- There are/are not duplicated values in the two arrays
- One or two input list head nodes are NULL

Loop in List

■ **Question 16**   How do you check whether there is a loop in a linked list? For example, the list in Figure 3-9 contains a loop.

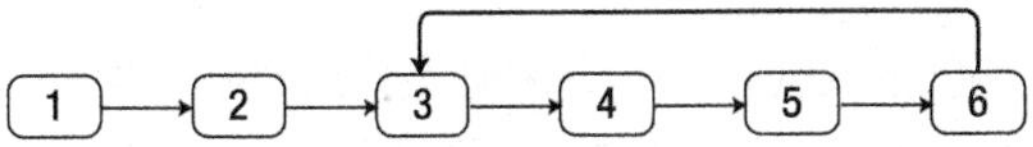

Figure 3-9. A list with a loop

This is a popular interview question. It can be solved with two pointers, which are initialized at the head of list. One pointer advances once at each step, and the other advances twice at each step. If the faster pointer meets the slower one again, there is a loop in the list. Otherwise, there is no loop if the faster one reaches the end of list.

The sample code in Listing 3-21 is implemented based on this solution. The faster pointer is pFast, and the slower one is pSlow.

Listing 3-21. *C++ Code to Check Whether a List Contains a Loop*

```cpp
bool HasLoop(ListNode* pHead) {
    if(pHead == NULL)
        return false;

    ListNode* pSlow = pHead->m_pNext;
    if(pSlow == NULL)
        return false;

    ListNode* pFast = pSlow->m_pNext;
    while(pFast != NULL && pSlow != NULL) {
        if(pFast == pSlow)
            return true;

        pSlow = pSlow->m_pNext;

        pFast = pFast->m_pNext;
        if(pFast != NULL)
            pFast = pFast->m_pNext;
    }

    return false;
}
```

Source Code:

    016_LoopsInLists.cpp

Test Cases:

- There is a loop in a list (including cases where there are one/multiple nodes in a loop, or a loop contains all nodes in a list)

- There is not a loop in a list

- The input node of the list head is NULL

▓ **Question 17**   If there is a loop in a linked list, how do you get the entry node of the loop? The entry node is the first node in the loop from the head of a list. For instance, the entry node of the loop in the list of Figure 3-9 is the node with value 3.

Inspired by the solution of the preceding problem, we can also solve this problem with two pointers.

Two pointers P_1 and P_2 are initialized to point to the head of a list. If there are *n* nodes in the loop, the first pointer move forward *n* steps, and then two pointers move together with same speed. When the second pointer reaches the entry node of the loop, the first one travels around the loop and returns back to the entry node.

Let's take the list in Figure 3-9 as an example. P_1 and P_2 are first initialized to point to the head node of the list (Figure 3-10(a)). There are four nodes in the loop of the list, so P_1 moves four steps ahead and reaches the node with value 5 (Figure 3-10(b)). Then these two pointers move two steps, and they meet at the node with value 3, which is the entry node of the loop, as shown in Figure 3-10(c).

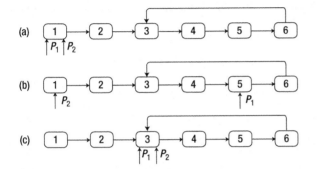

Figure 3-10. *Process to find the entry node of a loop in a list. (a) Pointers* P_1 *and* P_2 *are initialized at the head of list. (b) The pointer* P_1 *moves four steps ahead since there are four nodes in the loop. (c) Both* P_1 *and* P_2 *move ahead till they meet at the entry node of the loop.*

The only problem is how to figure out the number of nodes inside a loop. Let's go back to the solution of the previous question. Two pointers are employed, and the faster one meets the slower one if there is a loop. The meeting node should be inside the loop. Therefore, we can move forward from the meeting node and count nodes in the loop until we arrive at the meeting node again.

The function MeetingNode in Listing 3-22 finds the meeting node of two pointers if there is a loop in a list, which is a minor modification of the previous HasLoop.

Listing 3-22. *C++ Code to Get a Meeting Node in a Loop*

```cpp
ListNode* MeetingNode(ListNode* pHead) {
    if(pHead == NULL)
        return NULL;

    ListNode* pSlow = pHead->m_pNext;
    if(pSlow == NULL)
        return NULL;

    ListNode* pFast = pSlow->m_pNext;
    while(pFast != NULL && pSlow != NULL) {
        if(pFast == pSlow)
            return pFast;

        pSlow = pSlow->m_pNext;

        pFast = pFast->m_pNext;
```

```
        if(pFast != NULL)
            pFast = pFast->m_pNext;
    }

    return NULL;
}
```

The function MeetingNode returns a node in the loop when there is a loop in the list. Otherwise, it returns NULL.

After finding the meeting node, it counts nodes in a loop of a list, as well as finding the entry node of the loop with the sample code, as shown in Listing 3-23.

Listing 3-23. *C++ Code to Get a Meeting Node in a Loop*

```
ListNode* EntryNodeOfLoop(ListNode* pHead) {
    ListNode* meetingNode = MeetingNode(pHead);
    if(meetingNode == NULL)
        return NULL;

    // get the number of nodes in loop
    int nodesInLoop = 1;
    ListNode* pNode1 = meetingNode;
    while(pNode1->m_pNext != meetingNode) {
        pNode1 = pNode1->m_pNext;
        ++nodesInLoop;
    }

    // move pNode1
    pNode1 = pHead;
    for(int i = 0; i < nodesInLoop; ++i)
        pNode1 = pNode1->m_pNext;

    // move pNode1 and pNode2
    ListNode* pNode2 = pHead;
    while(pNode1 != pNode2){
        pNode1 = pNode1->m_pNext;
        pNode2 = pNode2->m_pNext;
    }

    return pNode1;
}
```

Source Code:

    017_EntryNodeInLoopsInLists.cpp

Test Cases:

- There is a loop in a list (including cases where there are one/multiple nodes in a loop, or a loop contains all nodes in a list)

- There is not a loop in a list

- The input node of the list head is NULL

Trees

Both arrays and lists are linear data structures, so it is difficult to utilize them to organize a hierarchical representation of objects. To overcome this limitation, a new data type named a tree was introduced, which consists of a set of nodes and links among them.

Trees are commonly used during our daily programming. In trees, all nodes except the root node have a parent node, and all nodes except leaves have one or more children nodes.

Interview questions about trees are usually not easy because there are many pointer operations on trees. If interviewers would like to examine candidates' capacity to handle complex pointer operations, they are likely to employ questions about trees.

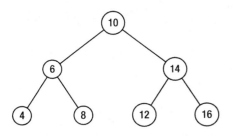

Figure 3-11. *A sample binary tree with seven nodes*

Most trees referred to during interviews are binary trees, where every node has two children at most. The most important operation on trees is traversal, which is to visit nodes in some order. The most common traversal algorithms include the following:

- *Pre-order traversal:* The root of a binary tree is visited first, then its left children, and finally its right children. The pre-order traversal sequence of the binary tree in Figure 3-11 is 10, 6, 4, 8, 14, 12, 16.

- *In-order traversal:* Left children of a binary tree are visited first, then its root, and finally its right children. The in-order traversal sequence of the binary tree in Figure 3-11 is 4, 6, 8, 10, 12, 14, 16.

- *Post-order traversal:* Left children of a binary tree are visited first, then its right children, and finally its root. The post-order traversal sequence of the binary tree in Figure 3-11 is 4, 8, 6, 12, 16, 14, 10.

- *Breadth-first traversal:* Nodes in the first level are traversed, then nodes in the second level, ..., and finally nodes in the bottom level. Nodes in the same level are usually traversed from left to right. The breadth-first traversal sequence of the binary tree in Figure 3-11 is 10, 6, 14, 4, 8, 12, 16.

The first three traversal algorithms in the preceding list can be implemented with both recursion and iteration, and recursive implementations are more concise than iterative ones. Candidates should be very familiar with these six implementations and be able to implement them with bug-free code in a short period of time.

There are many interview questions about tree traversal. For example, questions about "Subtrees" (Question 50), "Path with Sum in Binary Trees" (Question 60), and "Depth of Binary Trees" (Question 85) are in this category. The interview question "Build a Binary Tree from Traversal Sequences" (Question 61) is about the characteristics of traversals.

Usually, a queue is utilized for breadth-first traversal algorithms. There are also many interesting interview questions on this topic, which are discussed in the section *Print Binary Trees Level by Level*.

There are some special binary trees such as binary search trees. In a binary search tree, all nodes in the left subtree are not greater than the root node, and all nodes in the right subtree are not less than the root node. Binary search trees are closely related to the binary search algorithm, where it costs $O(\log n)$ time to find a value among n nodes.

The tree in Figure 3-11 is actually a binary search tree. "Binary Search Tree Verification" (Question 19) and "Binary Search Tree and Double-Lined List" (Question 64) are examples of interview questions about binary search trees.

Another category of binary trees is the heap. There are two kinds of heaps: max heaps and min heaps. The value in the root node is the maximum in a max heap, while the value in the root node is the minimum in a min heap. If it is required to find the maximal or minimal value, you may consider employing heaps. Please refer to interview questions "Median in a Stream" (Question 69) and "Minimal k Numbers" (Question 70) for more details.

Next Nodes in Binary Trees

■ **Question 18**   Given a node in a binary tree, please implement a function to retrieve its next node in the in-order traversal sequence. There is a pointer to the parent node in each tree node.

The tree in Figure 3-12 is a binary tree whose in-order traversal sequence is *d, b, h, e, i, a, f, c, g*. Let's take it as an example to analyze how to get the next node in a binary tree.

If a node has a right child, its next node is the most left child in its right subtree. That is to say, it moves to the right child and then traverses along the links to the left child as much as possible. For example, the next node of node *b* is node *h*, and the next node of node *a* is node *f*.

If a node does not have a right child, its next node is its parent if it is the left child of its parent. For instance, the next node of node *d* is node *b*, and the next node of node *f* is node *c*.

It is more complex to get the next node of a node that does not have a right child and is the right child of its parent. It traverses along the links to parents until it reaches a node that is the left child of its parent. The parent is the next node if such a node exists.

In order to get the next node of node *i*, it traverses along the link to the parent and reaches node *e* at first. Since node *e* is not the left child of its parent, it continues to traverse and reaches at node *b*, which is the left child of its parent. Therefore, the parent of node *b*, which is node *a*, is the next node after node *i*.

It is a similar process to get the next node of node g. It first traverses the link to the parent and reaches node *c*. It continues to traverse because node *c* is not a left child of its parent, and it reaches node *a*. Because node *a* does not have a parent, node *g* is the last in the binary tree and it does not have a next node.

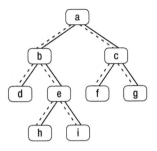

Figure 3-12. *A binary tree with nine nodes. Links from children to parents are drawn with dashed arrows.*

The C++ code to get the next node of a given node is found in Listing 3-24.

Listing 3-24. *C++ Code to Get the Next Node in a Binary Tree*

```cpp
BinaryTreeNode* GetNext(BinaryTreeNode* pNode) {
    if(pNode == NULL)
        return NULL;

    BinaryTreeNode* pNext = NULL;
    if(pNode->m_pRight != NULL) {
        BinaryTreeNode* pRight = pNode->m_pRight;
        while(pRight->m_pLeft != NULL)
            pRight = pRight->m_pLeft;

        pNext = pRight;
    }
    else if(pNode->m_pParent != NULL) {
        BinaryTreeNode* pCurrent = pNode;
        BinaryTreeNode* pParent = pNode->m_pParent;
        while(pParent != NULL && pCurrent == pParent->m_pRight) {
            pCurrent = pParent;
            pParent = pParent->m_pParent;
        }

        pNext = pParent;
    }

    return pNext;
}
```

Source Code:

    `018_NextNode.cpp`

Test Cases:

- Input different kinds of binary trees, such as full binary trees or binary trees, in which all nodes only have right subtrees or left subtrees

- The next node is in the right subtree of the input node, the parent, or the skip-level ancestors

- The input node does not have a next node

- The input node of tree root is NULL

Binary Search Tree Verification

■ **Question 19**   How do you verify whether a binary tree is a binary search tree? For example, the tree in Figure 3-13 is a binary search tree.

The binary search tree is a specific type of binary tree that has an important characteristic: each node is greater than or equal to nodes in its left subtree, and less than or equal to nodes in its right subtree. We can verify binary search trees bases on this characteristic, as shown in Figure 3-13.

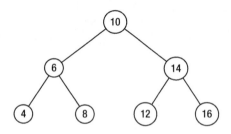

Figure 3-13. *A sample binary search tree with seven nodes*

Verify Value Range of Each Node

If a binary search tree is scanned with a pre-order traversal algorithm, the value in a root node is accessed first. After the root node is visited, it begins to scan nodes in the left subtree. The value of left subtree nodes should be less than or equal to the value of the root node. If a value of a left subtree node is greater than the value of the root node, it violates the definition of the binary search tree. Similarly, it also violates the definition of the binary search tree when a value of a right subtree node is less than the root node value because the value of the right subtree nodes should be greater than or equal to the root node value.

Therefore, when it visits a node in binary search tree, it narrows the value range of the left subtree and right subtree under the current visited node. All nodes are visited with the pre-order traversal algorithm, and their value is verified. If a value in any node is beyond its corresponding range, it is not a binary search tree.

The code in Listing 3-25 is implemented based on this pre-order traversal solution.

Listing 3-25. *C++ Code for Binary Search Tree Verification (Version 1)*

```
bool isBST_Solution1(BinaryTreeNode* pRoot) {
```

```
    int min = numeric_limits<int>::min();
    int max = numeric_limits<int>::max();
    return isBSTCore_Solution1(pRoot, min, max);
}

bool isBSTCore_Solution1(BinaryTreeNode* pRoot, int min, int max) {
    if(pRoot == NULL)
        return true;

    if(pRoot->nValue < min || pRoot->nValue > max)
        return false;

    return isBSTCore_Solution1(pRoot->pLeft, min, pRoot->nValue)
        && isBSTCore_Solution1(pRoot->pRight, pRoot->nValue, max);
}
```

In this code, the value of each node should be in the range between min and max. The value of the current visited node is the maximal value of its left subtree and the minimal value of its right subtree, so it updates the min and max parameters and verifies subtrees recursively.

Increasing In-Order Traversal Sequence

The first solution is based on the pre-order traversal algorithm. Let's have another try using in-order traversal. The in-order traversal sequence of the binary search tree in Figure 3-13 is 4, 6, 8, 10, 12, 14, and 16. It is noticeable that the sequence is increasingly sorted.

Therefore, a new solution is available: nodes in a binary tree are scanned with the in-order traversal algorithm and compare values of each node against the value of the previously visited node. If the value of the previously visited node is greater than the value of the current node, it breaks the definition of a binary search tree.

This solution might be implemented in C++, as shown in Listing 3-26.

Listing 3-26. *C++ Code for Binary Search Tree Verification (Version 2)*

```
bool isBST_Solution2(BinaryTreeNode* pRoot) {
    int prev = numeric_limits<int>::min();
    return isBSTCore_Solution2(pRoot, prev);
}

bool isBSTCore_Solution2(BinaryTreeNode* pRoot, int& prev) {
    if(pRoot == NULL)
        return true;

        // previous node
    return isBSTCore_Solution2(pRoot->pLeft, prev)
        // current node
        && (pRoot->nValue >= prev)
        // next node
        && isBSTCore_Solution2(pRoot->pRight, prev = pRoot->nValue);
}
```

The parameter `prev` of the function `isBSTCore_Solution2` is the value of the previously visited node in the pre-order traversal sequence.

Source Code:

`019_VerrifyBinarySearchTrees.cpp`

Test Cases:

- Binary trees (such as full binary trees or binary trees in which all nodes only have right subtrees or left subtrees) are binary search trees

- Binary trees (such as full binary trees or binary trees in which all nodes only have right subtrees or left subtrees) are not binary search trees

- Special binary trees, including a binary tree that has only one node, or the input node of tree root is `NULL`

■ **Question 20**   Please implement a function to get the largest size of all binary search subtrees in a given binary tree. A subtree inside a tree *t* is a tree consisting of a node and all of its descendants in *t*. The size of a tree is defined as the number of nodes in the tree.

For example, the largest binary search subtree in the binary tree of Figure 3-14 contains three nodes, which are node 9, node 8, and node 10.

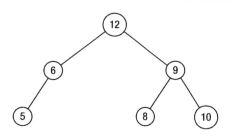

Figure 3-14. *A sample binary tree with six nodes in which the largest binary search subtree has three nodes (node 9, node 8, and node 10)*

There are two subproblems in this problem. One subproblem is how to verify whether a subtree is a binary search tree, and the other is how to find the size of a binary search subtree.

The whole tree may not be a binary tree even though some subtrees are binary search trees. Therefore, the solution has to verify binary search subtrees in bottom-up order. When the left subtree or right subtree under a node is not a binary search tree, the tree under the node cannot be a binary search. If both left subtree and right subtree are binary search trees and the value of the node is between the maximum in the left subtree and the minimum in the right subtree, the node and its descendants compose a binary search tree.

For example, node 6 and its children compose a binary search tree, and node 9 and its children compose another binary search tree in Figure 3-14. However, the tree rooted at node 12 is not a binary search tree because its value is greater than the minimal value in its right children.

The solution finds the size of a binary search subtree also in bottom-up order. When it visits a node, it finds the largest size of binary search trees in its left subtree (*size1*) and right subtree (*size2*). If both left and right subtrees are binary search trees and the value of the current visited node is inside the corresponding range, the node and its descendants compose a binary search tree whose size is *size1+size2+1*. If the current visited node and its descendants cannot compose a binary search tree, the largest size of binary search subtree is the maximal value between *size1* and *size2*.

The size of the subtree rooted at node 6 in Figure 3-14 is 2, and the size of the subtree rooted at node 9 is 3. Because the whole tree rooted at node 12 is not a binary search tree, the largest size of the binary search subtree is 3, the maximum between 2 and 3. (See Listing 3-27.)

Listing 3-27. C++ Code to Get the Largest Size of Binary Search Subtrees

```cpp
int LargestBST(BinaryTreeNode* pRoot) {
    int min, max, largestSize;
    LargestBST(pRoot, min, max, largestSize);

    return largestSize;
}

bool LargestBST(BinaryTreeNode* pRoot, int& min, int& max, int& largestSize) {
    if(pRoot == NULL) {
        max = 0x80000000;
        min = 0x7FFFFFFF;
        largestSize = 0;
        return true;
    }

    int minLeft, maxLeft, leftSize;
    bool left = LargestBST(pRoot->pLeft, minLeft, maxLeft, leftSize);

    int minRight, maxRight, rightSize;
    bool right  = LargestBST(pRoot->pRight, minRight, maxRight, rightSize);

    bool overall = false;
    if(left && right && pRoot->nValue >= maxLeft && pRoot->nValue <= minRight)
    {
        largestSize = leftSize + rightSize + 1;
        overall = true;

        min = (pRoot->nValue < minLeft) ? pRoot->nValue : minLeft;
        max = (pRoot->nValue > maxRight) ? pRoot->nValue : maxRight;
    }
    else
        largestSize = (leftSize > rightSize) ? leftSize : rightSize;

    return overall;
}
```

Source Code:

    020_LargestBinarySearchSubtrees.cpp

Test Cases:

- A whole binary tree is a binary search tree

- The left or right subtree under a certain node is a binary search tree, but the node, the left subtree, and the right subtree do not form a binary search tree as a whole

- Special binary trees, including a binary tree that has only one node, or the input node of tree root is NULL

Stack and Queue

A stack is a linear data structure that can be accessed only at one of its ends for storing and retrieving data, which follows the rule "Last In, First Out." That is to say, the last element pushed into a stack will be the first one to be popped. Because of this rule, stacks are very useful when data have to be stored and then retrieved in reverse order. The stack is a common data structure in computer-related domains. For instance, operating systems create a stack for each thread to store function parameters, return addresses, and local variables.

We will discuss the characteristics of push and pop sequences in the interview question "Push and Pop Sequence of Stacks" (Question 56). Moreover, stacks are closely related to recursion. More details will be covered in the section *Recursion and Iteration*.

A queue is another important data structure where both ends are used: one for inserting new elements and the other for removing them. Different from stacks, queues follow the rule "First in, First Out," where the first enqueued element will be the first one to be dequeued. It is necessary to utilize queues for breadth-first traversal algorithms.

Usually, elements in stacks or queues are not sorted and it costs O(*n*) time to get the minimal or maximal element. Special design and implementation are needed if it is required to get the minimum or maximum in O(1) time. A detailed discussion is available in the sections *Stack with min Function* and *Maximum in a Queue*.

Even though the rules for stacks and queues are opposite, what is interesting is that a stack can be implemented with two queues, and a queue can be implemented with two stacks.

Build a Queue with Two Stacks

■ **Question 21**   Please design a queue with two stacks and implement methods to enqueue and dequeue items.

It is necessary to implement a queue that follows the rule "First In, First Out" with two stacks that follow the rule of "Last In, First Out." The two stacks inside a queue are denoted as *stack1* and *stack2*.

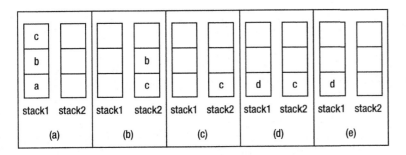

Figure 3-15. *The operations on a queue with two stacks. (a) Enqueue the three elements* a, b, c *one by one. (b) Dequeue the element* a. *(c) Dequeue the element* b *from the front end. (d) Enqueue another element* d. *(e) Dequeue the element* c.

Let us analyze the process required to enqueue and dequeue elements via some examples. First, an element *a* is appended. Let's push it into *stack1*. There is an element {*a*} in *stack1* and *stack2* that is empty. It continues to append two more elements, *b* and *c*, pushing them into *stack1*. There are three elements {*a*, *b*, *c*} in *stack1* now, where *c* is on top and *stack2* is still empty (as shown in Figure 3-15(a)).

We then delete an element from the queue. According to the "First in, First out" rule, the first element to be deleted is *a* since it was appended before *b* and *c*. The element *a* is stored in *stack1*, and it is not on the top of a stack. Therefore, it cannot be popped off directly. Note that *stack2* has not been used, and it is time for us to utilize it. If elements are popped from *stack1* and pushed into *stack2* one by one, the order of elements in *stack2* is in the reverse order of *stack1*. After three popping and pushing operations, *stack1* becomes empty and there are three elements {*c*, *b*, *a*} in *stack2*. The element *a* can be popped off now since it is on top of *stack2*. Now there are two elements left {*c*, *b*} in *stack2* and *b* is on top (as shown in Figure 3-15(b)).

How do we continue deleting more elements from the tail of the queue? The element *b* was inserted into the queue before *c*, so it should be deleted when there are two elements *b* and *c* left in queue. It can be popped off since it is on top of *stack2*. After the popping operation, *stack1* remains empty and there is only an element *c* in *stack2*, as shown in Figure 3-15(c).

It is time to summarize the steps to delete an element from a queue. The top of *stack2* can be popped off when *stack2* is not empty since it is the first element inserted into the queue. When *stack2* is empty, we pop all elements from *stack1* and push them into *stack2* one by one. The first element in a queue is pushed into the bottom of *stack1*. It can be popped out directly after popping and pushing operations since it is on top of *stack2*.

Let us enqueue another element, *d*, and it is pushed into *stack1*, as shown in Figure 3-15(d). If we are going to dequeue an element, the element on top of *stack2*, which is *c*, needs to be deleted. The element *c* is indeed inserted into the queue before the element *d*, so it is a reasonable operation to delete *c* before *d*. The final status of the queue is shown in Figure 3-15(e).

We can write code after we have gotten clear ideas about the process necessary to enqueue and dequeue elements. Some sample code in C# is shown in Listing 3-28.

Listing 3-28. *C# Code to Implement a Queue with Two Stacks*

```
public class QueueWithTwoStacks<T> {
    public void Enqueue(T item) {
        stack1.Push(item);
    }
```

```
    public T Dequeue() {
        if (stack2.Count == 0) {
            while (stack1.Count > 0) {
                T item = stack1.Peek();
                stack1.Pop();
                stack2.Push(item);
            }
        }

        if (stack2.Count == 0)
            throw new InvalidOperationException("Queue is Empty");

        T head = stack2.Peek();
        stack2.Pop();

        return head;
    }

    private Stack<T> stack1 = new Stack<T>();
    private Stack<T> stack2 = new Stack<T>();
}
```

Source Code:

021_QueueWithTwoStacks.cs

Test Cases:

- Insert elements into an empty queue and then delete them

- Insert elements into a non-empty queue and then delete them

- Enqueue and dequeue multiple elements continuously

Build a Stack with Two Queues

■ **Question 22**   Please design a stack with two queues and implement the methods to push and pop items.

Similar to the analysis for the previous question, we employ some examples to simulate a stack with two queues, denoted as *queue1* and *queue2*.

An element *a* is pushed into the stack at first. Since its two queues are empty, we could choose any one of them to hold the first element. Supposing *a* is enqueued into *queue1*. It continues to enqueue two more elements, *b* and *c*, into *queue1*. *queue1* has three elements {*a*, *b*, *c*}, and *a* is at its head, *c* is at its tail, as shown in Figure 3-16(a).

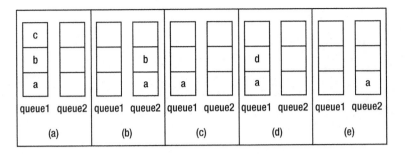

Figure 3-16. *The operations on a stack with two queues. (a) Push the three elements* a, b *and* c *one by one. (b) Pop the element* c. *(c) Pop the element* b *from the top. (d) Push another element* d. *(e) Pop the element* d.

Let us pop an element from the stack. The last element *c* should be popped according to the "Last In, First Out" rule. Only an element at the head of a queue can be deleted, but *c* is at the tail of *queue1*, so it can't be dequeued directly. The two elements *a* and *b* are deleted from queue1 one by one and inserted into *queue2*. Because elements before *c* have been dequeued from *queue1* and *c* is at the head, it can be dequeued now. The status of the stack after *c* is popped is shown in Figure 3-16(b). Similarly, the status of the stack after *b* is popped is shown in Figure 3-16(c).

How about pushing the element *d* into the stack? The item *d* is at the tail of *queue1* after it is enqueued (Figure 3-16(d)). The item *d* is inserted into *queue1* because it is not empty. We should keep one queue empty to accommodate elements of the other queue during popping operations.

If we are going to pop another element, the last pushed element *d* will be popped. Since *d* is not at the head of *queue1*, elements before it have to be dequeued and then enqueued into *queue2*. When *d* is at the head of *queue1*, it is deleted, as shown in Figure 3-16(e).

After we have clear ideas about how to handle pushing and popping operations in a stack with two queues, we can implement such a data structure. The sample code in C# is shown in Listing 3-29.

Listing 3-29. *C# Code to Implement a Stack with Two Queues*

```
public class StackWithTwoQueues<T> {
    public void Push(T item) {
        if (queue2.Count != 0)
            queue2.Enqueue(item);
        else
            queue1.Enqueue(item);
    }

    public T Pop() {
        if (queue1.Count == 0 && queue2.Count == 0)
            throw new InvalidOperationException("Stack is Empty");

        Queue<T> emptyQueue = queue1;
        Queue<T> nonemptyQueue = queue2;
        if (queue1.Count > 0) {
            emptyQueue = queue2;
            nonemptyQueue = queue1;
        }
```

73

```
        while (nonemptyQueue.Count > 1)
            emptyQueue.Enqueue(nonemptyQueue.Dequeue());

        return nonemptyQueue.Dequeue();
    }

    private Queue<T> queue1 = new Queue<T>();
    private Queue<T> queue2 = new Queue<T>();
}
```

Source Code:

    022_StackWithTwoQueues.cs

Test Cases:

- Insert elements into an empty stack and then delete them

- Insert elements into a non-empty stack and then delete them

- Push and pop multiple elements continuously

Summary

This chapter discusses many coding interview questions about data structures, which are always the focus of technical interviews. It covers common data structures, such as arrays, strings, linked lists, trees, stacks, and queues. It is necessary for candidates to master these structures.

Arrays and strings are two fundamental data structures that store numbers and characters in continuous memory. Many interview questions about arrays are related to search and sort algorithms. Linked lists and trees may be the most frequently discussed data structures during interviews. Candidates should pay much attention to robustness since there are many pointer operations on lists and trees. Stacks are related to recursion, and queues are related to bread-first-search in graphs. Stacks and queues can help us solve many algorithm problems if we have a deep understanding of them.

CHAPTER 4

■ ■ ■

Algorithms

In addition to data structures, algorithms are also quite common topics in interviews. There are many interview questions about search and sort algorithms. Backtracking, dynamic programming, and greedy algorithms are useful tools to solve many problems posed in coding interviews. Additionally, bit operations can be viewed as special algorithms to manipulate binary integers. All of these algorithms will be discussed in this chapter.

Recursion and Iteration

Repeated operations are handled either by recursion or iteration with loops. Recursion is a function (method) that invokes itself, directly or indirectly. One of the fundamental structures of programming is loops, which are built-in structures of most languages. For example, there are two strategies to calculate $1+2+\ldots+n$. The first strategy is a utilization of recursion, as shown in Listing 4-1.

Listing 4-1. Recursive C Code to Calculate 1+2+...+n

```
int AddFrom1ToN_Recursive(int n) {
    return n <= 0 ? 0 : n + AddFrom1ToN_Recursive(n - 1);
}
```

The second strategy is based on iteration, as shown in Listing 4-2.

Listing 4-2. Iterative C Code to Calculate 1+2+...+n

```
int AddFrom1ToN_Iterative(int n) {
  int i;
  int result = 0;
    for(i = 1; i <= n; ++ i)
        result += i;

    return result;
}
```

Usually, the code with recursion is more concise than the code with iteration. There is only one statement inside the recursive function, and there are more inside the iterative one. Additionally, loops, especially complex ones that involve nesting, are difficult to read and understand. Recursion may be clearer and simpler to divide a complex problem into manageable pieces. For instance, recursive implementations of pre-order, in-order, and post-order traversal algorithms on binary trees are much simpler than iterative implementations.

■ **Tip**   In most cases, recursive solutions are more concise as well as easier to implement than iterative solutions. Candidates may prefer to use recursion during interviews if it is not explicitly required to utilize iteration.

Recursion has some disadvantages even though it looks more concise and simpler than iteration. It is recursion when a function invokes itself, and function invokes consume time and space: it has to allocate memory on the stack for arguments, return address, and local variables. It also costs time to push and pop data on the stack. Therefore, the recursive solution to calculate 1+2+...+n is not as efficient as the iterative one.

Recursion has more negative impacts on performance if there are duplicated calculations. Recursion is essentially a technique to divide a problem into two or more subproblems. There are duplicated calculations if there are overlaps among subproblems. More details on the performance issue in recursion are discussed in the following subsection on the Fibonacci Sequence.

A more serious problem with recursion other than inefficiency is that it causes errors due to call stack overflows. As mentioned earlier, it consumes some memory on the stack for each recursive call, so it may use up all memory on the stack if recursive levels are very deep, and cause call stack overflow. For instance, when the input *n* to calculate 1+2+...+n is a relatively small number, such as 10, both recursive and iterative solution can get the correct result 55. However, if the input is 5000, the recursive solution crashes, but the iterative solution still gets the correct result 12502500. Therefore, iteration is more robust for large input data.

Fibonacci Sequence

■ **Question 23**   Given a number *n*, please find the nth element in the Fibonacci Sequence, which is defined as the following equation:

$$f(n) = \begin{cases} 0 & n = 0 \\ 1 & n = 1 \\ f(n-1) + f(n-2) & n > 1 \end{cases}$$

Recursive and Inefficient

In many textbooks, the Fibonacci Sequence is taken as an example to illustrate recursive functions, so many candidates are quite familiar with the recursive solution and can write code quickly, as shown in Listing 4-3.

Listing 4-3. *Recursive C Code for Fibonacci Sequence*

```
long long Fibonacci(unsigned int n) {
    if(n <= 0)
        return 0;

    if(n == 1)
        return 1;

    return Fibonacci(n - 1) + Fibonacci(n - 2);
}
```

However, recursion is not the best solution for this problem since it has serious performance issues. Let's take $f(10)$ as an example to analyze the recursive process. The element $f(10)$ is calculated based on $f(9)$ and $f(8)$. Similarly, $f(9)$ is based on $f(8)$ and $f(7)$, and so on. The dependency can be visualized as a tree (Figure 4-1).

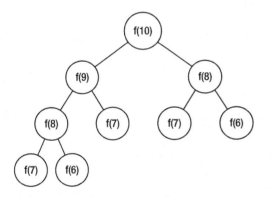

Figure 4-1. *The recursive process to calculate the 10th element in the Fibonacci Sequence*

It is noticeable that there are many duplicated nodes in the tree. The number of duplication increases dramatically when n increases. It can be proven that its time complexity grows exponentially with n.

Iterative Solution with O(*n*) Time Complexity

It is not difficult to improve this performance. Since the slowness is caused by duplicated calculations, let's try to void the duplications. A solution is to cache the calculated elements. Before an element is calculated, we first check whether it is cached. It is not calculated again if an element is already in the cache.

A simpler solution is to calculate using a bottom-up process. The elements $f(0)$ and $f(1)$ are already known, and $f(2)$ can be calculated based on them. Similarly, $f(3)$ can be calculated based on $f(2)$ and $f(1)$, and so on. It iterates until $f(n)$ is calculated. The code for this iterative solution is shown in Listing 4-4.

Listing 4-4. *Iterative C Code for Fibonacci Sequence*

```
long long Fibonacci_Solution2(unsigned int n) {
    int result[2] = {0, 1};
    long long  fibNMinusOne = 1;
    long long  fibNMinusTwo = 0;
    long long  fibN = 0;
    unsigned int i;

    if(n < 2)
        return result[n];

    for(i = 2; i <= n; ++ i) {
        fibN = fibNMinusOne + fibNMinusTwo;

        fibNMinusTwo = fibNMinusOne;
        fibNMinusOne = fibN;
    }

    return fibN;
}
```

Obviously, the time complexity for this iterative solution is O(*n*).

More Efficient in O(log*n*) Time

Usually, the solution costing O(*n*) time is the expected solution. However, interviewers may require a solution with O(log*n*) time complexity if they have higher expectation on performance.

There is an equation for the Fibonacci Sequence:

$$\begin{bmatrix} f(n) & f(n-1) \\ f(n-1) & f(n-2) \end{bmatrix} = \begin{bmatrix} 1 & 1 \\ 1 & 0 \end{bmatrix}^{n-1}$$

If you are interested, you can prove it with mathematical induction.

With the equation above, it finds f(*n*) if it finds $\begin{bmatrix} 1 & 1 \\ 1 & 0 \end{bmatrix}^{n-1}$. Additionally, an element (including a number, a matrix, and so on) to the power of *n* can be calculated recursively based on the following equation:

$$a^n = \begin{cases} a^{n/2} \cdot a^{n/2} & n \text{ is even} \\ a^{(n-1)/2} \cdot a^{(n-1)/2} \cdot a & n \text{ is odd} \end{cases}$$

It can get a^n in O(log*n*) time with the equation above, so the nth element in the Fibonacci Sequence can also be calculated in O(log*n*) time. The corresponding implementation is shown in Listing 4-5.

Listing 4-5. *C Code to Calculate Fibonacci Sequence in O(logn) Time*

```
struct Matrix2By2 {
    long long m_00;
    long long m_01;
```

```
        long long m_10;
        long long m_11;
};

struct Matrix2By2 MatrixMultiply(const struct Matrix2By2* matrix1, const struct Matrix2By2*
matrix2) {
        struct Matrix2By2 result;
        result.m_00 = matrix1->m_00 * matrix2->m_00 + matrix1->m_01 * matrix2->m_10;
        result.m_01 = matrix1->m_00 * matrix2->m_01 + matrix1->m_01 * matrix2->m_11;
        result.m_10 = matrix1->m_10 * matrix2->m_00 + matrix1->m_11 * matrix2->m_10;
        result.m_11 = matrix1->m_10 * matrix2->m_01 + matrix1->m_11 * matrix2->m_11;

        return result;
}

struct Matrix2By2 MatrixPower(unsigned int n) {
        struct Matrix2By2 result;
        struct Matrix2By2 unit = {1, 1, 1, 0};

        assert(n > 0);
        if(n == 1) {
                result = unit;
        }
        else if(n % 2 == 0) {
                result = MatrixPower(n / 2);
                result = MatrixMultiply(&result, &result);
        }
        else if(n % 2 == 1) {
                result = MatrixPower((n - 1) / 2);
                result = MatrixMultiply(&result, &result);
                result = MatrixMultiply(&result, &unit);
        }

        return result;
}

long long Fibonacci_Solution3(unsigned int n) {
        struct Matrix2By2 PowerNMinus2;
        int result[2] = {0, 1};

        if(n < 2)
                return result[n];

        PowerNMinus2 = MatrixPower(n - 1);
        return PowerNMinus2.m_00;
}
```

Source Code:

```
    023_Fibonacci.c
```

Test Cases:

- Normal case: 3, 5, 10

- Boundary case: 0, 1, 2

- Big numbers for performance tests, such as 40, 50, 100

■ **Question 24**   There is a stair with n levels. A frog can jump up one level or two levels at one time on the stair. How many ways are there for the frog to jump from the bottom of the stairs to the top?

For example, there are three choices for the frog to jump up a stair with three levels: (1) it jumps in three steps, one level for each jump; (2) it jumps in two steps, one level for the first jump and two levels for the second jump; or (3) it jumps with two steps, two levels for the first step and one level for the last jump.

Let's define a function $f(n)$ for the number of choices available on a stair with n levels. There are two choices for the frog at the first step. One choice is to jump only one level, and it has $f(n\text{-}1)$ choices for the remaining $n\text{-}1$ levels. The other one is to jump two levels at the first step, and it has $f(n\text{-}2)$ choices for the remaining $n\text{-}2$ levels. Therefore, the total number of choices on a stair with n levels is $f(n) = f(n\text{-}1) + f(n\text{-}2)$, which is the Fibonacci Sequence.

■ **Question 25**   There is a stair with n levels. A frog can jump up 1, 2, …, $n\text{-}1$, n levels at each step on the stair. How many approaches are there for this frog to jump from the bottom of the stair to the top?

For example, there are four approaches for the frog to jump on a stair with three levels: (1) it jumps with three steps, one level for each step; (2) it jumps with two steps, one level for the first step and two levels for the second step; (3) it jumps with two steps, two levels for the first step and one level for the second step; or (4) it jumps in only one step from the bottom to the top directly.

Similar to Question 24, a function $f(n)$ can be defined for the number of choices on a stair with n levels. Inspired by the solution of the previous problem, it is easy to get $f(n) = f(n\text{-}1)+f(n\text{-}2)+…+f(1)+1$. Since $f(n\text{-}1)=f(n\text{-}2)+…+f(1)+1$, $f(n)=2f(n\text{-}1)$. It is not difficult to get $f(n) = 2^{n\text{-}1}$.

What is the most efficient method to get $f(n)$? It costs $O(n)$ time if it is calculated sequentially with a loop, and it costs $O(\log n)$ time with recursion, as shown in the third solution for the Fibonacci Sequence.

Actually, there is an even faster solution available. Because $f(n)$ is 2 to the power of $n\text{-}1$, there is only one bit of 1 in the binary representation of the number. Therefore, $f(n)$ can be calculated with a left-shift operator, 1 << (n - 1), in $O(1)$ time.

■ **Question 26**   Rectangles with size 2×1 are utilized to cover other rectangles, horizontally or vertically. How many approaches are available to cover a 2×8 rectangle with eight 2×1 rectangles (Figure 4-2)?

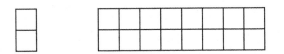

Figure 4-2. A 2×1 rectangle and a 2×8 rectangle

The number of choices to cover a 2×8 rectangle is denoted as $f(8)$. There are two choices to cover with the first 2×1 rectangle. One is to lay it vertically to the left side of the 2×8 rectangle, and the number of choices to cover the remaining 2×7 rectangle is $f(7)$. The other choice is to lay the first 2×1 at the top left corner horizontally. It has to lay another 2×1 rectangle at the lower left corner. The number of choices to cover the remaining 2×6 rectangle is $f(6)$.

We can see that $f(8)=f(7)+f(6)$, so it is also a Fibonacci Sequence.

Search and Sort

The most common search algorithms are sequential search and binary search. If an input array is not sorted, or input elements are accommodated by dynamic containers such as lists, it has to be searched sequentially. If the input is a sorted array, usually the binary search algorithm is a good choice. For example, the problems "Minimum of a Rotated Array" (Question 27), "Turning Number in a Sorted Array" (Question 28), and the "Time of Occurrences in a Sorted Array" (Question 83) can all be solved by the binary search algorithm.

■ **Tip**   If it is required to search or count a number in a sorted array (even the array is only partially sorted), we may try with the binary search algorithm.

If it is allowed to use auxiliary memory, a hash table might facilitate searching, with which a value can be located in O(1) time with a key. Some common interview questions, such as "First Character Appearing Once in a String" (Question 76) and "Delete Duplication in a String" (Question 79), are all solved with hash tables.

There are many sort algorithms available, such as insert sort, bubble sort, merge sort, and quicksort. Candidates should be familiar with each one's pros and cons in terms of space consumption, time efficiency on average, and in worst cases.

Many interviewers like to ask candidates to implement their own quicksort. The key step of the quicksort algorithm is to partition an array into two parts. It selects a pivot number and moves numbers less than the pivot to the left side, and it moves numbers greater than the pivot to the right side. The partition method can be implemented in Java, as shown in Listing 4-6.

Listing 4-6. Java Code to Partition an Array

```java
int partition(int[] numbers, int start, int end) {
    Random random = new Random();
    int pivot = random.nextInt(end - start + 1) + start;
    swap(numbers, pivot, end);

    int small = start - 1;
    for(int i = start; i <= end; ++i) {
        if(numbers[i] < numbers[end]) {
            ++small;
            if(i != small)
                swap(numbers, small, i);
        }
    }

    ++small;
    if(small != end)
        swap(numbers, small, end);

    return small;
}
```

The method `swap` is to swap two elements in an array. After the array is partitioned into two parts, they are sorted recursively, as shown in Listing 4-7.

Listing 4-7. Java Code for Quicksort

```java
void quicksort(int[] numbers, int start, int end) {
    if(start >= end)
        return;

    int index = partition(numbers, start, end);
    quicksort(numbers, start, index);
    quicksort(numbers, index + 1, end);
}
```

The method `quicksort` sorts an array with n elements with the parameter `start` as 0 and `end` as n-1.

Quicksort might be the most efficient sort algorithm in general, but it is not the best one for all cases. The time complexity is $O(n^2)$ in the worst cases, when the pivot is the least or greatest number in each round of partition. In order to avoid the worst cases, we randomize the choice of the pivot number in the method `partition`.

The method `partition` is useful not only to sort, but also to find the arbitrary k^{th} number from an array. The interview question "Majorities in Arrays" (Question 29) and "Minimal k Numbers" (Question 70) are both solved with the `partition` method.

Different sort algorithms work for different scenarios. If it is required to implement an algorithm to sort, it is critical to know the details about the input data as well as limitations about time and space. For example, the following is a piece of dialog during an interview:

Interviewer: How do you implement a sort algorithm in $O(n)$ time?

Candidate: What are the elements to be sorted, and how many?

Interviewer:	I am going to sort ages of all employees in our company. The total number is tens of thousands.
Candidate:	Does it mean all the elements are in some narrow range?
Interviewer:	Yes.
Candidate:	Is it allowed to use auxiliary memory?
Interviewer:	It depends on how much memory is used. You can only utilize space less than O(n).

It is encouraged for candidates to ask questions of their interviewers. With questions and answers, we know the numbers to be sorted are in a narrow range and an auxiliary space less than O(n) can be employed. Therefore, this problem can be solved with the count sort algorithm, which is implemented in Listing 4-8.

Listing 4-8. *Java Code of Count Sort*

```java
void countSort(int ages[]) {
    int oldestAge = 99;
    int timesOfAge[] = new int[oldestAge+1];
    for(int i = 0; i <= oldestAge; ++ i)
        timesOfAge[i] = 0;

    for(int i = 0; i < ages.length; ++ i) {
        int age = ages[i];
        if(age < 0 || age > oldestAge)
            throw new IllegalArgumentException("Out of range.");
        ++ timesOfAge[age];
    }

    int index = 0;
    for(int i = 0; i <= oldestAge; ++ i) {
        for(int j = 0; j < timesOfAge[i]; ++ j) {
            ages[index] = i;
            ++ index;
        }
    }
}
```

The method countSort assumes all ages are in the range between 0 and 99. It counts the occurrence of each age in the array. If an age occurs m times in the array, it writes the age for m time continuously in the array.

It reads and writes the input array once, so the overall time complexity is O(n) to sort an array with size n. No matter how large n is, it only allocates an auxiliary array timesOfAge with size 100, so the space complexity is O(1).

All the sort algorithms above are about arrays. Lists are sorted with other algorithms, which are discussed in the section *Sort Lists*.

Binary Search in Partially Sorted Arrays

■ **Question 27**   When some elements at the beginning of an array are moved to the end, it becomes a rotation of the original array. Please implement a function to get the minimum number in a rotation of an increasingly sorted array. For example, the array {3, 4, 5, 1, 2} is a rotation of array {1, 2, 3, 4, 5}, of which the minimum is 1.

Binary search is suitable for sorted arrays. Let's try to utilize it on a rotation of a sorted array. It is noticeable that a rotation of a sorted array can be partitioned into two sorted sub-arrays, where numbers in the first sub-array are greater than numbers in the second one. Additionally, the minimum is on the boundary of two sub-arrays.

Two pointers P_1 and P_2 are utilized. P_1 references the first element in the array, and P_2 references the last element. According to the rotation rule, the first element should be greater than or equal to the last one.

The algorithm always compares the number in the middle with the numbers pointed to by P_1 and P_2 during binary search. If the middle number is in the first increasingly sorted sub-array, it is greater than or equal to the number pointed to by P_1. In such cases, the minimal number is behind the middle number in the array. Therefore, it moves P_1 to the middle, which is also in the first sub-array. It continues to search numbers between P_1 and P_2 recursively.

If the middle number is in the second sub-array, it is less than or equal to the number pointed to by P_2. The minimal number is before the middle number in the array in such cases, so it moves P_2 to the middle. It can continue to search recursively too because P_1 still points to a number in the first sub-array, and P_2 points to a number in the second sub-array.

No matter if it moves P_1 or P_2 for the next round of search, half of the array is excluded. It stops searching when P_1 points to the last number of the first sub-array and P_2 points to the first number of the second sub-array, which is also the minimum of the array.

Let's take the sample array {3, 4, 5, 1, 2} as an example. P_1 is initialized pointing to the first element (with index 0), and P_2 points to the last element (with index 4), as shown in Figure 4-3(a). The middle element 5 (with index 2) is greater than the number pointed by P_1, so it is in the first increasingly sorted sub-array. Therefore, P_1 is moved to the middle of the array, as shown in Figure 4-3(b).

The middle element 1 (with index 3) at this time is less than the number pointed by P_2, so it is in the second sub-array. It moves P_2 to the middle and continues the next round of search (Figure 4-3(c)).

Now the distance between two pointers is 1. It means that P_1 already points to the last element in the first sub-array, and P_2 points to the first element in the second sub-array. Therefore, the number pointed to by P_2 is the minimum in the array.

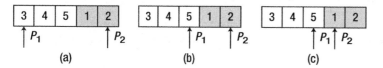

Figure 4-3. *Search the minimal element in an array {3, 4, 5, 1, 2}. Elements in the gray background are in the second increasingly sorted sub-array. (a) P_1 points to the first element, and P_2 points to the last element. Since the middle number 5 is greater than the number pointed to by P_1, it moves P_1 to the middle number for the next round of search. (b) The middle number 1 is less than the number pointed to by P_2, so it moves*

P_2 to the middle number for the next round of search. (c) Since P_1 and P_2 point to two adjacent numbers, the number pointed to by P_2 is the minimum.

In the analysis above, the middle element is in the first sub-array if it is greater than the element pointed to by P_1, and it is in the second sub-array if it is less than the element pointed to by P_2. However, the middle element and elements pointed to by P_1 and P_2 may be equal when there are duplicated elements in the array. Does binary search work for such cases?

Let's look at other examples. Two arrays {1, 0, 1, 1, 1} and {1, 1, 1, 0, 1} are both rotations of an increasingly sorted array {0, 1, 1, 1, 1}, which are visualized in Figure 4-4.

In these two cases of Figure 4-4, the elements pointed to by P_1 and P_2, as well as the middle element, are all 1. The middle element with index 2 is in the second sub-array in Figure 4-4(a), while the middle element is in the first sub-array in Figure 4-4(b).

Therefore, the algorithm cannot determine if the middle element belongs to the first or second sub-array when the middle element and the two numbers pointed to by P_1 and P_2 are equal, and it cannot move pointers to narrow the search range. It has to search sequentially in such a scenario.

Figure 4-4. *Two rotations of an increasingly sorted array {0, 1, 1, 1, 1}: {1, 0, 1, 1, 1} and {1, 1, 1, 0, 1}. Elements with gray background are in the second increasingly sorted sub-array. In both cases, the first, last, and middle numbers are equal. (a) The middle element is in the second sub-array. (b) The middle element is in the first sub-array.*

The sample code to get the minimum from a rotation of a sorted array is shown in Listing 4-9.

Listing 4-9. *Java Code to Get the Minimum from a Rotation of a Sorted Array*

```java
int getMin(int numbers[]) {
    int index1 = 0;
    int index2 = numbers.length - 1;
    int indexMid = index1;

    while(numbers[index1] >= numbers[index2]) {
        if(index2 - index1 == 1) {
            indexMid = index2;
            break;
        }

        indexMid = (index1 + index2) / 2;

        // if numbers with indexes index1, index2, indexMid
        // are equal, search sequentially
        if(numbers[index1] == numbers[index2]
                && numbers[indexMid] == numbers[index1])
            return getMinSequentially(numbers, index1, index2);

        if(numbers[indexMid] >= numbers[index1])
```

```
            index1 = indexMid;
        else if(numbers[indexMid] <= numbers[index2])
            index2 = indexMid;

    }

    return numbers[indexMid];
}

int getMinSequentially(int numbers[], int index1, int index2) {
    int result = numbers[index1];
    for(int i = index1 + 1; i <= index2; ++i) {
        if(result > numbers[i])
            result = numbers[i];
    }

    return result;
}
```

Source Code:

> 027_ArrayRotation.java

Test Cases:

- Functional cases: rotations of an increasingly sorted array, with/without duplicated numbers

- Boundary cases: An increasingly sorted array (rotating 0 number in the array), an array with only one number

---

▨ **Question 28**   A turning number is the maximum number in a unimodal array that increases and then decreases. Please write a function (or a method) that finds the index of the turning number in a unimodal array. For example, the turning number in the array {1, 2, 3, 4, 5, 10, 9, 8, 7, 6} is 10, so its index 5 is the expected output.

As we know, the binary search algorithm is suitable for search of a number in a sorted array. Since the input array for this problem is partially sorted, we may also try with binary search.

Let's try to get the middle number in an array. The middle number of the array {1, 2, 3, 4, 5, 10, 9, 8, 7, 6} is 5. It is greater than its previous number 4 and less than its next number 10, so it is in the increasing sub-array. Therefore, numbers before 5 can be discarded in the next round of the search.

The remaining numbers for the next round of search are {5, 10, 9, 8, 7, 6}, and the number 9 is in the middle of them. Since 9 is less than its previous number 10 and greater than its next number 8, it is in the decreasing sub-array. Therefore, numbers after 9 can be discarded in the next round of search.

The remaining numbers for the next round of search are {5, 10, 9}, and the number 10 is in the middle. Notice that the number 10 is greater than the previous number 5 and greater than the next number 9, so it is the maximal number. That is to say, the number 10 is the turning number in the input array.

We can see the process above is actually a classic binary search. Therefore, we can implement the required functionality based on the binary search algorithm, as shown in Listing 4-10.

Listing 4-10. Java Code for Turning Number in Array

```java
int getTurningIndex(int numbers[]) {
    if(numbers.length <= 2)
        return -1;

    int left = 0;
    int right = numbers.length - 1;
    while(right > left + 1) {
        int middle = (left + right) / 2;
        if(middle == 0 || middle == numbers.length - 1)
            return -1;

        if(numbers[middle] > numbers[middle - 1]
            && numbers[middle] > numbers[middle + 1])
            return middle;
        else if(numbers[middle] > numbers[middle - 1]
            && numbers[middle] < numbers[middle + 1])
            left = middle;
        else
            right = middle;
    }

    return -1;
}
```

Source Code:

028_TurningNumber.java

Test Cases:

- Functional cases: Unimodal arrays with turning numbers

- Boundary cases: A unimodal array with only three numbers

Majorities in Arrays

■ **Question 29**   How do you find the majority element in an array when it exists? The majority is an element that occurs for more than half of the size of the array.

For example, the number 2 in the array {1, 2, 3, 2, 2, 2, 5, 4, 2} is the majority element because it appears five times and the size of the array is 9.

It is easy to get the majority element if the array is sorted because it is not difficult to count the occurrence of each number in a sorted array. It takes O($n$log$n$) time to sort an array with n elements as well as O(n) time to count, so the time efficiency of this intuitive solution is O($n$log$n$). Let's explore more efficient solutions.

Based on the Partition Method

The intuitive solution above does not utilize the characteristic of a majority element, which occurs for more than half of the size of an array. If there is a majority element in an array, the majority should occur in the middle of the array when it is sorted. That is to say, the majority of an array is also the median of the array, which is the $(n/2)^{th}$ number in an array with n elements. There is an algorithm available to get the arbitrary k^{th} ($0 \leq k < n$) number in an array in O(n) time.

This algorithm is closely related to the quicksort algorithm, where a pivot is selected to partition an array into two parts. All numbers less than the pivot are located to the left side, and others are located to the right side. If the index of the pivot is $n/2$, it is done because the median is found. If the index is greater than $n/2$, the median should be in the left side of the pivot, so it continues to partition in the left side. Similarly, it continues to partition in the right side if the index is less than $n/2$. It is a typical recursive process, which might be implemented as shown in Listing 4-11.

Listing 4-11. Java Code to Get the Majority (Version 1)

```java
int getMajority_1(int[] numbers) {
    int length = numbers.length;
    int middle = length >> 1;
    int start = 0;
    int end = length - 1;

    int index = partition(numbers, start, end);
    while(index != middle) {
        if(index > middle) {
            end = index - 1;
            index = partition(numbers, start, end);
        }
        else {
            start = index + 1;
            index = partition(numbers, start, end);
        }
    }

    int result = numbers[middle];
    if(!checkMajorityExistence(numbers, result))
        throw new IllegalArgumentException("No majority exisits.");

    return result;
}
```

The method `partition` was discussed before for quicksort.

The majority is the element that occurs for more than half of the size of the array. How about the scenario where the element occurring most frequently does not meet the bar? That is why a method checkMajorityExistence is defined. It is important to handle invalid inputs during interviews, as shown in Listing 4-12.

Listing 4-12. *Java Code to Check Existence of Majority*

```java
boolean checkMajorityExistence(int[] numbers, int number) {
    int times = 0;
    for(int i = 0; i < numbers.length; ++i) {
        if(numbers[i] == number)
            times++;
    }

    return (times * 2 > numbers.length);
}
```

Based on the Definition of Majority

According to the definition of the majority, the occurrence of a majority element is greater than the total occurrences of all other elements. Therefore, this problem can be solved with a new strategy. It scans the array from the beginning to the end, and saves and updates an element of the array as well as a number for occurrences. When an element is visited, the occurrence number is incremented if the currently visited element is the same as the saved one. Otherwise, it decreases the occurrence number when the visited element is different from the saved one. When the occurrence number becomes 0, it saves the currently visited element and sets the occurrence number as 1. The last element that sets the occurrence number to 1 is the majority element.

This solution might be implemented as the code in Listing 4-13, where the method checkMajorityExistence is the same as in the preceding solution.

Listing 4-13. *Java Code to Get the Majority (Version 2)*

```java
int getMajority_2(int[] numbers) {
    int result = numbers[0];
    int times = 1;
    for(int i = 1; i < numbers.length; ++i) {
        if(times == 0) {
            result = numbers[i];
            times = 1;
        }
        else if(numbers[i] == result)
            times++;
        else
            times--;
    }

    if(!checkMajorityExistence(numbers, result))
        throw new IllegalArgumentException("No majority exisits.");

    return result;
}
```

Comparison

The time efficiencies for these two solutions are both O(n). They differ from each other in whether you are allowed to alter the array. It is noticeable that elements in the input array are reordered in the first solution, so it modifies the input array. Is it allowed to modify the input? It depends on the requirement. Therefore, it is necessary to ask the interviewer for clarification. If it is disallowed to modify, we have to take the second solution or make a copy of the input array and swap numbers in the copy while applying the first solution.

Source Code:

    029_MajorityElement.java

Test Cases:

- Functional cases: Arrays with/without majority elements

- Boundary cases: An array with only one element

Backtracking

Backtracking is a refinement of the brute-force approach, which systematically searches for a solution to a problem among all available options. It is suitable for scenarios where there is a set of options available at each step, and we must choose one from these. After a choice is made, there is a new set of options for the next step. This procedure is repeated over and over until we reach a final state.

Conceptually, all options compose a tree structure. Leaves in the tree correspond to solution states, some of which might be the final acceptable state, but others might not. The backtracking algorithm traverses this tree recursively, from the root down and in depth-first order.

When it reaches a leaf that corresponds to a non-acceptable state, it backtracks to continue the search for another leaf by revoking the most recent choice and tries out the next option. If it runs out of options, it revokes again and tries another choice at that node. If it ends up at the root with no options left, there are no acceptable states to be found.

As shown in Figure 4-5, there are two options available at each step. The backtracking algorithm starts at the root node A, and it selects the node B from the two options. It chooses D for the second step, and the state is not acceptable. Therefore, it backtracks to node B and then selects the next option and advances to node E. It reaches a non-acceptable state again, and it has to return back to node B again. Since it has tried all options on node B, it returns back to the parent node A. It selects the next option of node A, which is node C. It then selects node F. It stops traversal since it reaches an acceptable state.

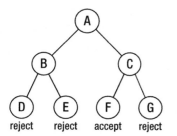

Figure 4-5. *Tree structure to visualize options for certain problems. There are two options available at each step.*

Usually the backtracking algorithm is implemented with recursion. When it reaches a node, it tries all options for the next step recursively if the state is not rejected.

String Path in Matrix

■ **Question 30**   How do you implement a function to check whether there is a path for a string in a matrix of characters? It moves to left, right, up, and down in a matrix, and a cell for a step. The path can start from any cell in a matrix. If a cell is occupied by a character of a string on the path, it cannot be occupied by another character again.

For example, the matrix below with three rows and four columns has a path for the string "bcced" (as highlighted in the matrix). It does not have a path for the string "abcb", because the first "b" in the string occupies the "b" cell in the matrix, and the second "b" in the string cannot enter the same cell again.

a *b c* e

s f *c* s

a *d e* e

It is a typical problem that can be solved by the backtracking algorithm. First, we choose any entry in the matrix to start a path. Suppose the character value in an entry is *ch* and the entry is for the ith node on the path. If the ith character in the string is also *ch*, it tries all options available at that entry for the next step. All entries except those on boundaries have four options. It continues until all characters in the string have been found on a path.

The path of a string can be defined as a stack because of the recursive nature of the backtracking algorithm. When the algorithm enters a rejecting state where the character on the path is not the same as the corresponding character in the string, it returns back to the preceding state and pops a character off the stack.

Because a path can enter an entry in the matrix only once at most, a set of Boolean flags are defined to mark whether an entry has been occupied by a previous step on the path.

The solution can be implemented with recursion, as depicted in Listing 4-14.

Listing 4-14. C++ Code for String Paths

```
bool hasPath(char* matrix, int rows, int cols, char* str) {
    if(matrix == NULL || rows < 1 || cols < 1 || str == NULL)
        return false;

    bool *visited = new bool[rows * cols];
    memset(visited, 0, rows * cols);

    int pathLength = 0;
    for(int row = 0; row < rows; ++row) {
        for(int col = 0; col < cols; ++col) {
            if(hasPathCore(matrix, rows, cols, row, col, str, pathLength, visited))
```

```
                        return true;
            }
        }

        delete[] visited;

        return false;
}
bool hasPathCore(char* matrix, int rows, int cols, int row, int col, char* str, int&
pathLength, bool* visited) {
        if(str[pathLength] == '\0')
            return true;

        bool hasPath = false;
        if(row >= 0 && row < rows && col >= 0 && col < cols
                && matrix[row * cols + col] == str[pathLength]
                && !visited[row * cols + col]) {
            ++pathLength;
            visited[row * cols + col] = true;

            hasPath = hasPathCore(matrix, rows, cols, row, col - 1, str, pathLength, visited)
                    || hasPathCore(matrix, rows, cols, row - 1, col, str, pathLength, visited)
                    || hasPathCore(matrix, rows, cols, row, col + 1, str, pathLength, visited)
                    || hasPathCore(matrix, rows, cols, row + 1, col, str, pathLength, visited);

            if(!hasPath) {
                --pathLength;
                visited[row * cols + col] = false;
            }
        }

        return hasPath;
}
```

When an entry with index (row, col) is not a rejecting state, the function hasPathCore has a try at the four neighbors with index (row, col - 1), (row - 1, col), (row, col + 1), and (row + 1, col). It continues until it reaches the final acceptable state when the statement str[length] == '\0' gets true, which indicates that all characters in the string have been matched in a path.

Source Code:

030_StringPath.cpp

Test Cases:

- Functional cases: A 2-D matrix has/does not have a path for a string

- Boundary cases: (1) A 2-D matrix has only a row, a column, or even an element. (2) A path for a string occupies all elements in a matrix.

Robot Move

___

■ **Question 31**   A robot starts at cell (0, 0) of a grid with *m* rows and *n* columns. It can move to the left, right, up, and down, and moves one cell for a step. It cannot enter cells where the digit sum of the row index and column index are greater than a given *k*.

For example, when *k* is 18, the robot can reach cell (35, 37) because 3+5+3+7=18. However, it cannot reach cell (35, 38) because 3+5+3+8=19 and that is greater than *k*. How many cells can the robot reach?

___

Similar to the preceding problem, a grid can also be viewed as a 2-D matrix, where all cells except those on boundaries have four neighbors.

The robot starts to move from the cell (0,0). When it reaches a cell (*i,j*), we check whether it is a valid move according to the digits sum of the indexes. If the move is valid, we continue to move to the four neighboring cells (*i,j*-1), (*i*-1,*j*), (*i,j*+1), and (*i*+1,*j*). Therefore, the problem can be solved with the recursive code in Listing 4-15.

Listing 4-15. C++ Code for Moving Robots

```
int movingCount(int threshold, int rows, int cols){
    bool *visited = new bool[rows * cols];
    for(int i = 0; i < rows * cols; ++i)
        visited[i] = false;

    int count = movingCountCore(threshold, rows, cols, 0, 0, visited);

    delete[] visited;

    return count;
}

int movingCountCore(int threshold, int rows, int cols, int row, int col, bool* visited){
    int count = 0;
    if(check(threshold, rows, cols, row, col, visited)) {
        visited[row * cols + col] = true;

        count = 1 + movingCountCore(threshold, rows, cols, row - 1, col, visited)
                + movingCountCore(threshold, rows, cols, row, col - 1, visited)
                + movingCountCore(threshold, rows, cols, row + 1, col, visited)
                + movingCountCore(threshold, rows, cols, row, col + 1, visited);
    }

    return count;
}
```

Similar to the previous problem, a set of Boolean flags is defined in order to avoid duplicated moves.

The function check in Listing 4-16 checks whether a move to the cell (row, col) is valid, and the function getDigitSum finds the sum of all digits of a given number.

Listing 4-16. *C++ Code for Moving Robots*

```
bool check(int threshold, int rows, int cols, int row, int col, bool* visited){
    if(row >=0 && row < rows && col >= 0 && col < cols
        && getDigitSum(row) + getDigitSum(col) <= threshold
        && !visited[row* cols + col])
        return true;

    return false;
}

int getDigitSum(int number){
    int sum = 0;
    while(number > 0){
        sum += number % 10;
        number /= 10;
    }

    return sum;
}
```

Source Code:

> 031_RobotMove.cpp

Test Cases:

- Functional cases: Counting moves on a normal grid

- Boundary cases: Counting moves on a grid with only a row, a column, or even an element

Dynamic Programming and Greedy Algorithms

A popular topic during interviews is dynamic programming, which simplifies a complicated problem by breaking it down into simpler subproblems by means of recursion. If an interview problem has optimal substructure and overlapping subproblems, it might be solved by dynamic programming.

The ingredient optimal substructure means that the solution to a given optimization problem can be obtained by a combination of optimal solutions to its subproblems. Therefore, the first step to utilize dynamic programming is to check whether the problem exhibits such optimal substructures.

For example, the problem to find the minimal number of coins to make change for a value *t* exhibits optimal substructures. If a set of coins that has the minimal number of coins to make change for the value *t* contains a coin v_i, the set of coins excluding v_i should have the minimal number of coins to make change for value $t-v_i$.

The other ingredient, overlapping subproblems, means a recursive algorithm solves subproblems over and over, rather than always generating new subproblems. Dynamic programming algorithms typically take advantage of overlapping subproblems by solving each subproblem once and then storing the solution in a table where it can be retrieved when necessary.

Let's take the problem of making change as an example again, assuming we are going to make change for value 15 with a set of coins with value 1, 3, 9, 10. $f(t)$ is defined as the optimal solution to get the minimum number of coins to make change for the value t. There are four subproblems for the overall problem $f(15)$: $f(14)$, $f(12)$, $f(6)$, and $f(5)$. It is noticeable that $f(11)$ is a subproblem of both $f(14)$ and $f(12)$, and $f(5)$ is a subproblem of both $f(14)$ and $f(6)$, so there are many overlapping subproblems. Solutions of subproblems are stored in a 2-D table to avoid duplicated calculations. More details about the problem to make change are discussed in the section *Minimal Number of Coins for Change*.

A choice is made at each step in dynamic programming, and the choice usually depends on the solutions to subproblems. Consequently, dynamic programming problems are typically solved in a bottom-up manner, progressing from smaller subproblems to larger subproblems.

Greedy algorithms are different from dynamic programming solutions, in which a greedy choice is made that seems best at the moment and then you solve the subproblem arising after the choice is made. Therefore, a greedy strategy usually progresses in a top-down order, making one greedy choice after another and reducing each given problem instance to a smaller one.

For example, in order to minimize the number of key presses on a cell-phone keyboard, we choose the most frequent character at the first step and locate it as the first character on a key, and then choose the next most frequent character and locate it as the first character on another key. If the first locations of all keys are already occupied, a character is located as the second one on a key, and so on. Actually, it is a greedy choice to select the most frequent character of the remaining characters and locate it in a key with the lowest index. More details about this problem are discussed in the section *Minimal Times of Presses on Keyboards*.

Edit Distance

Question 32   Implement a function that finds the edit distance of two input strings. There are three types of edit operations: insertion, deletion, and substitution. Edit distance is the minimal number of edit operations to modify a string from one state to the other.

For example, the edit distance between "Saturday" and "Sunday" is 3 since the following three edit operations are required to modify one into another:

(1) Saturday → Sturday (deletion of 'a')

(2) Sturday → Surday (deletion of 't')

(3) Surday → Sunday (substitution of 'n' for 'r')

There is no way to achieve it with fewer than three operations.

If a function $f(i,j)$ is defined to indicate the edit distance between the substring of the first string ending with the jth character and the substring of the second string ending with the ith character, it is obvious that $f(i,0)=i$ because when we delete i characters from the substring of the first string ending with the ith character, we get an empty string. (It is also the substring of the second string ending with the 0th character.) Similarly, $f(0,j)=j$.

Let's analyze the cases when both i and j are greater than 0. If the ith character of the second string is the same as the jth character of the first string, no edit operations are necessary. Therefore, $f(i,j) = f(i-1,j-1)$ in such a case.

When the jth character of the first string is different from the ith character of the second string, there are three options available:

- Insert the ith character of the second string into the first string. In this case, $f(i,j)=f(i-1,j)+1$.

- Delete the jth character of the first string. In this case, $f(i,j)=f(i,j-1)+1$.

- Replace the jth character of the first string with the ith character of the second string. In this case, $f(i,j)=f(i-1,j-1)+1$.

What is the final value for $f(i,j)$? It should be the minimum value of the three cases. A formal equation can be defined for this problem:

$$f(i,j) = \begin{cases} i & j = 0 \\ j & i = 0 \\ f(i-1,j-1) & string1[j] = string2[i] \\ min(f(i-1,j), f(i,j-1), f(i-1,j-1))+1 & string1[j] \neq string2[i] \end{cases}$$

If we draw a table to show the edit distance values $f(i,j)$ between "Saturday" and "Sunday," it looks like Table 4-1. The edit distance of two strings is at the right-bottom corner of the table for edit distance values.

Table 4-1. *Edit Distance Value* f(i,j) *between "Saturday" and "Sunday"*

		S	a	t	u	r	d	a	y
	0	1	2	3	4	5	6	7	8
S	1	0	1	2	3	4	5	6	7
u	2	1	1	2	2	3	4	5	6
n	3	2	2	2	3	3	4	5	6
d	4	3	3	3	3	4	3	4	5
a	5	4	3	4	4	4	4	3	4
y	6	5	4	4	5	5	5	4	3

A table of edit distance values can be implemented as a 2-D array to simulate Table 4-1, which is the variable `distances` in the code found in Listing 4-17.

Listing 4-17. *C# Code for Moving Robots*

```csharp
int GetEditDistance(String str1, String str2) {
    int len1 = str1.Length;;
    int len2 = str2.Length;
```

```
    int[,] distances = new int[len2 + 1, len1 + 1];

    int editDistance = GetEditDistance(str1, str2, distances, len1, len2);

    return editDistance;
}

int GetEditDistance(String str1, String str2, int[,] distances, int len1, int len2) {
    for (int i = 0; i < len2 + 1; ++i)
        distances[i, 0] = i;
    for (int j = 0; j < len1 + 1; ++j)
        distances[0, j] = j;

    for (int i = 1; i < len2 + 1; ++i) {
        for (int j = 1; j < len1 + 1; ++j) {
            if (str1[j - 1] == str2[i - 1])
                distances[i, j] = distances[i - 1, j - 1];
            else {
                int deletion = distances[i, j - 1] + 1;
                int insertion = distances[i - 1, j] + 1;
                int substitution = distances[i - 1, j - 1] + 1;
                distances[i, j] = Min(deletion, insertion, substitution);
            }
        }
    }

    return distances[len2, len1];
}

int Min(int num1, int num2, int num3) {
    int less = (num1 < num2) ? num1 : num2;
    return (less < num3) ? less : num3;
}
```

Source Code:

    032_EditDistance.cs

Test Cases:

- Functional cases: Finding edit distances of normal strings, including two identical strings, or a string is a substring of the other

- Boundary cases: One or two strings are empty

Minimal Number of Coins for Change

■ **Question 33**   Please implement a function that gets the minimal number of coins with values v_1, v_2, ..., v_n, to make change for an amount of money with value t. There are an infinite number of coins for each value v_i.

For example, the minimum number of coins to make change for 15 out of a set of coins with values 1, 3, 9, 10 is 3. We can choose two coins with value 3 and a coin with value 9. The number of coins for other choices should be greater than 3.

First, let's define a function $f(t)$, which is the minimum number of coins to make change for the total value t. If there are n different coins, we have n choices to make change for the value t. We can add a coin with value v_1 to a set of coins whose total value is t-v_1. The minimum number of coins to get a value t-v_1 is $f(t$-$v_1)$. Similarly, we can add a coin with value v_2 into a set of coins whose total value is t-v_2. The minimal number of coins to get value t-v_2 is f(t-v_2). It is similar for other coins.

Therefore, a problem to calculate $f(t)$ is divided into n sub-problems: $f(t$-$v_1)$, $f(t$-$v_2)$, ..., $f(t$-$v_n)$. We can get a formal equation for $f(t)$ as the following accordingly:

$$f(t) = min(f(t - v_i)) + 1, where 0 < i \le n$$

This equation can be implemented with recursion easily. However, the recursive solution may cause serious performance issues since there are overlaps when we divide this problem into n subproblems. A better solution is to utilize iteration and store the result of subproblems into a table (as in Table 4-2).

Table 4-2. *The Iterative Process to Calculate the Minimal Number of Coins to Make Changes for 15*

	1	2	3	4	5	6	7	8	9	10	11	12	13	14	15
1	1	2	3	2	3	4	3	4	5	2	2	3	3	4	5
3	-	-	1	2	3	2	3	4	3	4	5	2	2	3	3
9	-	-	-	-	-	-	-	-	1	2	3	2	3	4	3
10	-	-	-	-	-	-	-	-	-	1	2	3	2	3	4

In Table 4-2, each column denotes the number of coins to make change for a specific value. We can calculate the numbers in Table 4-2 from left to right to simulate the iterative process to get the result of $f(15)$.

For instance, there are two numbers 4 and 2 under the column titled "6". We have two alternatives to make change for 6: the first one is to add a coin with value 1 to a set of coins whose total value is 5. Since the minimal number of coins to get value 5 is 3 (*highlighted* number under the column titled "5"), the number in the first cell under column titled "6" is 4 (4=3+1). The second choice is to add a coin with value 3 to a set of coins whose total value is 3. Since the minimal number of coins to get a value of 3 is 1 (the *highlighted* number under the column tile "3"), the number in the second cell under column title "6" is 2 (2=1+1). We highlight the number 2 in the column under title "6" because 2 is less than 4.

Even though we have a 2-D matrix to show the iterative process, it only requires a 1-D array for coding because it is only necessary to store the minimum number of coins to make change for each total value. The sample code is shown in Listing 4-18.

Listing 4-18. C# Code for Coin Changes

```
int GetMinCount(int total, int[] coins) {
    int[] counts = new int[total + 1];
    counts[0] = 0;

    const int MAX = Int32.MaxValue;

    for (int i = 1; i <= total; ++i) {
        int count = MAX;
        for (int j = 0; j < coins.Length; ++j) {
            if (i - coins[j] >= 0 && count > counts[i - coins[j]])
                count = counts[i - coins[j]];
        }

        if (count < MAX)
            counts[i] = count + 1;
        else
            counts[i] = MAX;
    }

    return counts[total];
}
```

Source Code:

033_CoinChanges.cs

Test Cases:

- There are multiple choices to make change for a total value

- There is only one choice to make change for a total value

- It is not possible to make change for a total value

Minimal Times of Presses on Keyboards

■ **Question 34**   Please design an efficient algorithm to lay out cells on phone keyboards in order to minimize key presses.

The current phone keyboard looks like the following layout:

```
              key 2: abc   key 3: def
key 4: ghi    key 5: jkl   key 6: mno
key 7: pqrs   key 8: tuv   key 9: wxyz
```

The first press of a key types the first letter. Each subsequent press advances to the next letter. For example, to type the word "snow", we have to press the key 7 four times, followed by the 6 key twice, followed by the 6 key three times, followed by the 9 key once. The total number of key presses is 10.

This typical solution is not an efficient one. The letter 'i' is used much more frequently than the letter 'w' in English. However, we have to press the 4 key three times to get an 'i', and press the 9 key only once to get a 'w'. If these two letters are interchanged on the keyboard, it will reduce the overall press times.

Let's place letters on a keyboard one by one. It is a greedy choice at each step to select the most frequent letter from the remaining letters and locate it on a key with the lowest index. That is to say, we choose the most frequent letter at the first step and place it as the first letter on a key, and then choose the next most frequent letter and place it as the first letter on another key. If the first locations of all keys are already occupied, a letter is placed as the second one on a key, and so on.

When given the number of keys on a keyboard, as well the frequency of every letter in an alphabet (which is not necessarily English), we may implement the greedy algorithm with the C# code shown in Listing 4-19.

Listing 4-19. C# Code to Get the Minimal Number Of Key Touches

```csharp
int MinKeyPress(int keys, int[] frequencies) {
    Array.Sort(frequencies);

    int letters = frequencies.Length;
    int presses = 0;

    // The last element has the highest frequency in
    // an increasingly sorted array
    for(int i = letters - 1; i >= 0; --i) {
        int j = letters - 1 - i;
        presses += frequencies[i] * (j / keys + 1);
    }

    return presses;
}
```

Letters are sorted based on their frequencies in this code. The most frequent letter is the last one in the sorted array, so we begin to select and place letters from the end of the array.

Source Code:

```
034_MinimalPresses.cs
```

Test Cases:

- Functional Tests: Given different sets of characters and various numbers of keys

Bit Operations

People get accustomed to the decimal system in daily life. However, a number is stored as a binary in computers, which is a sequence of 0s and 1s. For example, the decimal 2 is 10 in binary, and decimal 10 is 1010 in binary.

Besides 2 and 10, numbers can be converted with other bases. For instance, the time system has 60 as its base to record seconds, minutes, and hours. The following problem is an interesting interview question about numbers with uncommon bases: in Microsoft Excel, "A" stands for the first column, "B" for the second column, ..., "Z" for the 26th column, "AA" for the 27th column, "AB" for the 28th column, and so on. Please write a function to get the column index according to a given string.

A column index in Excel is converted with base 26, so it essentially requires converting a number with base 26 to a decimal number.

Each bit in a binary number, 0 or 1, can be manipulated. Bit operations can be divided into two categories. The first category contains bitwise operations, which include AND, OR, XOR, and NOT. The first three are binary operators taking two input bits, which are summarized in Table 4-3.

Table 4-3. *Bitwise AND, OR, and XOR*

Bitwise AND (&)	0 & 0 = 0	1 & 0 = 0	0 & 1 = 0	1 & 1 = 1
Bitwise OR (|)	0 | 0 = 0	1 | 0 = 1	0 | 1 = 1	1 | 1 = 1
Bitwise XOR(^)	0 ^ 0 = 0	1 ^ 0 = 1	0 ^ 1 = 1	1 ^ 1 = 0

The bitwise NOT is a unary operator, which has only one argument. It produces the opposite of the input bit: a 1 if the input is a 0, or a 0 if the input is a 1.

The second category of bit operations contains shift operations. The left-shift operator in $m << n$ shifts m to the left by n bits and inserts n 0s at the lower-order bits. For example:

```
00001010 << 2 = 00101000
10001010 << 3 = 01010000
```

The right-shift operator in $m >> n$ shifts m to the right by n bits. It inserts n 0s at the higher-order bits if m is positive and inserts n 1s if m is negative. In the following examples, it takes signed 8-bit numbers as the left operand for simplicity:

```
00001010 >> 2 = 00000010
10001010 >> 3 = 11110001
```

The right operator >> is called a signed right-shift in Java, and a new operator >>> named unsigned right-shift is introduced. The operator in $m >>> n$ also shifts m to the right by n bits, and it always inserts 0s at the higher-order bits no matter what the sign of m is. In the following two examples, it takes signed 8-bit numbers as the left operand for simplicity again:

```
00001010 >>> 2 = 00000010
10001010 >>> 3 = 00010001
```

The unsigned right-shift operator >>> is available only in Java, but unavailable in C/C++/C#.

Number of 1s in Binary

■ **Question 35**   Please implement a function to get the number of 1s in the binary representation of an integer. For example, the integer 9 is 1001 in binary, so it returns 2 since there are two bits of 1.

It looks like a simple question about binary numbers, and we have many solutions for it. Unfortunately, the most intuitive solution for many candidates is incorrect. We should be careful.

Check the Rightmost Bit with Endless Loop

When candidates are given this problem during an interview, many of them find a solution in a short time: the solution checks whether the rightmost bit is 0 or 1, and then right-shifts the integer one bit and checks the rightmost bit again. It continues in a loop until the integer becomes 0.

How do you check whether the rightmost bit of an integer is 0 or 1? It is simple since we have the AND operation. There is only one bit of 1 in the binary representation of the integer 1, which is the rightmost bit. When we have the bitwise AND operation on an integer and 1, we can check whether the rightmost bit is 0 or 1. When the result of the AND operation is 1, it indicates the rightmost bit is 1; otherwise, it is 0. We can implement a function based on this solution quickly, as shown in Listing 4-20.

Listing 4-20. C Code for Number of 1 in Binary (Version 1)

```c
int NumberOf1(int n) {
    int count = 0;
    while(n) {
        if(n & 1)
            count ++;

        n = n >> 1;
    }

    return count;
}
```

Interviewers may ask a question when they are told this solution: What is the result when the input integer is a negative number such as 0x80000000? When we right-shift the negative number 0x80000000 for a bit, it becomes 0xC0000000 rather than 0x40000000. The integer 0x8000000 is negative before the shift, so it is guaranteed to be negative after the shift. Therefore, when a negative integer is right-shifted, the first bit is set as 1 after the right-shift operation. If we continue to shift to the right side, a negative integer will be 0xFFFFFFFF eventually and it is trapped in an endless loop.

Left-Shift Operation on 1

If we are using Java, the unsigned right-shift operator >>> can be utilized to eliminate the problem of negative numbers.

We have to utilize other strategies if we are developing in C/C++. Instead of shifting the input integer *n* to right, we may shift the number 1 to left. We may check first the least important bit of the input number *n*, and then shift the number 1 to the left and continue to check the second least important bit of *n*. The code can be revised as shown in Listing 4-21.

Listing 4-21. C Code for Number of 1 in Binary (Version 2)

```
int NumberOf1(int n) {
    int count = 0;
    unsigned int flag = 1;
    while(flag) {
        if(n & flag)
            count ++;

        flag = flag << 1;
    }

    return count;
}
```

Minus One and Then Bitwise AND

Let's analyze what happens when you have a binary number minus 1. There is at least one bit 1 in a non-zero number. We first assume the rightmost bit is 1. It becomes 0 if you subtract 1 and other bits then keep unchanged.

Second, we assume the rightmost bit is 0. Since there is at least one 1 bit in a non-zero number, we suppose the mth bit is the rightmost bit of 1. When it is minus 1, the mth bit becomes 0, and all 0 bits behind the mth bit become 1. For instance, the second bit of binary number 1100 is the rightmost 1 bit. When you take 1100 minus 1, the second bit becomes 0, and the third and fourth bits become 1, so the result is 1011.

In both situations above, the rightmost 1 bit becomes 0 when you subtract the 1. When there are some 0 bits on the right side, all of them become 1. The result of the bitwise AND operation on the original number and the minus 1 result is identical to the result gotten by modifying the rightmost 1 to 0. Take the binary number 1100 as an example again. Its result is 1011 when you apply minus 1. The result of the bitwise AND operation on 1100 and 1011 is 1000. If we change the rightmost 1 bit in the number 1100, it also becomes 1000 (Figure 4-6).

```
        1  1  0  0
(−)                 1
        1  0  1  1
(&)     1  1  0  0
        1  0  0  0
```

Figure 4-6. If we take 1100 minus 1 and then take the bitwise AND operation of the minus result 1011 and the original number 1100, the final result 1000 is the same as changing the rightmost 1 bit of the number 1100 to 0. (Numbers are in the binary representation.)

The analysis can be summarized as follows: if we first apply minus 1 to a number and apply the bitwise AND operation to the original number and the minus result, the rightmost 1 bit becomes 0. We repeat these operations until the number becomes 0. We can develop the code in Listing 4-22 accordingly.

Listing 4-22. *C Code for Number of 1 in Binary (Version 3)*

```c
int NumberOf1(int n) {
    int count = 0;

    while (n) {
        ++ count;
        n = (n - 1) & n;
    }

    return count;
}
```

The number of times in the while loops equals to the number of 1 in the binary format of input n.

Source Code:

035_NumberOf1.c

Test Cases:

- Positive integers (including the maximum integer as a boundary test case)

- Zero

- Negative integers (including the minimum integer as a boundary test case)

■ **Question 36**   Please check whether a number is a power product of 2 in only one C statement.

When a number is 2 to the power of k ($k \geq 0$), there is only one 1 bit in its binary representation. As discussed above, a statement $(n-1)\&n$ removes the only 1 bit in the number if n is 2^k. Therefore, the Boolean value of the statement n != 0 && (n - 1) & n == 0 indicates whether n is 2^k.

■ **Question 37**   Given two integers, *m* and *n*, please calculate the number of bits in binary that need to be modified to change *m* to *n*. For example, the number 10 is 1010 in binary, and 13 is 1101 in binary. We can modify 3 bits of 1010 to get 1101 in binary.

We can modify three bits of 1010 to get 1101 in binary because their last three bits are different. According to the definition of the bitwise XOR operation, it gets 1 when two input bits are different and gets 0 when they are same. Therefore, the result of XOR indicates the bit difference between *m* and *n*. For example, the XOR result of 1010 and 1101 is 0111. Three bits are different between these two numbers, and there are three 1 bits in their XOR result.

After we get the XOR result, the remaining task is to count 1s in a number that has been discussed already, as shown in Listing 4-23.

Listing 4-23. *C Code to Modify a Number to Another*

```c
int bitsToModify(int number1, int number2) {
    int temp = number1 ^ number2;

    // the number of 1 bits in temp
    int bits = 0;
    while(temp != 0) {
        ++bits;
        temp = (temp - 1) & temp;
    }

    return bits;
}
```

Source Code:

037_ModifyANumberToAnother.c

Test Cases:

- One or two numbers are positive, zero, or negative

Numbers Occurring Only Once

■ **Question 38**   Let's assume all numbers except two occur twice in an array. How do you get those two numbers to occur only once in O(n) time and O(1) space?

For example, only two numbers, 4 and 6, in the array {2, 4, 3, 6, 3, 2, 5, 5} occur once, and the others numbers occur twice. Therefore, the output should be 4 and 6.

This is a very difficult interview question. When an interviewer notices that a candidate does not have any ideas after a few minutes, it is possible for the interviewer to modify the question a little bit: If all numbers except one occur twice in the array, how do you find the only number occurring only once?

Why does the interviewer emphasize the times a number occurs (once or twice)? It reminds us of the characteristic of the bitwise XOR operation: it gets 1 when two input bits are different and gets 0 when they are same. Therefore, XOR gets 0 on a pair of duplicated numbers. If numbers in an array where all numbers except one occur twice are XORed, the result is exactly the number occurring only once.

With the simplified problem solved, let's return back to the original one. We know how to solve it if we could partition the array into two sub-arrays, where only one number appears once and the others appear twice. The only problem is how to partition the array into two.

Supposing the two numbers occurring once in the array are *num1* and *num2*. If we take XOR operations on all numbers in the array, the result should be the same as the result of *num1^num2* because XOR gets 0 on pairs of duplicated numbers. The result of *num1*^*num2* is not 0 because *num1* and *num2* are two different numbers. There is a 1 bit at least in the XOR result.

Let's denote the first 1 bit in the XOR result as the ith bit. Numbers in the array are partitioned according to their i^{th} bits. The ith bits of all numbers in the first sub-array are 1s, and the ith bits of all numbers in the second sub-array are 0s. Two duplicated numbers in a pair are in either the first or the second sub-array, but *num1* and *num2* cannot be in the same sub-array.

Take the sample array {2, 4, 3, 6, 3, 2, 5, 5} as an example. The XOR result of all numbers in the array is 0010 in binary, of which the second bit from the right is 1. Numbers in the array are partitioned into two sub-arrays: the first one is {2, 3, 6, 3, 2} where the numbers all have the property that the second bit from the right is 1, and the second one is {4, 5, 5}, which are numbers where the second bit from the right is 0. If we use XOR operations on these two sub-arrays, we can get the two numbers 6 and 4 occurring only once.

It is time to write code after we have confirmed our ideas about how to partition an array, as shown in 4-24.

Listing 4-24. *Java Code to Get Numbers Occurring Only Once*

```java
void getOnce(int numbers[], NumbersOccurringOnce once){
    if (numbers.length < 2)
        return;

    int resultExclusiveOR = 0;
    for (int i = 0; i < numbers.length; ++ i)
        resultExclusiveOR ^= numbers[i];

    int indexOf1 = findFirstBitIs1(resultExclusiveOR);

    once.num1 = once.num2 = 0;
    for (int j = 0; j < numbers.length; ++ j) {
        if(isBit1(numbers[j], indexOf1))
            once.num1 ^= numbers[j];
        else
            once.num2 ^= numbers[j];
    }
}

// The first 1 bit from the rightmost
int findFirstBitIs1(int num){
    int indexBit = 0;
    while (((num & 1) == 0) && (indexBit < 32)) {
        num = num >> 1;
        ++ indexBit;
    }

    return indexBit;
}

// check whether the bit with index indexBit is 1
boolean isBit1(int num, int indexBit) {
    num = num >> indexBit;
    return (num & 1) == 1;
```

```
}

class NumbersOccurringOnce {
    public int num1;
    public int num2;
}
```

Source Code:

    038_NumbersOccuringOnce.java

Test Cases:

- Functional cases: Numbers in a array appear twice/four times except two numbers occurring once

- Boundary cases: An array only has two unique numbers

■ **Question 39**   Two numbers out of n numbers from 1 to n are missing. The remaining $n-2$ numbers are restored in an array, not in any particular order. Please write a method (or a function) to find the missing two numbers.

Based on Arithmetic Calculation

Supposing the two missing numbers are *num1* and *num2*. It is easy to get the sum when adding all numbers in the array denoted as S_1 as well as the result of $1+2+...+n$ denoted as S_2. Let's denote $S_2 - S_1$ as s. It is also easy to get the product when multiplying all numbers in the array denoted as P_1 as well as the result of $1 \times 2 \times ... \times n$ denoted as P_2. Similarly, we denote P_2 / P_1 as p.

Now we have the following pair of linear equations:

$$\begin{cases} num1 + num2 = s \\ num1 \times num2 = p \end{cases}$$

After solving this linear equations, we get *num1*=$\frac{s+\sqrt{s^2-4p}}{2}$ and *num2*=$\frac{s-\sqrt{s^2-4p}}{2}$. Therefore, this solution can be implemented with the code shown in Listing 4-25.

Listing 4-25. Java Code to Get Two Missing Numbers (Version 1)

```
void findMissing_solution1(int numbers[], NumbersOccurringOnce missing){
    int sum1 = 0;
    int product1 = 1;
    for(int i = 0; i < numbers.length; ++i){
        sum1 += numbers[i];
        product1 *= numbers[i];
    }

    int sum2 = 0;
```

```
    int product2 = 1;
    for(int i = 1; i <= numbers.length + 2; ++i){
        sum2 += i;
        product2 *= i;
    }

    int s = sum2 - sum1;
    int p = product2 / product1;

    missing.num1 = (s + (int)(Math.sqrt(s * s - 4 * p))) / 2;
    missing.num2 = s - missing.num1;
}
```

This solutions works when the range of numbers from 1 to n is relatively narrow. However, it causes overflow errors to calculate $1+2+...+n$ and $1×2×...×n$ when n is large. Let's look for a more robust solution.

Based on Bit Operations

There are n-2 numbers in an array in the range from 1 to n missing two numbers *num1* and *num2*. We define another array with size $2n$-2, of which the first n-2 numbers are copies of numbers in the original array and others are numbers from 1 to n. All numbers except two numbers, *num1* and *num2*, occur twice in the new array, and *num1* and *num2* occur only once. Therefore, this problem is equivalent to the preceding problem: find two numbers occurring once in an array where others occur twice. Let's solve it based on bit operations with the method getOnce, borrowed from the solution of the preceding problem, as shown in Listing 4-26.

Listing 4-26. Java Code to Get Two Missing Numbers (Version 2)

```
void findMissing_solution2(int numbers[], NumbersOccurringOnce missing){
    int originalLength = numbers.length;
    int extendedLength = originalLength * 2 + 2;
    int extention[] = new int[extendedLength];

    for(int i = 0; i < originalLength; ++i)
        extention[i] = numbers[i];
    for(int i = originalLength; i < extendedLength; ++i)
        extention[i] = i - originalLength;

    getOnce(extention, missing);
}
```

Source Code:

    039_FindTwoMissingNumbers.java

Test Cases:

- Functional tests: Two numbers out of n numbers from 1 to n are missing in an array

- Boundary tests: An array only has one or two numbers

- Robust tests: The maximum number n is very big

Summary

Similar to data structures, there are many coding interview questions about common algorithms. Many algorithms can be implemented based on both recursion and iteration. Usually, recursion looks more concise, but iteration is more efficient and robust with big data inputs.

When it is required to find or count a number in a sorted array, binary search might be the right choice. Merge sort and quicksort are the most important sort algorithms for interviews. The `Partition` method is useful not only in quicksort, but also to select the arbitrary k^{th} number out of an array.

The backtracking algorithm is used to search for a solution to a problem among all available options in depth-first order. A backtracking solution is implemented with recursion in most cases.

Two hot interview topics are dynamic programming and greedy algorithms, which are quite helpful tools to get an optimized solution (the minimum or maximum value) to a problem. If there is a greedy choice available at each step, the greedy algorithm works; otherwise, we may have a try dynamic programming.

Bit operations can be viewed as special algorithms on binary numbers. There are four bitwise operators, AND, OR, XOR, and NOT, as well as right-shift and left-shift to manipulate bits.

CHAPTER 5

■ ■ ■

High-Quality Code

Interview candidates will want to write code of high quality during interviews, but many of them cannot meet their interviewers' expectations. This chapter provides detailed instructions on how to write clean, complete, and robust code. While solving a set of sample coding interview problems, we will illustrate how functional, boundary, and negative test cases, as well as defensive programming, are used to produce complete and robust code.

Clearness

Interviewers make their hiring decisions based on candidates' code. Code clearness has an important impact on the decision. As shown in Figure 5-1, handwriting, layout, and naming are three factors of code clearness important in interviews.

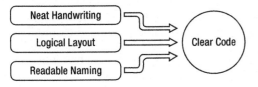

Figure 5-1. *Three factors of clear code: handwriting, layout, and naming*

First, clear code is written neatly. Engineers write code with keyboards for their daily development, but they have to write code on paper or whiteboards in most interviews. It is a good idea to practice writing code on paper during interview preparation and, if you have a whiteboard, a little practice can make a big difference. Many candidates' handwriting is illegible when they feel rushed, especially when they find problems in their own code and have to make some changes. The number of lines of code for interview problems is usually less than 50, so it does not take too much time to write. In other words, candidates should take their time, within reason, while writing code. The key factor is to form clear solutions and express them with neat and readable code.

Second, clear layout shows logical structure. Programmers usually write code in an integrated development environment, such as Visual Studio or Eclipse, which facilitates layout greatly. Candidates should pay attention to layout when such tools are unavailable in interviews. Candidates shouldn't write too large on a whiteboard or they may not have room to finish their code and then have to worry about cramming it in somewhere, interrupting their thinking about the code itself. Similarly, indentation level increases when there are many loops and conditional checks. Complex code without clear layout makes an interviewer confused if indentation does not show the logical structures, or curly brackets do not appear in pairs.

Last but not least, names in clear code are easy to read and understand. Many novices like the shortest names. They name variables as i, j, k, and name functions as f, g, h. Since such names do not show the meaning and purpose of variables and functions, they are very difficult to understand when a function gets long. It is recommended that you use word concatenations for names. For example, if a function takes a root node of a binary tree as a parameter, the parameter can be declared as BinaryTreeNode* pRoot in C/C++. Readable variables and function names make it simpler for interviewers to understand candidates' code. Otherwise, interviewers have to guess. For instance, is a variable m the maximum or minimum in an array?

■ **Tip**   In order to improve code readability, it is a good practice to name variables and functions (methods) with English words or word concatenations.

Completeness

The ability to write complete code is a core competence of software developers, and it is also a key factor impacting interview results. Code is complete when it fulfills basic functional requirements, performs well on boundary inputs, and handles invalid input gracefully.

Test Cases for Completeness

In order to prevent bugs from occurring during interviews, it is a good practice for candidates to figure out a complete set of unit test cases before they begin to write code. After finishing coding, the candidate can test the code with the test cases in mind, which include functional test cases, boundary test cases, and negative test cases (Figure 5-2). If all cases pass, the candidate should feel confident in handing his or her code to the interviewer.

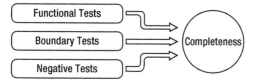

Figure 5-2. Three types of tests to guarantee complete code

The first type of test case is about functionality because candidates' code has to fulfill basic functional requirements. For example, if a candidate is asked to convert a string to a number, he or she may test with input strings "123", "0", and "-123". The function is expected to be able to convert strings for positive and negative numbers as well as zero.

Candidates have to break through the limit of conventional thinking while designing functional test cases. Sometimes functional requirements are ignored because of conventional thinking. For example, many candidates think the coding interview problem to print from 1 to the maximal numbers with n digits is quite easy—or is it? The maximum with three digits is 999, and the maximum with four digits is 9999. These maximal values are not difficult to calculate. However, the int or long type cannot accommodate numbers with n digits when n is large. If it is required that the program is able to handle arbitrarily large *n*, some data structures for big numbers, such as strings or arrays, may be utilized to solve this problem.

Boundary values should also be covered during unit tests. It is not rare to utilize iteration and recursion in code. What are the boundary values to end loops or recursion? Candidates may design some test cases based on these boundary values. Take the problem to convert a string to a number as an example again. Candidates should make sure their code can convert the maximal and minimal integers as expected.

Invalid inputs should also be considered while designing test cases. Cases about negative tests should be included to make sure that the program handles errors gracefully when given invalid inputs. When developing a function to convert a string to a number, strings with non-digit characters such as "1a2b3c" should be taken into consideration.

The points above are presented to consider all possible inputs according to the current requirements. In software engineering, what never changes is the fact that the requirements always change. If candidates take potential requirement changes into consideration to reduce risks in the future, they demonstrate their understanding of scalability and maintainability. Scalability and maintainability will be discussed in detail later for the question "*Partition Numbers in Arrays*" (Question 45).

Strategies to Handle Errors

When given inputs are invalid, they cause errors and the normal execution flow in a function cannot continue. It is necessary to handle errors in the function and pass error messages to the function caller. There are three common strategies to pass error messages to the caller of a function.

The first strategy is to use the return value. Many Windows APIs return 0 when they execute smoothly and return non-zero values when they fail. Microsoft defines different return values for different types of errors, so API callers have the opportunity to know the reason for failure according to the return values. The disadvantage is that the calculation result cannot be assigned to variables or passed to other functions as a parameter directly.

The second strategy is to pass calculation results via return values and set a global variable when an error occurs. Callers may assign results to variables or pass results to other functions directly with this strategy. When errors occur in many Windows APIs, they update a global variable that is accessible by the function `GetLastError`. It leaves in risks if a caller forgets to check the global variable and fails to handle the corresponding errors.

The third strategy is to throw exceptions when errors occur. Different types of exceptions are defined for different types of errors, so callers are able to handle the specific error according to the type of a caught exception. Additionally, code structure looks clear because the exception mechanism partitions a function into a `try` block for normal execution, a `catch` block to handle errors, and a `finally` block to make sure resources are cleaned up whether an exception happens or not. Some programming languages, such as C, do not support the exception mechanism. The execution flow is interrupted when an exception is thrown, and it has a negative impact on performance.

Every error-handling mechanism has its own pros and cons (Table 5-1). Which one is suitable for interviews? It depends on interviewers' requirements. When candidates are asked to solve a certain coding problem, they should figure out all possible invalid inputs and discuss how to handle errors with their interviewers.

Table 5-1. *Pros and Cons of Three Strategies to Handle Errors via Return Values, Global Variables, and Exceptions*

	Advantages	Disadvantages
Return Values	Consistent with system APIs	Inconvenient to use results
Global Variables	Convenient to use results	Possible for callers to forget to check the variable
Exceptions	Clear code structure isolating blocks for normal execution and error handling	Some languages don't support exceptions, and exceptions impact performance negatively

Power of Integers

■ **Question 40**   Please implement the function double Power(double base, int exponent) to raise a number base to power of exponent. You are not allowed to call library functions, and it is not necessary to take care of overflow issues.

As we know, there is a pow function in the C/C++ library for power calculation. You will try to simulate the functionality of pow here. Similarly, there are many interview questions simulating library functions, especially functions about numeric calculations and string operations. In order to solve such problems, candidates should not only be familiar with the usages of library functions, but also understand the functional implementation inside of them.

Incomplete

It looks like a simple problem because it does not require taking care of overflow issues. Some candidates finish writing code in a minute, as shown in Listing 5-1.

Listing 5-1. C++ Code to Calculate Power (Version 1)

```cpp
double Power(double baseNumber, int exponent) {
    double result = 1.0;

    for(int i = 1; i <= exponent; ++i)
        result *= baseNumber;

    return result;
}
```

A fast solution is not necessarily a good one. The code in Listing 5-1 underestimates the complexity of the problem because it only handles cases where an exponent is positive. What happens when it is negative? Or zero? Incomplete solutions are not acceptable to almost all interviewers.

Complete but Inefficient

When the exponent is negative, it calculates power with absolute value of the exponent first and then gets the reciprocal of the power result. It raises an error when it tries to get the reciprocal of zero. Therefore, the scenario with a negative base and zero as the exponent should be handled specially. How do you handle the error in such scenarios? As discussed before, there are three choices available. Candidates can describe the pros and cons of each choice to the interviewers and select a solution based on the requirements. The solution in Listing 5-2 sets the global variable errno when an error occurs, which is defined in the standard C library.

Listing 5-2. C++ Code to Calculate Power (Version 2)

```
double Power(double base, int exponent) {
    errno = 0;

    if(Equal(base, 0.0) && exponent < 0) {
        errno = EDOM;
        return 0.0;
    }

    unsigned int absExponent = (unsigned int)(exponent);
    if(exponent < 0)
        absExponent = (unsigned int)(-exponent);

    double result = PowerWithUnsignedExponent(base, absExponent);
    if(exponent < 0)
        result = 1.0 / result;

    return result;
}

double PowerWithUnsignedExponent(double base, unsigned int exponent) {
    double result = 1.0;

    for(int i = 1; i <= exponent; ++i)
        result *= base;

    return result;
}

bool Equal(double num1, double num2) {
    if((num1 - num2 > -0.0000001)
        && (num1 - num2 < 0.0000001))
        return true;
    else
        return false;
}
```

A corner case is worthy of attention: it is undefined in mathematics when both base and exponent are zero, so the corresponding power result is acceptable if it is one or zero. Candidates should explain this to interviewers to show that they have considered such a boundary value.

A function `Equal` is defined to check whether the base is equal to zero. Comparing float numbers with the == operator can be problematic because of the precision issue of the floating-point representation. When the difference between two float numbers is in a narrow range, these two numbers are equal to each other.

■ **Tip**   Checking the equality of decimals (including float and double numbers) with the == operator is error-prone. Two decimals are treated as equal when the difference between them is in a narrow range, such as a range between 0 and 0.0000001.

The solution is already comprehensive and it is acceptable to many interviewers. However, if an interviewer is very passionate about performance, he or she may give you some hints that the efficiency of the function `PowerWithUnsignedExponent` can be improved.

Complete and Efficient

When the parameters `baseNumber` and `exponent` of the function `PowerWithUnsignedExponent` are n and 32 respectively, it requires 31 multiplications to get n^{32}. However, it only requires five multiplications with another strategy: it calculates n^2 first, and then calculates $n^4 = n^2 \times n^2$, and similarly calculates n^8, n^{16}, and finally n^{32}.

That is to say, a^n can be calculated with the following equation efficiently:

$$a^n = \begin{cases} a^{n/2} \cdot a^{n/2} & n \text{ is even} \\ a^{(n-1)/2} \cdot a^{(n-1)/2} & n \text{ is odd} \end{cases}$$

It is easy to implement such an equation recursively, so the function `PowerWithUnsignedExponent` can be updated, as shown in Listing 5-3.

Listing 5-3. C++ Code to Calculate Power (Version 3)

```cpp
double PowerWithUnsignedExponent(double base, unsigned int exponent) {
    if(exponent == 0)
        return 1;
    if(exponent == 1)
        return base;

    double result = PowerWithUnsignedExponent(base, exponent >> 1);
    result *= result;
    if((exponent & 0x1) == 1)
        result *= base;

    return result;
}
```

Some details are worthy of attention. This program replaces a division operation (/) with a right-shift (>>), and replaces a modulo operation (%) with a bitwise AND (&). Right-shift and bitwise AND operations are more efficient than arithmetic division and modulo operations.

Source Code:

    040_Power.cpp

Test Cases:

- The exponent is positive/negative/zero

- The base is positive/negative/zero

Big Numbers as Strings

■ **Question 41**   Given a number *n*, please print all numbers from 1 to the maximum *n* digit number in order. For example, if the input is 3, it prints 1, 2, 3, …, 999, which is the maximum number with three digits.

Underestimating Complexity

This problem looks simple. An intuitive solution is to get the maximum number with *n* digits, which is $10^n - 1$, and print numbers from 1 one by one. Many candidates can create the code in Listing 5-4 in a very short time.

Listing 5-4. C++ Code to Print Numbers (Version 1)

```
void Print1ToMaxOfNDigits_1(int n) {
    int number = 1;
    int i = 0;
    while(i++ < n)
        number *= 10;

    for(i = 1; i < number; ++i)
        printf("%d\t", i);
}
```

If candidates scrutinize the requirement carefully, they may find that the range of *n* is unspecified. When the input *n* is quite large, it causes overflow on the variable number, even if it is declared as long long. Therefore, it is necessary to handle big numbers.

■ **Tip**   If the range of input numbers is not specified explicitly in an interview question, it might be necessary to handle big numbers. Candidates can ask for more clarification on the requirement. Utilizing strings or arrays is a simple solution to handling big numbers.

Simulating Increment on a String

There are many methods available to express big numbers. The most common method, also the simplest one, is to utilize arrays or strings to express big numbers. The following solution is based on strings.

When a number is expressed as a string, each character in the string is in the range '0' to '9'. A string with length $n+1$ is created to accommodate numbers with n digits at most (there is a '\0' and the end of string). When the number of digits is less than n, some leading characters are set to '0'. For example, when the input n is 3, the number 98 is expressed as the string "098".

First, all characters in the string are set as '0', and then a number in the string is increased by 1 and printed in each step of an iteration. There are two tasks to be finished: simulating addition on a string and printing a number in a string. Therefore, the skeleton function to solve this problem can be implemented as shown in Listing 5-5.

Listing 5-5. C++ Code to Print Numbers (Version 2)

```
void Print1ToMaxOfNDigits_2(int n) {
    if(n <= 0)
        return;

    char *number = new char[n + 1];
    memset(number, '0', n);
    number[n] = '\0';

    while(!Increment(number, n))
        PrintNumber(number);

    delete []number;
}
```

This solution increases a number in a string by one in the function `Increment` and prints the number in the function `PrintNumber`. Let's consider the implementation details of these two functions.

The return type of the function `Increment` is `bool`. It returns `true` when it reaches the maximum number with n digits to stop the `while` loop in its caller. Otherwise, it returns `false`. How do you check if it reaches the maximum number? A straightforward method is to compare the string with "999...99"(n 9s) with the library function `strcmp`. It is done if they are equal. It costs O(n) time to compare two strings with length n.

There is a more efficient solution available for the `Increment` function. It carries the first digit (with index 0) when it adds 1 to the number "999...99", but it does not carry the first digit for other numbers. Therefore, it reaches the maximal number with n digits when it carries the first digit during an increment. The sample code of `Increment` is shown in Listing 5-6.

Listing 5-6. C++ Code to Increase on a String

```cpp
bool Increment(char* number, int length) {
    bool isOverflow = false;
    int carry = 0;

    for(int i = length - 1; i >= 0; i --) {
        int sum = number[i] - '0' + carry;
        if(i == length - 1)
            sum ++;

        if(sum >= 10) {
            if(i == 0)
                isOverflow = true;
            else {
                sum -= 10;
                carry = 1;
                number[i] = '0' + sum;
            }
        }
        else {
            number[i] = '0' + sum;
            break;
        }
    }

    return isOverflow;
}
```

It only takes O(1) time to check whether a number is increased to "999...99" in the function `Increment`, which is faster than utilizing the function `strcmp`.

Now let's consider how to print the number in a string. The library function `printf` is a handy tool to print a string, but it is not the best choice for this scenario. As mentioned earlier, the leading characters are 0s when the number of digits is less than n. The leading 0s in a number usually are not printed. Therefore, the function `PrintNumber` skips the leading 0s, as shown in Listing 5-7.

Listing 5-7. *C++ Code to Increase on a String*

```cpp
void PrintNumber(char* number) {
    char* pChar = number;
    while(*pChar == '0')
        ++pChar;

    if(*pChar != '\0')
        printf("%s\t", pChar);
}
```

Simulating Permutation

The permutations of *n* digits ranging from 0 to 9 compose all numbers between 1 and 10^n-1. It is easy to implement the permutation recursively. Each digit is set as a value between 0 and 9, and then the next digit is set. It exits the recursion when all digits are set, as shown in Listing 5-8.

Listing 5-8. *C++ Code to Print Numbers (Version 3)*

```cpp
void Print1ToMaxOfNDigits_3(int n) {
    if(n <= 0)
        return;

    char* number = new char[n + 1];
    number[n] = '\0';
    Print1ToMaxOfNDigitsCore(number, n, -1);

    delete[] number;
}

void Print1ToMaxOfNDigitsCore(char* number, int length, int index) {
    if(index == length - 1) {
        PrintNumber(number);
        return;
    }

    for(int i = 0; i < 10; ++i) {
        number[index + 1] = i + '0';
        Print1ToMaxOfNDigitsCore(number, length, index + 1);
    }
}
```

The function `PrintNumber` is the same as before, which skips the leading 0s and prints a number in a string.

More discussion about permutation is available in the section *Permutation and Combination*.

Source Code:

  `041_Print1ToMaxOfNDigits.cpp`

Test Cases:

- Functional Cases (2, 3, 4, ...)

- Boundary Cases (1, 0, -1)

■ **Question 42**   Please design a function to add two arbitrary positive integers.

The problem requires you to add two arbitrary positive numbers, of which ranges are not specified. Therefore, you have to handle huge numbers beyond the range of the type int and even long long. Inspired by the solution of the preceding problem, strings are employed to express huge numbers.

What is the signature of the function? Your intuition might suggest that you pass the addition result in the return value, and the signature is defined as char* add(char* num1, char* num2). It returns a NULL pointer for invalid inputs (including strings with non-digital characters and NULL pointers for numbers). Otherwise, it returns a string containing the addition result.

The problem with this solution is that the add function allocates a string containing the addition result on the heap, and it expects its caller to release the memory. However, it is highly possible that the caller will forget to release memory because the memory is allocated by others. Usually, a function that allocates memory is responsible for release.

Therefore, the signature of the function can be defined as int add(char* num1, char* num2, char* sum). It returns a non-zero value such as -1 when given invalid inputs; otherwise, it returns 0. It takes a pointer to a string for the addition result as the last parameter, which is passed from the caller. Therefore, the caller is responsible for allocating sufficient memory to accommodate the result and to release it afterward.

After the signature is figured out, it is time to implement the addition functionality. The sample code is shown in Listing 5-9.

Listing 5-9. *C Code to Add Two Numbers in Strings*

```c
/* It returns -1 if the input invalid, otherwise returns 0. */
int add(char* num1, char* num2, char* sum) {
    int index1, index2, indexSum;
    int sumDigit, carry, digit1, digit2;

    if(checkInvalidInput(num1, num2, sum) != 0)
        return -1;

    reverse(num1);
    reverse(num2);

    index1 = index2 = indexSum = 0;
    carry = 0;
    while(num1[index1] != '\0' || num2[index2] != '\0') {
        digit1 = (num1[index1] == '\0') ? 0 : num1[index1] - '0';
        digit2 = (num2[index2] == '\0') ? 0 : num2[index2] - '0';

        sumDigit = digit1 + digit2 + carry;
        carry = (sumDigit >= 10) ? 1 : 0;
        sumDigit = (sumDigit >= 10) ? sumDigit - 10 : sumDigit;

        sum[indexSum++] = sumDigit + '0';

        if(num1[index1] != '\0')
            ++index1;
        if(num2[index2] != '\0')
            ++index2;
    }

    if(carry != 0)
```

```
            sum[indexSum++] = carry + '0';

        sum[indexSum] = '\0';

        reverse(sum);
}
```

Usually, addition begins from the last digits (also the least significant digits). However, it reverses numbers at first in the previous code and then adds numbers from the first digits. The reason is about simplicity. If it begins to add from the last digit, the index of the last digit in the sum is unknown before addition completes. For example, the sum of two numbers with two digits 33 and 44 is 77, which also has two digits. However, the sum of two other numbers with two digits 88 and 99 is 187, which has three digits. The index of the least significant digit is different even if it adds two numbers with two digits in both cases. When numbers are reversed, it begins to add from the first digits and set the first digit in the sum, no matter how many digits the sum will have finally.

Strings with non-digital characters are treated as invalid inputs. Additionally, NULL pointers to numbers should also be excluded from inputs in order to avoid execution crashes. The helper function checkInvalidInput in Listing 5-10 is defined to validate inputs.

Listing 5-10. *C Code to Validate Inputs*

```c
int checkInvalidInput(char* num1, char* num2, char* sum) {
    int length1, length2, i;

    if(num1 == NULL || num2 == NULL || sum == NULL)
        return -1;

    length1 = strlen(num1);
    for(i = 0; i < length1; ++i) {
        if(num1[i] < '0' || num1[i] > '9')
            return -1;
    }

    length2 = strlen(num2);
    for(i = 0; i < length2; ++i) {
        if(num2[i] < '0' || num2[i] > '9')
            return -1;
    }

    return 0;
}
```

The use of the following **reverse** function in Listing 5-11 reverses a given string.

Listing 5-11. *C Code to Validate Inputs*

```c
void reverse(char* str) {
    int i, length;
    char temp;
```

```
        length = strlen(str);
        for(i = 0; i < length / 2; ++i) {
            temp = str[i];
            str[i] = str[length - 1 - i];
            str[length - 1 - i] = temp;
        }
    }
```

Source Code:

042_AddNumericStrings.c

Test Cases:

- Add numbers with/without a carry

- One or two numbers are very large

- One or two numbers are invalid inputs (with non-numeric characters, or NULL pointers)

Delete Nodes from a List

■ **Question 43**   How to delete a given node from a single-linked list in O(1) time?

The most straightforward way to delete a node from a single-linked list is to scan all nodes in it and to find the target node to be deleted. It updates the next pointer in the preceding node and deletes the target.

Suppose node *i* in the list in Figure 5-3(a) is going to be deleted. It scans the list from its head node *a*. When it reaches node *h* (the preceding node of the target node *i*), the next pointer is updated to reference to node *j* (the next node of *i*). After reconnecting the link, node *i* is deleted. Nodes in the list remain connected, as shown in Figure 5-3(b). It costs O(*n*) time on a list with *n* nodes because it has to scan the list.

The reason it has to scan the list from its head is that it needs to get the node preceding the target. There is not a pointer to the preceding node in a single-linked list, so it has to traverse the list.

Is it absolutely necessary to get the preceding node of the target to be removed? The answer is no. It is easy to get the next node of the target in a single-linked list. If the target node data is replaced with the data in the next node and then the next node is deleted, it is equivalent to deleting the target node. Only the data in the target node gets removed, and the data in the next node is stored.

Let's take the list in Figure 5-3(a) as an example again. The node *i* is the target node to be removed. The new solution copies the data in node *j*, pastes it into node *i*, and then sets the next node of node *j* as the next node of node *i*. When node *j* is deleted, it looks like node *i* is deleted, as shown in Figure 5-3(c).

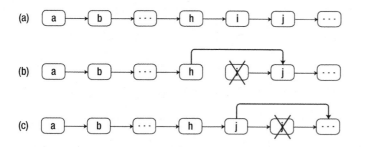

Figure 5-3. *Two methods to remove a node from a list. (a) A sample list. (b) It scans the list from its head node. When it reaches node h, the preceding node of the target node i, it updates the next pointer in h to node j, which is the next node of node i. And then node i is deleted. (c) It replaces the data in node i with the data in node j and then deletes node j.*

Notice that the tail node of the list does not have a next node. How do you delete it? We have to traverse the whole list, get the preceding node of the tail, and then delete the tail.

The last scenario is worthy of consideration when there is only one node in the list. When the only node is deleted, the pointer for the head node should be set as a NULL pointer, as shown in Listing 5-12.

Listing 5-12. *C++ Code to Delete a Node from a List*

```cpp
void DeleteNode(ListNode** pListHead, ListNode* pToBeDeleted) {
    if(!pListHead || !pToBeDeleted)
        return;

    // The node to be deleted is not the tail of the list.
    if(pToBeDeleted->m_pNext != NULL) {
        ListNode* pNext = pToBeDeleted->m_pNext;
        pToBeDeleted->m_nValue = pNext->m_nValue;
        pToBeDeleted->m_pNext = pNext->m_pNext;

        delete pNext;
        pNext = NULL;
    }
    // The list has only one note. Delete the only node.
    else if(*pListHead == pToBeDeleted) {
        delete pToBeDeleted;
        pToBeDeleted = NULL;
        *pListHead = NULL;
    }
    // Delete the tail node of a list with multiple nodes
    else {
        ListNode* pNode = *pListHead;
        while(pNode->m_pNext != pToBeDeleted) {
            pNode = pNode->m_pNext;
        }

        pNode->m_pNext = NULL;
        delete pToBeDeleted;
```

```
            pToBeDeleted = NULL;
    }
}
```

Now let's analyze the time efficiency of this solution. It only costs O(1) time to copy the data from the next node and delete the next node for the n-1 nodes, which are not at the end of the list. It costs O(n) time to delete the tail node because it has to scan the whole list. Therefore, the time efficiency on average is $[(n$-1$)\times O(1)+O(n)]/n$, and so is O(1).

Source Code:

043_DeleteNodeInList.cpp

Test Cases:

- Functional Cases (Delete the head/tail node from a list or delete a node inside a list)

- Boundary Cases (Delete the only node in a list)

- Cases about Robustness (The pointer to the head node is NULL, or the pointer to the target node is NULL)

▨ **Question 44**   Given a sorted linked list, please delete all duplicated numbers and leave only distinct numbers from the original list. For example, when the duplicated numbers in the list in Figure 5-4(a) are removed, it becomes the list in Figure 5-4(b).

The first step to solve this problem is to figure out the signature of the required function. The head of the original list will be deleted if it is duplicated in the following nodes. Therefore, the function should be declared as void deleteDuplication(ListNode** pHead) rather than void deleteDuplication(ListNode* pHead).

We traverse the list beginning from the head of the list. When the value in the current visited node (pNode in the node below) is the same as the value in the next node, the current visited node and its duplicate will be deleted. In order to make sure the list is still connected, the node prior to the current visited node (pPreNode in the code) is linked to the node with value greater than the current visited value. It should be guaranteed that pPreNode always points to the last node having a distinct value in the visited list so far.

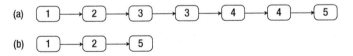

(a)   1 → 2 → 3 → 3 → 4 → 4 → 5

(b)   1 → 2 → 5

Figure 5-4. Remove duplicate numbers in a list. (a) A list with seven elements. (b) Three elements are left when duplications are removed.

Take the sample list as an example. When it visits the first node with value 3, pPreNode points to the node with value 2. Since the next node also has value 3, both nodes with value 3 should be deleted, and then the node pointed to by **pPreNode** is linked to the first node with value 4. Since the node with value 4 also has a duplicate, the node pointed by **pPreNode** is linked to the node with value 5 after nodes with value 4 are deleted. (See Listing 5-13.)

Listing 5-13. *C++ Code to Delete Duplicated Nodes*

```cpp
void deleteDuplication(ListNode** pHead) {
    if(pHead == NULL || *pHead == NULL)
        return;

    ListNode* pPreNode = NULL;
    ListNode* pNode = *pHead;
    while(pNode != NULL) {
        ListNode *pNext = pNode->m_pNext;
        bool needDelete = false;
        if(pNext != NULL && pNext->m_nValue == pNode->m_nValue)
            needDelete = true;

        if(!needDelete) {
            pPreNode = pNode;
            pNode = pNode->m_pNext;
        }
        else {
            int value = pNode->m_nValue;
            ListNode* pToBeDeleted = pNode;
            while(pToBeDeleted != NULL && pToBeDeleted->m_nValue == value) {
                pNext = pToBeDeleted->m_pNext;

                delete pToBeDeleted;
                pToBeDeleted = NULL;

                pToBeDeleted = pNext;
            }

            if(pPreNode == NULL)
                *pHead = pNext;
            else
                pPreNode->m_pNext = pNext;
            pNode = pNext;
        }
    }
}
```

Source Code:

> 044_DeleteDuplicationInList.cpp

Test Cases:

- Functional Cases (Groups of duplicated nodes are at the head/tail of a list, or groups of duplicated nodes are inside a list, or groups of duplicated nodes are continuous)

- Boundary Cases (All nodes in a list are duplicated, either in a duplication group or in multiple duplication groups)

- Cases Involving Robustness (The pointer to the head node is NULL)

Partition Numbers in Arrays

■ **Question 45**   Please reorder an input array to place all odds before evens. For example, after numbers in the array {1, 2, 3, 4, 5} are reordered, it looks like {1, 5, 3, 4, 2}. The result is not unique, and there are multiple arrays meeting the reordering criteria.

The brute-force solution is to scan the array sequentially and relocate every even number. Move all numbers behind the even number backward and then place it at the end of array. Since it has to shift $O(n)$ numbers for an even number, the overall time complexity is $O(n^2)$.

Workable but Not Scalable

The problem asks you to place all odd numbers before even numbers. Therefore, we have to swap all pairs of numbers in which an even number is before an odd one.

Two pointers are defined to find such pairs. The first pointer P_1 is initialized at the first number, which moves forward, and the second one P_2 is initialized at the last number, which moves backward. When the number pointed to by P_1 is even and the number pointed by P_2 is odd, we have to swap these two numbers.

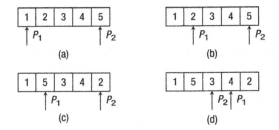

Figure 5-5. *The process to place all odd numbers before even numbers in an array {1, 2, 3, 4, 5}. (a) P$_1$ points to the first number, and P$_2$ points to the last one in the array. (b) P$_1$ moves forward until it reaches the first even number, 2. Since P$_2$ already points to an odd number, it does not move. (c) Numbers pointed to by P$_1$ and P$_2$ are swapped. (d) P$_1$ moves forward until it reaches an even number, 4, and P$_2$ moves backward until it reaches an odd number, 3. All odd numbers have been moved before even numbers because P$_2$ is before P$_1$.*

Let's take the sample array {1, 2, 3, 4, 5} as an example to simulate the process to reorder numbers step-by-step. During the initialization phase, P_1 points to the first number in the array, and P_2 points to the last one (Figure 5-5(a)). The pointer P_1 moves forward until it reaches an even number 2, but P_2 does not move because it already points to an odd number 5 (Figure 5-5(b)). A pair of numbers in which an even number is before an odd one has been found. The state of the array is shown in Figure 5-5(c) after swapping.

It continues to move P_1 forward until reaching another even number, 4, and moves P_2 backward until reaching another odd number, 3 (Figure 5-5(d)). Since P_2 is now before P_1, all odd numbers have been placed before even numbers in the array {1, 5, 3, 4, 2}.

We are able to implement this solution in Java with the step-by-step analysis above, as shown in Listing 5-14.

Listing 5-14. *Java Code to Reorder Numbers in an Array (Version 1)*

```java
void reorderOddEven_solution1(int nums[]) {
    int begin = 0;
    int end = nums.length - 1;
    while(begin < end) {
        // Move begin forward until it meets an even number
        while(begin < end && (nums[begin] & 0x1) != 0)
            begin++;

        // Move end backward until it meets an odd number
        while(begin < end && (nums[end] & 0x1) == 0)
            end--;

        if(begin < end) {
            int temp = nums[begin];
            nums[begin] = nums[end];
            nums[end] = temp;
        }
    }
}
```

Scalable to Handle Similar Scenarios

The solution in Listing 5-13 is acceptable for a graduate or a junior engineer. However, an interviewer may follow up with more questions if the candidate applies for a senior position as demonstrated in the following dialogue:

Interviewer: Let's change the requirement to place all negative numbers before non-negative ones. How do you do it?

Candidate: It's easy. Just define a method similar to before and modify the conditions in the second and third `while` loop.

Interviewer: Let's change the requirement again. We are going to partition an array into two parts where primes are placed before others.

Candidate: Define another new method of which the conditions …

Interviewer: (Interrupting the candidate's words): Are there any better choices?

The candidate should get the interviewer's point: what he or she expects is a scalable solution to a series of similar problems.

Let's take a close look at those two new problems. In order to solve them, it is only necessary to modify conditions in the second and third `while` loop and leave the overall code structure untouched. Therefore, we can decouple the method into two parts: one is the criterion to place an element and the other is about how to partition an array into two sub-arrays. Let's define an interface `Criterion` and a method `reorder` corresponding to these two purposes, as shown in Listing 5-15.

Listing 5-15. *Java Code to Decouple Partitioning Criterion and Process*

```java
public interface Criterion{
    boolean check(int num);
}

void reorder(int nums[], Criterion criterion) {
    int begin = 0;
    int end = nums.length - 1;
    while(begin < end) {
        while(begin < end && !criterion.check(nums[begin]))
            begin++;

        while(begin < end && criterion.check(nums[end]))
            end--;

        if(begin < end) {
            int temp = nums[begin];
            nums[begin] = nums[end];
            nums[end] = temp;
        }
    }
}
```

In order to place odd numbers before even ones, a specific criterion `isEven` is defined, as shown in Listing 5-16.

Listing 5-16. *Java Code to Reorder Numbers in an Array (Version 2)*

```java
void reorderOddEven_solution2(int nums[]) {
    Criterion isEven = new Criterion() {
        public boolean check(int num) {
            if((num & 0x1) == 0)
                return true;

            return false;
        }
    };

    reorder(nums, isEven);
}
```

If you must reorder numbers with other criteria, it is only necessary to implement new classes from the interface `Criterion`, but keep the method `reorder` untouched. Therefore, our decoupling strategy minimizes modification and potential risks to fulfill new requirements.

Source Code:

> `045_ReorderNumbers.java`

Test Cases:

- Functional Cases (Including cases where all odd numbers are before even numbers in the original array, or all even numbers are before odd numbers, or numbers do not appear in any particular order)

- Boundary Cases (There is only an odd/even number in the array)

■ **Question 46**   Given an array and a value, how do you implement a function to remove all instances of that value in place and return the new length of the array? It is not required that you keep the order of the remaining numbers. It doesn't matter what you leave beyond the new length.

For example, if the input array is {4, 3, 2, 1, 2, 3, 6}, the resulting array after removing value 2 contains the numbers {4, 3, 1, 3, 6}, and the new length of the remaining array is 5.

Move Numbers for O(n) Times

The most straightforward solution for this problem is to scan the whole array from the beginning to the end. When a target number is scanned, it is skipped and numbers behind it are moved backward, as shown in Listing 5-17.

Listing 5-17. Java Code to Remove Numbers in an Array (Version 1)

```java
int remove_solution1(int numbers[], int n) {
    int i = 0;
    for (int j = 0; j < numbers.length; j++) {
        if (numbers[j] != n)
            numbers[i++] = numbers[j];
    }

    return i;
}
```

Obviously, the time complexity of this solution is O(n). It is also noticeable that it has to move numbers for O(n) times even if the target number occurs only once in the original array because there are O(n) numbers behind it. Is it possible to reduce the times needed to move numbers? Let's explore alternatives.

Move Numbers for O(*k*) Times

Notice that it is not required to keep the order for the remaining numbers, and the problem does not care about what numbers are left except the new length. Therefore, this problem is essentially the same as the previous one. We partition the array into two parts: the left part contains all non-target values, and the right part contains target values to be removed.

Two pointers are defined to solve this problem. The first pointer (denoted as P_1) moves forward until it reaches a number equal to the target value, which is initialized at the beginning of the array. The other pointer (denoted as P_2) moves backward until it reaches a number different from the target value, which is initialized at the end of the array. Two numbers pointed to by P_1 and P_2 are swapped. We repeat the moving and swapping operations until all target numbers are scanned.

The sample code is shown in Listing 5-18.

Listing 5-18. *Java Code to Remove Numbers in an Array (Version 2)*

```java
int remove_solution2(int numbers[], int n) {
    int p1 = 0;
    while(p1 < numbers.length && numbers[p1] != n)
        ++p1;

    int p2 = numbers.length - 1;
    while(p1 < p2){
        while(p1 < numbers.length && numbers[p1] != n)
            ++p1;
        while(p2 > 0 && numbers[p2] == n)
            --p2;

        if(p1 < p2){
            numbers[p1] = numbers[p2];
            numbers[p2] = n;
        }
    }

    return p1;
}
```

Since it is only necessary to scan the whole array once and it costs O(1) time to swap a target value, the overall time complexity is O(*n*) for an array with *n* numbers. Additionally, it swaps a pair of numbers only when a target number to be removed is scanned. If there are *k* target numbers in the array, it swaps O(*k*) times. Therefore, it is more efficient in terms of data moving.

Source Code:

    046_RemoveNumbers.java

Test Cases:

- Functional Cases (There is a single target number to be removed in the array, there are multiple target numbers in the array, or there are no target numbers in the array)

- Boundary Cases (There is only one number in the array, which is/is not the target number to be removed; all numbers in the array are to be removed; the first/last number is/is not the target number)

Robustness

Robust applications are able to check whether inputs are valid and handle invalid inputs appropriately. If applications are not robust, they might behave in unpredictable ways or crash when unexpected things happen, such as cases when users input incorrect user names, files to be opened do not exist, or servers cannot be connected. User experiences with such applications are almost surely disasters.

It is necessary for candidates to pay careful attention to code robustness. Defensive programming is an effective method of improving robustness, which predicts where it is possible to have problems, and handles problems gracefully. For example, it prompts users to check the file name when the file to be opened does not exist, or it tries a backup server when the server is inaccessible. The behavior of a robust application is predictable.

The most simple and effective defensive programming technique during interviews is to check whether inputs are valid at the entry of each function. When a function has a pointer argument, what is the expected behavior when the pointer is NULL? When a function takes a string as an argument, what is the expected behavior when the string is empty? If all problems have been considered in advance, it is a strong demonstration of defensive programming habits and a candidate's ability to develop robust applications.

Not all problems related to robustness are as simple as validating inputs at function entries. It is better to ask questions in the pattern of "how to handle it when … is not …". For instance, it assumes that there are more than k nodes in a list for the interview problem "k^{th} Node from End" (Question 47). Candidates should ask themselves what the expected behavior is when the number of nodes is less than k. This kind of question helps to find potential problems and handle them in advance.

k^{th} Node from End

■ **Question 47**   Please implement a function to get the kth node from tail of a single linked list. For example, if a list has six nodes whose values are 1, 2, 3, 4, 5, 6 in order from head, the third node from tail contains the value 4.

The program can only move forward in a single-linked list from the head node, but it cannot move backward from the tail. Supposing a list has n nodes. The kth node from the tail is the $(n-k+1)^{th}$ node from the head. It reaches the target node if it moves $n-k+1$ steps along links to the next nodes. How do you find the total number of nodes n in a list? Just traverse the whole list and count.

As a result, it gets the kth node from the tail after it traverses the list twice: it traverses the whole list to get the number of nodes n in the list, and then it moves along the links between nodes for $n-k+1$ steps.

This solution works. However, usually interviewers prefer a solution that traverses the list only once.

In order to solve this problem with only one traversal, two pointers are employed. The first pointer (P_1) moves $k-1$ steps from the head of the list. The second pointer (P_2) begins to move from the head and

P_1 continues to move. Since the distance between these two pointers keeps at k-1, the second pointer reaches the kth node from the tail when the first one reaches the tail of the list.

Figure 5-6 simulates the process of finding the third node from the end of a list with six nodes. The pointer P_1 moves 2 steps (2=3-1) in the list (Figure 5-6(a)). The pointer P_2 is initialized at the head of the list (Figure 5-6(b)). Then these two pointers move at the same speed. When P_1 reaches the tail of the list, P_2 arrives at the third node from the end (Figure 5-6(c)).

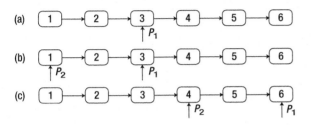

Figure 5-6. *The process to get the third node from the tail of a list with six nodes. (a) Pointer* P_1 *moves two steps on the list. (b) The pointer* P_2 *is initialized at the head of the list. (c) Both* P_1 *and* P_2 *move ahead until* P_1 *reaches the tail of the list. The node pointed to by* P_2 *is the third node from the tail.*

Some candidates implement a solution with two pointers quickly, as shown in Listing 5-19.

Listing 5-19. *C++ Code to Get the* k^{th} *Node from End (Version 1)*

```cpp
ListNode* FindKthToTail(ListNode* pListHead, unsigned int k) {
    ListNode *pAhead = pListHead;
    ListNode *pBehind = NULL;

    for(unsigned int i = 0; i < k - 1; ++ i) {
        pAhead = pAhead->m_pNext;
    }

    pBehind = pListHead;
    while(pAhead->m_pNext != NULL){
        pAhead = pAhead->m_pNext;
        pBehind = pBehind->m_pNext;
    }

    return pBehind;
}
```

Many candidates read web pages about the solution with two pointers during interview preparation. When they meet such a problem in interviews, they feel lucky and write code similar to the code in Listing 5-19 quickly. Unfortunately, they may receive a rejection letter rather than an offer. Is it unfair? It is a fair result because the code has three potential risks for crash:

- The head of the list `pListHead` is a `NULL` pointer. An application crashes when it tries to access the `NULL` address in memory.

- The number of nodes in the list with head pListHead is less than k. It crashes because it tries to move k-1 steps in the for loop.

- The input parameter k is 0. Because k is an unsigned integer, the value of k-1 is 4294967295 (unsigned 0xFFFFFFFF) rather than -1. It iterates in the for loop many more times than expected.

There are too many risks of a crash in such a simple piece of code, so it is reasonable for the writer of this code to be rejected.

■ **Tip**   Robustness is worthy of attention in interviews. Rejection is quite likely if there are many potential risks of crash in code.

Let's fix the listed problems one by one:

- If the pointer of the head node is NULL, the whole list is empty, so naturally the kth node from the tail is also NULL.

- An if statement can be inserted to check whether it reaches a NULL address when it tries to move k steps on the list. When the total number of nodes in the list is less than k, it returns NULL.

- It counts from 1 here, and the first node from the tail is the tail node itself. It is an invalid input if k is 0 because it is meaningless to find the zeroth node from the tail. It returns NULL too in such a case.

The revised version of the code is shown in Listing 5-20.

Listing 5-20. C++ Code to Get the kth Node from End (Version 2)

```cpp
ListNode* FindKthToTail(ListNode* pListHead, unsigned int k) {
    if(pListHead == NULL || k == 0)
        return NULL;

    ListNode *pAhead = pListHead;
    ListNode *pBehind = NULL;

    for(unsigned int i = 0; i < k - 1; ++ i) {
        if(pAhead->m_pNext != NULL)
            pAhead = pAhead->m_pNext;
        else {
            return NULL;
        }
    }

    pBehind = pListHead;
    while(pAhead->m_pNext != NULL) {
        pAhead = pAhead->m_pNext;
        pBehind = pBehind->m_pNext;
```

```
    }

    return pBehind;
}
```

Source Code:

> `047_KthNodeFromEnd.cpp`

Test Cases:

- Functional Cases (The kth node is the head/tail of a list or inside a list)
- Cases for Robustness (The pointer to the list head is `NULL`; the number of a list is less than k; k is 0)

Reverse a List

■ **Question 48**   Please implement a function to reverse a list.

Lots of pointer operations are involved in solving problems related to linked lists. Interviewers know that many candidates are prone to making mistakes on pointer operations, so they like problems related to linked lists to qualify candidates' programming capabilities. Candidates should analyze and design carefully before they begin to write code. It is much better to write robust code with comprehensive analysis than to write code quickly with many bugs.

The direction of pointers should be reversed in order to reverse a linked list. Let's utilize figures to analyze visually the complex steps to reverse pointers. As shown in the list in Figure 5-7(a), node h, i, and j are three adjacent nodes. Supposing pointers to all nodes prior to h have been reversed after some operations and all next pointers are linked to their preceding nodes. The next step is to reverse the next pointer in node i. The status of the list is shown in Figure 5-7(b).

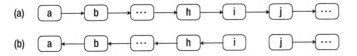

Figure 5-7. *A list gets broken when it is reversed. (a) A list. (b) All next pointers in nodes prior to the node* i *are reversed to reference their preceding nodes. The link between the nodes* i *and* j *gets disconnected.*

Notice that the next pointer in node i references its preceding node h, so the list is broken and node j is inaccessible (Figure 5-7(b)). Node j should be saved before the next pointer of node i is adjusted in order to prevent the list from becoming broken.

When the next pointer in node i is reversed, we need access to node h since the pointer is adjusted to reference node h. It also needs to access node j; otherwise, the list will be broken. Therefore, three pointers should be declared in our code that point to the current visited node, its preceding node, and its next node respectively.

Lastly, the head node of the reversed list should be returned. Obviously, the head in the reversed list should be the tail of the original list. Which pointer is the tail? It should be the node whose next pointer is NULL.

With comprehensive analysis above, we are ready to write code, which is shown in Listing 5-21.

Listing 5-21. *C++ Code to Reverse a List*

```
ListNode* ReverseList(ListNode* pHead) {
    ListNode* pReversedHead = NULL;
    ListNode* pNode = pHead;
    ListNode* pPrev = NULL;
    while(pNode != NULL) {
        ListNode* pNext = pNode->m_pNext;

        if(pNext == NULL)
            pReversedHead = pNode;

        pNode->m_pNext = pPrev;

        pPrev = pNode;
        pNode = pNext;
    }

    return pReversedHead;
}
```

The common issues remaining in many candidates' code are in three categories:

- The program crashes when the pointer of the head node is NULL or there is only one node in the list.

- The reversed list is broken.

- The returned node is the head node of the original list rather than the head node of the reversed list.

How do you make sure there are no problems remaining in code during interviews? A good practice is to have comprehensive test cases. After finishing writing code, candidates can test their own code with the prepared cases. The code can be handed to interviewers only after all unit tests are passed. Actually, interviewers have their own test cases to verify candidates' code. If a candidate's test covers all test cases prepared by his or her interviewer, it is highly possible to pass this round of interviews.

Source Code:

048_ReverseList.cpp

Test Cases:

- Functional Cases (The number of nodes in a list is even/odd; there is only one node in a list)

- Cases for Robustness (The pointer to the list head is NULL)

■ **Question 49**   How do you design an algorithm to reverse every *k* nodes in a list? A list is divided into several groups, and each group has *k* nodes except the last group, where the number of nodes may be less than *k*. Please reverse the nodes in each group and connect all groups together.

For example, when groups with three nodes are reversed in the list of Figure 5-8(a), it becomes the list in Figure 5-8(b).

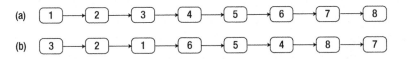

Figure 5-8. *Reverse every group with three nodes in a list with eight nodes.*

Three steps are necessary to reverse a list group by group. First, the process finds a group with *k* nodes (the number of nodes in the last group may be less than *k*). Then it reverses pointers to nodes inside the group. Finally, it connects reversed groups together. Therefore, the overall code structure looks like the function **Reverse**, as shown in Listing 5-22.

Listing 5-22. *C++ Code to Reverse Nodes in a List in Groups*

```
ListNode* Reverse(ListNode* pHead, unsigned int k) {
    if(pHead == NULL || k <= 1)
        return pHead;

    ListNode* pReversedHead = NULL;
    ListNode* pNode1 = pHead;
    ListNode* pPrev = NULL;
    while(pNode1 != NULL) {
        // find k nodes within a group
        ListNode* pNode2 = pNode1;
        ListNode* pNext = NULL;
        for(unsigned int i = 1; pNode2->m_pNext != NULL && i < k; ++i)
            pNode2 = pNode2->m_pNext;

        pNext = pNode2->m_pNext;

        // reverse nodes within a group
        ReverseGroup(pNode1, pNode2);

        // connect groups together
        if(pReversedHead == NULL)
            pReversedHead = pNode2;

        if(pPrev != NULL)
            pPrev->m_pNext = pNode2;
        pPrev = pNode1;
```

```
        pNode1 = pNext;
    }

    return pReversedHead;
}
```

The process required to reverse nodes inside a group is similar to the process discussed for the preceding problem, so it will not be analyzed step-by-step. The function ReverseGroup is used to reverse a group between two nodes, as shown in Listing 5-23.

Listing 5-23. *C++ Code to Reverse Nodes in a Group*

```
void ReverseGroup(ListNode* pNode1, ListNode* pNode2) {
    ListNode* pNode = pNode1;
    ListNode* pPrev = NULL;
    while(pNode != pNode2) {
        ListNode* pNext = pNode->m_pNext;
        pNode->m_pNext = pPrev;

        pPrev = pNode;
        pNode = pNext;
    }

    pNode->m_pNext = pPrev;
}
```

Source Code:

    049_ReverseListInGroups.cpp

Test Cases:

- Functional Cases (The number of nodes in the last group of a list is k or less than k; the number of nodes in a list is less than or equal to k)

- Cases for Robustness (The pointer to the list head is NULL; k is 0 or negative)

Substructures in Trees

■ **Question 50**   Given two binary trees, please check whether one is a substructure of the other. For example, the tree *b* on the right side of Figure 5-9 is a substructure of the tree *a* on the left side.

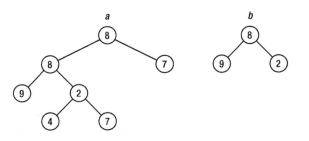

Figure 5-9. *Two binary trees of which tree* b *on the right side is a substructure of tree* a *on the left side.*

Similar to lists, pointer operations on trees are also quite complicated, so it is usually not easy to solve coding interview problems about trees. Candidates have to be very careful on pointer operations; otherwise, it is highly possible to leave crash risks.

Let's return to the problem itself. It can be solved in two steps. The first step is to find a node r in tree a whose value is the same as the value in the root node of tree b, and the second step is to check whether the subtree rooted at the node r has the same structure as tree b.

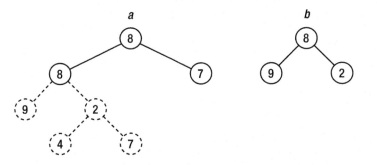

Figure 5-10. *Two root nodes in trees* a *and* b *have the same value, but their children are different.*

Take the two sample trees as an example. Our solution traverses tree a and finds a node with a value of 8 (the value in the root node of tree b). Since the value in the root of tree a is 8, the solution checks whether the subtree under the root node in tree a has the same structure as tree b. As shown in Figure 5-10, their structures are different.

It continues to traverse on tree a, and another node with value 8 is found in the second level. It checks the structure of the subtree again, and the left and right children have the same values as the children nodes in tree b (Figure 5-11). Therefore, a subtree in tree a with the same structure as tree b has been found, so tree b is a substructure of tree a.

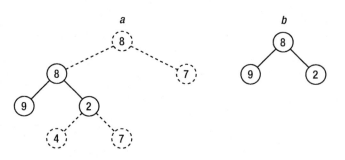

Figure 5-11. *The structure under the second node with value 8 in tree* a *is the same as the structure of tree* b.

The first step to find a node in tree *a* with the same value in the root node of tree *b* is actually a traversal process. There are different traversal algorithms available, and the following code is based on the pre-order traversal algorithm. The following function HasSubtree solves this problem recursively in Listing 5-24 because it is simpler to implement traversal algorithms with recursion.

Listing 5-24. *C++ Code Check Whether a Tree Is a Subtree of Another*

```cpp
bool HasSubtree(BinaryTreeNode* pRoot1, BinaryTreeNode* pRoot2) {
    bool result = false;

    if(pRoot1 != NULL && pRoot2 != NULL) {
        if(pRoot1->m_nValue == pRoot2->m_nValue)
            result = DoesTree1HaveTree2(pRoot1, pRoot2);
        if(!result)
            result = HasSubtree(pRoot1->m_pLeft, pRoot2);
        if(!result)
            result = HasSubtree(pRoot1->m_pRight, pRoot2);
    }

    return result;
}
```

In the function HasSubtree, it moves on to check whether a subtree in tree *a* has the same structure as tree *b* with the function DoesTree1HaveTree2, as shown in Listing 5-25.

Listing 5-25. *C++ Code Check Whether a Tree Is a Subtree of Another*

```cpp
bool DoesTree1HaveTree2(BinaryTreeNode* pRoot1, BinaryTreeNode* pRoot2) {
    if(pRoot2 == NULL)
        return true;

    if(pRoot1 == NULL)
        return false;

    if(pRoot1->m_nValue != pRoot2->m_nValue)
        return false;
```

```
    return DoesTree1HaveTree2(pRoot1->m_pLeft, pRoot2->m_pLeft) &&
        DoesTree1HaveTree2(pRoot1->m_pRight, pRoot2->m_pRight);
}
```

Notice that there are many places to check whether a pointer is NULL. Candidates have to be careful when writing code to traverse trees. They should ask themselves whether it is possible for a pointer to be NULL in every statement with pointers and how to handle it when the pointer is NULL. Programs are prone to crash when some NULL pointers are not handled appropriately.

▓ **Tip**   It is important to ask two questions when writing code with pointer operations: Is it possible for the pointer to be NULL? How do you handle it when the pointer is NULL?

Source Code:

   050_SubtreeInTree.cpp

Test Cases:

- Functional Cases (A binary tree is/is not a subtree of another)
- Cases for Robustness (The pointers to the head of one or two binary trees are NULL; some special binary trees where nodes do not have left/right subtrees)

Summary

This chapter has discussed how to improve code quality in interviews with clearness, completeness, and robustness.

Candidates write code on paper or whiteboards in most interviews. It improves code readability if code is written neatly with a clear layout and indentation, and variables and functions are named reasonably.

It is a good practice to figure out all possible inputs before writing code. Code is complete only when it fulfills functional requirements as well as when it handles boundary values and errors appropriately.

Defensive programming is a good habit to improve code robustness. Candidates should check input validity at the entry of each function and handle invalid inputs gracefully.

CHAPTER 6

∎ ∎ ∎

Approaches to Solutions

There are often tough situations where candidates are asked difficult interview questions. This chapter provides three strategies to solve complex problems:

- Figures may be helpful to visualize data structures problems such as lists and trees.
- Step-by-step analysis with examples may uncover hidden rules.
- The divide-and-conquer approach breaks down a problem into manageable pieces and solves them recursively.

Each strategy is illustrated with several sample coding interview questions.

Figures to Visualize Problems

Figures are helpful tools to analyze and solve problems. When interview problems are complex, it is a good practice for candidates to visualize them with figures, which may help uncover hidden rules. Many candidates get inspiration when drawing figures or say "Gotcha" while staring at figures.

Figures are extremely useful in analyzing problems about data structures such as binary trees, 2D matrices, and lists. Sometimes it is difficult to find a solution after meditating for a long time over the problem, but with a few figures you can get the hang of it. Take the problem "Mirror of Binary Trees" (Question 51) as an example. The operations to get a mirrored image of a binary tree are not simple. However, if we draw some figures using binary trees and their mirrored images, we may find that it is only necessary to swap the left and right children nodes of each node while traversing.

Figures are also quite helpful tools to facilitate communications with interviewers. It can be difficult to explain complicated solutions only with spoken words. However, as we know, a picture is worth a thousand words. It is much easier for interviewers to understand the candidates' ideas if candidates draw some figures while explaining their solutions. The habit of drawing intelligible figures while explaining solutions is a demonstration of strong communication skills during interviews.

Mirror of Binary Trees

∎ **Question 51**   Given a binary tree, how do you get its mirrored tree?

The mirrored tree is a new concept for many candidates. If you cannot find a solution in a short time, you may try to draw a binary tree and its mirrored image. The tree on the right of Figure 6-1 is the mirrored image of the tree on the left.

Let's try to figure out the steps needed to get a mirrored tree by scrutinizing these two trees. Their root nodes are the same, but their left and right children are swapped. Therefore, two nodes under the root are swapped and the result is shown as the second tree in Figure 6-2.

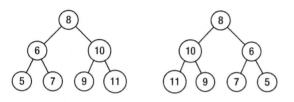

Figure 6-1. *Two binary trees of which one is the mirrored tree of the other*

After two nodes under the root have been swapped, notice that the order of children nodes under these two nodes is different from the mirrored target tree. Therefore, it continues to swap children nodes and gets the third and fourth trees in Figure 6-2. The fourth tree looks the same as the mirrored image of the original tree.

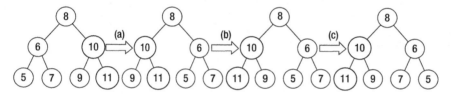

Figure 6-2. *The process to get a mirrored tree. (a) Swap the left and right subtrees of the root node. (b) Swap the left and right subtrees of the node with value 10. (c) Swap the left and right subtrees of the node with value 6.*

The process to get a mirrored tree can be summarized in a couple of sentences. Scan a binary tree with the pre-order traversal algorithm. When a node is visited, its children nodes are swapped.

This solution can be implemented based on recursion, as shown in Listing 6-1.

Listing 6-1. *C++ Code to Get a Mirrored Image of a Binary Tree*

```cpp
void MirrorRecursively(BinaryTreeNode *pNode) {
    if(pNode == NULL)
        return;
    if(pNode->m_pLeft == NULL && pNode->m_pRight == NULL)
        return;

    BinaryTreeNode *pTemp = pNode->m_pLeft;
    pNode->m_pLeft = pNode->m_pRight;
    pNode->m_pRight = pTemp;

    if(pNode->m_pLeft)
        MirrorRecursively(pNode->m_pLeft);
```

```
    if(pNode->m_pRight)
        MirrorRecursively(pNode->m_pRight);
}
```

Source Code:

051_MirrorOfBinaryTree.cpp

Test Cases:

- Functional Cases (Normal binary trees)
- Cases for Robustness (The pointer to the head of a binary tree is NULL; a binary tree with only one node; some special binary trees where nodes do not have left/right subtrees)

■ **Question 52**   Please implement a function to verify whether a binary tree is symmetrical. A tree is symmetrical if its mirrored image looks the same as the tree itself.

There are three binary trees in Figure 6-3. The first tree is symmetrical, but the second and the third are not.

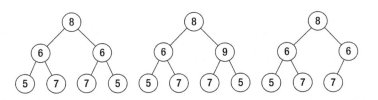

Figure 6-3. Three binary trees. The first tree is symmetrical, but the other two are not.

As we know, there are three common depth-first traversals, which are pre-order, in-order, and post-order traversals. Left children are visited prior to right children with these algorithms. What if we define a mirrored traversal algorithm that visits right children before left children? For example, it visits the root node first, then the left children, and finally the right children with the pre-order traversal algorithm. If the mirrored pre-order traversal algorithm is applied, it visits the root node first, then the right children, and finally the left children.

If the first tree in Figure 6-3 is scanned with the pre-order traversal algorithm, the traversal sequence is {8, 6, 5, 7, 6, 7, 5}. If the mirrored pre-order traversal is applied, its traversal sequence is {8, 6, 5, 7, 6, 7, 5}. Notice that these two sequences are identical to each other.

The traversal sequence of the second tree is {8, 6, 5, 7, 9, 7, 5} if the pre-order traversal algorithm is applied, and the sequence is {8, 9, 5, 7, 6, 7, 5} with the mirrored pre-order traversal. The second and fifth steps are different. Similarly, the traversal sequences are {8, 6, 5, 7, 6, 7} and {8, 6, 7, 6, 7, 5} for the third tree with the normal and mirrored pre-order traversals. They differ from each other starting with the third step.

We have found that the pre-order traversal sequence and mirrored pre-order traversal sequence are the same when a binary tree is symmetrical; otherwise, these two sequences are different. Therefore, we can verify whether a tree is symmetrical with the code shown in Listing 6-2.

Listing 6-2. *C++ Code to Verify Symmetrical Trees*

```cpp
bool isSymmetrical(BinaryTreeNode* pRoot) {
    return isSymmetrical(pRoot, pRoot);
}

bool isSymmetrical(BinaryTreeNode* pRoot1, BinaryTreeNode* pRoot2) {
    if(pRoot1 == NULL && pRoot2 == NULL)
        return true;

    if(pRoot1 == NULL || pRoot2 == NULL)
        return false;

    if(pRoot1->m_nValue != pRoot2->m_nValue)
        return false;

    return isSymmetrical(pRoot1->m_pLeft, pRoot2->m_pRight)
        && isSymmetrical(pRoot1->m_pRight, pRoot2->m_pLeft);
}
```

Source Code:

> 052_SymmetricalBinaryTrees.cpp

Test Cases:

- Functional Cases (Ordinary binary trees are/are not symmetrical)

- Cases for Robustness (The pointer to the head of a binary tree is NULL; a binary tree with only one node; some special binary trees where nodes do not have left/right subtrees)

Print Matrix in Spiral Order

■ **Question 53**   Please print a matrix in spiral order, clockwise from outer rings to inner rings. For example, the matrix below is printed in the sequence of 1, 2, 3, 4, 8, 12, 16, 15, 14, 13, 9, 5, 6, 7, 11, 10.

```
1  2  3  4
5  6  7  8
9  10 11 12
13 14 15 16
```

It looks like a simple problem because it is not about any complex data structures or advanced algorithms. However, the source code to solve this problem contains many loops with lots of boundary values. Many candidates find themselves in a pickle if they begin to write code before they get clear ideas of all the issues involved.

Figures are helpful tools to analyze problems. Since it is required to print to a matrix from outer rings to inner ones, a matrix is viewed as a set of concentric rings. Figure 6-4 shows a ring in a square matrix. A matrix can be printed in a `for` or `while` loop starting with outer rings and moving to the interior in each iteration.

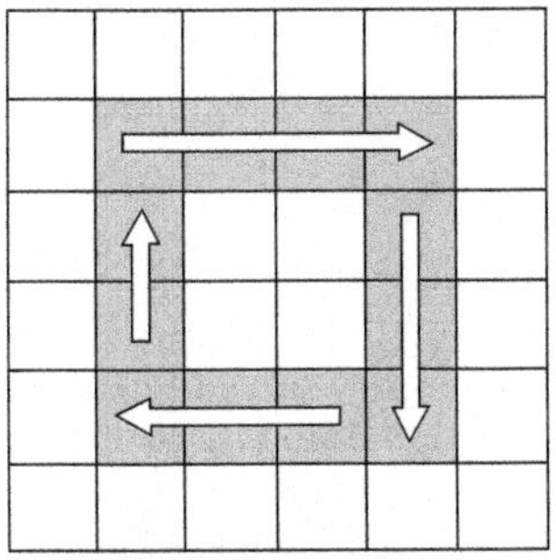

Figure 6-4. *A matrix is composed of a set of rings.*

Let's analyze when to end the iteration. Suppose there are r rows and c columns in a matrix. Notice the row index and column index are always identical in the beginning element in each ring at the top left corner. The index of the beginning element in the ith ring is denoted as (i, i). The statements $c > i \times 2$ and $r > i \times 2$ are always `true` for all rings in a matrix. Therefore, a matrix can be printed iteratively with the code shown in Listing 6-3.

Listing 6-3. *Java Code to Print a Matrix*

```java
void printMatrixClockwise(int numbers[][]) {
    int rows = numbers.length;
    int columns = numbers[0].length;
    int start = 0;

    while(columns > start * 2 && rows > start * 2) {
        printRing(numbers, start);

        ++start;
    }
}
```

Let's move on to implement the method `printRing` to print a ring in a matrix. As shown in Figure 6-4, a ring can be printed in four steps. It prints a row from left to right in the first step, a column in top down order in the second step, then another row from right to left in the third step, and finally a column bottom up.

There are many corner cases worthy of attention. The innermost ring in a matrix might only have a column, a row, or even an element. Some corner cases are included in Figure 6-5, where it only needs three steps, two steps, or even one step to print the innermost ring.

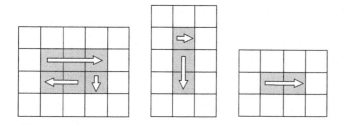

Figure 6-5. *It may take three, two, or even one step to print the last ring in a matrix.*

We have to analyze the prerequisites for each step. The first step is always necessary since there is at least one element in a ring. The second step is not needed if there is only one row remaining in the last ring. Similarly, the third step is needed when there are two rows and two columns at least in a ring, and the fourth step is needed when there are three rows and two columns. Therefore, the method `printRing` can be implemented as shown in Listing 6-4.

Listing 6-4. *Java Code to Print a Ring in a Matrix*

```
void printRing(int numbers[][], int start) {
    int rows = numbers.length;
    int columns = numbers[0].length;
    int endX = columns - 1 - start;
    int endY = rows - 1 - start;

    // Print a row from left to right
    for(int i = start; i <= endX; ++i) {
        int number = numbers[start][i];
        printNumber(number);
    }

    // print a column top down
    if(start < endY) {
        for(int i = start + 1; i <= endY; ++i) {
            int number = numbers[i][endX];
            printNumber(number);
        }
    }

    // print a row from right to left
    if(start < endX && start < endY) {
        for(int i = endX - 1; i >= start; --i) {
            int number = numbers[endY][i];
            printNumber(number);
        }
    }

    // print a column bottom up
    if(start < endX && start < endY - 1) {
        for(int i = endY - 1; i >= start + 1; --i) {
```

```
            int number = numbers[i][start];
            printNumber(number);
        }
    }
}
```

Source Code:

    053_PrintMatrix.java

Test Cases:

- Functional Cases (A matrix with multiple rows and columns)
- Boundary Cases (A matrix with only a row, a column, or even an element)

Clone Complex Lists

■ **Question 54**   Please implement a function to clone a complex list. Every node in a complex list has a link m_pSibling to an arbitrary node in the list besides the link m_pNext to the next node.
For example, there is a complex list in Figure 6-6 with five nodes. The dashed arrows are m_pSibling links, and the normal arrows are m_pNext links.

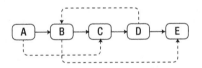

Figure 6-6. A complex list with five nodes. Normal arrows are links to the next nodes, and dashed arrows are links to arbitrary nodes. Pointers to NULL are not drawn for simplicity.

It is not difficult to get the brute-force solution in two steps. In the first step, clone every node in the original list and link all cloned nodes with m_pNext pointers. In the second step, set m_pSibling links on the cloned list. Let's suppose m_pSibling of node *N* points to node *S* in the original list, and the cloned node of *N* is *N'*. If the distance between the head node and node *S* in the original list is *s*, the distance between the head node and node *S'*, referenced by m_pSibling of *N'* in the cloned list, should also be *s*.

If there are *n* nodes in a list, this solution has to move O(*n*) steps beginning from the head node to locate the target of a m_pSibling link. Therefore, the overall time complexity of this solution is O(n^2).

Notice that most of the time is spent on locating targets of m_pSibling links. We can improve time efficiency with another solution. The new solution also clones a list in two steps. In the first step, it creates a node *N'* and clones data from every node *N* in the original list and links all cloned nodes together with m_pNext pointers. Additionally, all node pairs <*N, N'*> are saved in a hash table where *N* is a key and *N'* is a value. The second step is also to set m_pSibling links on the cloned list. Suppose m_pSibling of node *N* points to node *S* in the original list and their corresponding nodes are *N'* and *S'* in the cloned list. This solution can locate *S'* in O(1) time in the hash table with node *S*.

The second solution sacrifices space efficiency for time efficiency. It needs a hash table with $O(n)$ size if there are n nodes in a list, and it reduces the time complexity to $O(n)$ from $O(n^2)$.

Let's explore another solution with $O(n)$ time efficiency and without auxiliary space consumption. Similar to before, this solution also creates new nodes and clones the data of the original nodes. However, the cloned node N' is linked next to the original node N. The list in Figure 6-6 becomes longer after this step, as shown in Figure 6-7.

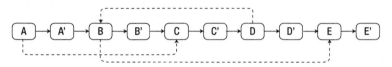

Figure 6-7. *The first step to clone a complex list. A node N' is created in order to clone a node N, and it is linked as the next node of N.*

The source code for the first step to clone a complex list is shown in Listing 6-5.

Listing 6-5. *C++ Code of the First Step to Clone a Complex List*

```cpp
void CloneNodes(ComplexListNode* pHead) {
    ComplexListNode* pNode = pHead;
    while(pNode != NULL) {
        ComplexListNode* pCloned = new ComplexListNode();
        pCloned->m_nValue = pNode->m_nValue;
        pCloned->m_pNext = pNode->m_pNext;
        pCloned->m_pSibling = NULL;

        pNode->m_pNext = pCloned;
        pNode = pCloned->m_pNext;
    }
}
```

Figure 6-8. *The second step to clone a complex list. If the m_pSlibling of a node N points to S, the m_pSlibling of the cloned node N' points to S', which is the next node of S.*

The second step is to set m_pSibling for each cloned node. Suppose that originally the m_pSibling in node N points to node S. Node N', the cloned node of N, is the next node of N, and node S' is also the next node of S. Therefore, it locates the m_pSibling target of node N' in $O(1)$ time. The list after setting all m_pSibling links is shown in Figure 6-8.

The code for the second step is shown in Listing 6-6.

Listing 6-6. *C++ Code of the Second Step to Clone a Complex List*

```cpp
void ConnectSiblingNodes(ComplexListNode* pHead) {
    ComplexListNode* pNode = pHead;
    while(pNode != NULL) {
        ComplexListNode* pCloned = pNode->m_pNext;
        if(pNode->m_pSibling != NULL) {
            pCloned->m_pSibling = pNode->m_pSibling->m_pNext;
        }
        pNode = pCloned->m_pNext;
    }
}
```

It splits the long list into two lists in the third step. The nodes with odd indexes are linked together with m_pNext pointers, which reform the original list. The nodes with even indexes are linked together with m_pNext pointers too, and they compose the cloned list, as shown in Figure 6-9.

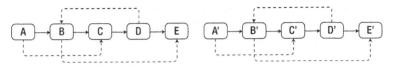

Figure 6-9. *The third step to clone a complex list, which splits the list in Figure 6-8 into two lists. The nodes with odd indexes (1ˢᵗ, 3ʳᵈ, 5ᵗʰ, and so on) compose the original list, while others compose the cloned list.*

The code for the third step is shown in Listing 6-7.

Listing 6-7. *C++ Code of the Third Step to Clone a Complex List*

```cpp
ComplexListNode* ReconnectNodes(ComplexListNode* pHead) {
    ComplexListNode* pNode = pHead;
    ComplexListNode* pClonedHead = NULL;
    ComplexListNode* pClonedNode = NULL;

    if(pNode != NULL) {
        pClonedHead = pClonedNode = pNode->m_pNext;
        pNode->m_pNext = pClonedNode->m_pNext;
        pNode = pNode->m_pNext;
    }

    while(pNode != NULL) {
        pClonedNode->m_pNext = pNode->m_pNext;
        pClonedNode = pClonedNode->m_pNext;
        pNode->m_pNext = pClonedNode->m_pNext;
        pNode = pNode->m_pNext;
    }

    return pClonedHead;
}
```

It is the whole process to clone a complex list when the three steps above are combined together, as shown in Listing 6-8.

Listing 6-8. *C++ Code of the Third Step to Clone a Complex List*

```
ComplexListNode* Clone(ComplexListNode* pHead) {
    CloneNodes(pHead);
    ConnectSiblingNodes(pHead);
    return ReconnectNodes(pHead);
}
```

Source Code:

```
054_CloneComplexList.cpp
```

Test Cases:

- Functional Cases (Lists with multiple nodes and m_pSibling links)

- Boundary Cases (There is only one node in a list; there are loops with m_pSibling links, or some of the m_pSibling links are connected to their owner nodes)

- Cases for Robustness (the pointer to the head node of a list is NULL)

Examples to Simplify Problems

Similar to figures, examples are also helpful tools to analyze and solve complex problems. It is quite common for candidates to find solutions when they utilize examples to simulate complicated processes step-by-step. For instance, many candidates cannot find rules to push and pop quickly for the interview question "Push and Pop Sequences of Stacks" (Question 56). When meeting such a problem, candidates may take one or two sequences as examples to simulate the pushing and popping operations. It is much easier to uncover the hidden rules with step-by-step analysis.

Examples can help candidates to communicate with interviewers. Abstract algorithms are usually difficult to explain only with oral words. In such situations, candidates may tell interviewers how their algorithms handle some sample inputs in a stepwise manner. Take the interview problem "Print Binary Trees in Zigzag Order" (Question 59) as an example. Candidates may take some sample binary trees with multiple levels as samples to illustrate why they need two stacks.

Examples are great tools to assure code quality during interviews. It is a good habit for candidates to review their code carefully and make sure that there are no bugs before they hand code to interviewers. How do you check for bugs? The answer is test cases. The examples utilized to analyze problems are test cases. Candidates can simulate execution in their minds. If operation results at every step on all examples are the same as expected, the code quality is assured.

Stack with Min Function

An intuitive solution for this problem might be that it sorts all numbers in the stack when it pushes a new element and keeps the minimum number on the top of stack. In this way, we can get the minimum number in O(1) time. However, it cannot be guaranteed that the last number pushed in to the container will be the first one to be popped off, so the data container is no longer a stack.

■ **Question 55** Define a stack in which we can get its minimum number with a function `min`. The time complexity of `min`, `push`, and `pop` on such stacks are all O(1).

A new field variable may be added in a stack to keep the minimum number. When a new number that is less than the minimum number is pushed, the minimum gets updated. It sounds good. However, how do you get the next minimum when the current minimum is popped? This naïve solution does not work either.

Let's explore other alternatives.

With an Auxiliary Stack

It is not enough just to keep a field variable as the minimum number. When the minimum is popped, the solution should be able to find the next minimum. Therefore, it is necessary to restore the next minimum number after the current minimum one is popped off.

How about storing each minimum number (the lesser value of the number to be pushed and the minimum number at that time) into an auxiliary stack? Let's analyze the process needed to push and pop numbers via some examples (Table 6-1).

At first, the solution pushes 3 into both data stack and auxiliary stack. The second number to be pushed into the data stack is the number 4. It pushes 3 again into the auxiliary stack because the number 4 is greater than 3. Third, it continues pushing 2 into the data stack. It updates the minimum number to 2 and pushes 2 into the auxiliary stack since 2 is less than the previous minimum number 3. The fourth step to push 1 is similar. The minimum number is updated to 1, and it is pushed into the auxiliary stack. Notice that the top of the auxiliary stack is always the minimum number in each step.

Table 6-1. *The Status of the Data Stack, Auxiliary Stack, and Minimum Number When It Pushes the Numbers 3, 4, 2, 1, Pops Twice, and Then Pushes 0*

Step	Operation	Data Stack	Auxiliary Stack	Minimum
1	Push 3	3	3	3
2	Push 4	3, 4	3, 3	3
3	Push 2	3, 4, 2	3, 3, 2	2
4	Push 1	3, 4, 2, 1	3, 3, 2, 1	1
5	Pop	3, 4, 2	3, 3, 2	2
6	Pop	3, 4	3, 3	3
7	Push 0	3, 4, 0	3, 3, 0	0

Whenever a number is popped from the data stack, a number is also popped from the auxiliary stack. If the minimum number is popped, the next minimum number should also be on the top of the auxiliary stack. In the fifth step, it pops 1 from the data stack, and it also pops the number on the top of the auxiliary, which is 1. The next minimum number, 2, is now on the top of the auxiliary stack. If it continues popping from both the data and auxiliary stacks, there are only two numbers, 3 and 4, left in the data stack. The minimum number, 3, is indeed on the top of the auxiliary stack. If a new number, 0, is pushed into the data stack, as well as the auxiliary stack, the number on top of the auxiliary stack is the minimum 0.

This step-by-step analysis demonstrates that our solution is correct. Now it is time to implement the required stack, which can be defined as the code found in Listing 6-8.

Listing 6-8. C++ Code for a Stack with Function Min (Version 1)

```cpp
template <typename T> class StackWithMin {
public:
    StackWithMin(void) {}
    virtual ~StackWithMin(void) {}

    T& top(void);

    void push(const T& value);
    void pop(void);

    const T& min(void) const;

private:
    std::stack<T>   m_data;     // data stack, to store numbers
    std::stack<T>   m_min;      // auxiliary stack, to store minimum numbers
};

template <typename T> void StackWithMin<T>::push(const T& value) {
    m_data.push(value);

    if(m_min.size() == 0 || value < m_min.top())
        m_min.push(value);
    else
        m_min.push(m_min.top());
}

template <typename T> void StackWithMin<T>::pop() {
    assert(m_data.size() > 0 && m_min.size() > 0);

    m_data.pop();
    m_min.pop();
}

template <typename T> const T& StackWithMin<T>::min() const {
    assert(m_data.size() > 0 && m_min.size() > 0);

    return m_min.top();
}

template <typename T> T& StackWithMin<T>::top() {
    return m_data.top();
}
```

The length of the auxiliary stack is n if it pushes n numbers into the data stack. Therefore, it takes O(n) auxiliary memory for this solution.

Without an Auxiliary Stack

The second solution is trickier without an auxiliary stack. It requires arithmetic before pushing rather than always pushing numbers into the data stack directly.

Suppose that the solution is going to push a number *value* into a stack with minimum number *min*. If *value* is greater than or equal to *min*, it is pushed directly into the data stack. If it is less than *min*, it pushes 2×*value*-*min* into the stack and updates *min* as *value* since a new minimum number is pushed.

How about pop? It pops directly if the number at the top of the data stack (denoted as *top*) is greater than or equal to *min*. Otherwise, the number on the top is not the real pushed number. The real pushed number is *min*. After the current minimum number is popped, it restores the previous minimum number, which is 2×*min*-*top*.

Now let's demonstrate the correctness of this solution. When *value* is greater than or equal to *min*, it is pushed into the data stack directly without updating *min*. Therefore, when the number on the top of the stack is greater than or equal to *min*, it is popped off directly without updating *min*.

However, if *value* is less than *min*, it pushes 2×*value*-*min*. Notice that 2×*value*-*min*=*value*+(*value*-*min*), and *value*+(*value*-*min*) should be less than *value* when *value* is less than *min*. Then the solution updates current *min* as *value*, so the new top of the data stack (*top*) is less than the current *min*. Therefore, when the number on the top of the data stack is less than *min*, the real pushed number value is stored in *min*. After the number on top of the stack is popped off, it has to restore the previous minimum number (denoted as *min'*). Since *top*=2×*value*-*min'* and *value* is the current *min*, the previous minimum number is restored with *min'*=2×*min*-*top*.

It sounds great. We now feel confident to write code with the correctness demonstrated. The code in Listing 6-10 is the sample code.

Listing 6-10. *C++ Code for a Stack with Function Min (Version 2)*

```cpp
template <typename T> class StackWithMin {
public:
    StackWithMin(void) {}
    virtual ~StackWithMin(void) {}

    T& top(void);

    void push(const T& value);
    void pop(void);

    const T& min(void) const;

private:
    std::stack<T>   m_data;      // data stack, to store numbers
    T               m_min;       // minimum number
};

template <typename T> void StackWithMin<T>::push(const T& value) {
    if(m_data.size() == 0) {
        m_data.push(value);
        m_min = value;
```

```
    }
    else if(value >= m_min) {
        m_data.push(value);
    }
    else {
        m_data.push(2 * value - m_min);
        m_min = value;
    }
}

template <typename T> void StackWithMin<T>::pop() {
    assert(m_data.size() > 0);

    if(m_data.top() < m_min)
        m_min = 2 * m_min - m_data.top();

    m_data.pop();
}

template <typename T> const T& StackWithMin<T>::min() const {
    assert(m_data.size() > 0);

    return m_min;
}

template <typename T> T& StackWithMin<T>::top() {
    T top = m_data.top();
    if(top < m_min)
        top = m_min;

    return top;
}
```

In this solution, it is not necessary to have an auxiliary stack with $O(n)$ elements, so it is more efficient from the perspective of memory utilization than the first solution.

Source Code:

```
055_MinInStack.cpp
```

Test Cases:

- The number to be pushed is less/greater than or equal to the current minimum number in a stack

- The number to be popped is/is not the current minimum number in a stack

Push and Pop Sequence of Stacks

■ **Question 56**   You are given two integer arrays, one of which is a sequence of numbers pushed into a stack (supposing all numbers are unique). Please check whether the other array is a corresponding sequence popped from the stack.

For example, if the pushing sequence is {1, 2, 3, 4, 5}, the sequence {4, 5, 3, 2, 1} is a corresponding popping sequence, but {4, 3, 5, 1, 2} is not.

An auxiliary stack is utilized to stimulate pushing and popping operations, and the order of operations is defined by the two pushing and popping sequences. Let's simulate pushing and popping operations step-by-step in the sample sequences.

The first number to be popped off is 4 in the popping sequence {4, 5, 3, 2, 1}. The number 4 should be pushed into the auxiliary stack before it is popped off. The pushing order is defined by the sequence {1, 2, 3, 4, 5}, so numbers 1, 2 and 3 are pushed into the stack before the number 4. Four numbers (1, 2, 3, and 4) are in the stack at this time, and the number 4 is on top.

After the number 4 is popped off, three numbers (1, 2, and 3) are left. The next number to be popped is 5, but 5 has not been pushed into the stack yet. Therefore, numbers left in the pushing sequence are pushed into the stack. When the number 5 is pushed, it can be popped, and three numbers (1, 2, and 3) are left in the stack.

The next numbers to be popped off are 3, 2, and 1, and they are on the top of the stack before popping operations, so there are no problems popping them off one by one.

The steps to push and pop numbers according the pushing sequence {1, 2, 3, 4, 5} and popping sequence {4, 5, 3, 2, 1} are summarized in Table 6-2.

Table 6-2. *The Process Used to Push and Pop Elements According to the Pushing Sequence {1, 2, 3, 4, 5} and Popping Sequence {4, 5, 3, 2, 1}*

Step	Operation	Stack	Popped	Step	Operation	Stack	Popped
1	Push 1	1		6	Push 5	1, 2, 3, 5	
2	Push 2	1, 2		7	Pop	1, 2, 3	5
3	Push 3	1, 2, 3		8	Pop	1, 2	3
4	Push 4	1, 2, 3, 4		9	Pop	1	2
5	Pop	1, 2, 3	4	10	Pop		1

Let's take the popping sequence {4, 3, 5, 1, 2} as another example. Similar to before, numbers prior to 4 in the pushing sequence should be pushed into the stack because the number 4 is the first number to be popped off. The next number to be popped is 3, and it is on the top of the stack, so it is popped directly.

At this time there are two numbers, 1 and 2, in the stack. The number 5 is not in the stack, which is the next number to be popped. Numbers remaining in the pushing sequence are pushed into the stack. The number 5 can be popped after it is pushed into the stack.

The next number to be popped off is 1, but it is not on the top of the stack. The number on the top of the stack is 2. Additionally, there are no numbers remaining in the pushing sequence, so no more numbers can be pushed into the stack. We cannot continue to pop numbers, as shown in Table 6-3.

Table 6-3. *The Process to Push and Pop Elements According to the Pushing Sequence {1, 2, 3, 4, 5} and Popping Sequence {4, 3, 5, 1, 2}*

Step	Operation	Stack	Popped	Step	Operation	Stack	Popped
1	Push 1	1		6	Pop	1, 2	3
2	Push 2	1, 2		7	Push 5	1, 2, 5	
3	Push 3	1, 2, 3		8	Pop	1, 2	5
4	Push 4	1, 2, 3, 4		The next number to be popped is 1, but 1 is not on the top of the stack.			
5	Pop	1, 2, 3	4				

Let's summarize the process analyzed in detail. When the next number to be popped is on top of the stack, it is popped off directly. If it is not, more numbers are pushed into the stack. If the next number to be popped is not found when all numbers have been pushed, the sequence cannot be a popping sequence.

We feel confident enough to write the code after we have clear ideas about the pushing and popping process. The sample code is shown in Listing 6-11.

Listing 6-11. *C++ Code for Pushing and Popping Sequences of Stacks*

```cpp
bool IsPopOrder(const int* pPush, const int* pPop, int nLength) {
    bool bPossible = false;

    if(pPush != NULL && pPop != NULL && nLength > 0) {
        const int* pNextPush = pPush;
        const int* pNextPop = pPop;
        std::stack<int> stackData;

        while(pNextPop - pPop < nLength) {
            // Push some numbers when the number to be popped is not
            // is not on the top of the stack
            while(stackData.empty() || stackData.top() != *pNextPop) {
                // Break when all numbers have been pushed
                if(pNextPush - pPush == nLength)
                    break;

                stackData.push(*pNextPush);
                pNextPush ++;
```

```
        }

        if(stackData.top() != *pNextPop)
            break;

        stackData.pop();
        pNextPop ++;
    }

    if(stackData.empty() && pNextPop - pPop == nLength)
        bPossible = true;
    }

    return bPossible;
}
```

Source Code:

    056_StackPushPopOrder.cpp

Test Cases:

- Functional Cases (The pushing and popping sequences contain one or more numbers; an array is/is not the popping sequence corresponding to the pushing sequence in the other array)

- Cases for Robustness (One or two pointers to the arrays are NULL)

Print Binary Trees Level by Level

■ **Question 57**   Please print a binary tree from its top level to bottom level, and print nodes at the same level from left to right.

For example, the binary tree in Figure 6-10 is printed in the sequence of 8, 6, 10, 5, 7, 9, 11.

This problem examines candidates' understanding of tree traversal algorithms, but the traversal here is not the common pre-order, in-order, or post-order traversals. If you are not familiar with it, you may analyze the printing process with some examples during the interview. Let's take the binary tree in Figure 6-10 as an example.

Since we begin to print from the top level of the tree in Figure 6-10, we can start our analysis from its root node. First, the value of the root node is printed, which is 8. You can store its children nodes with values 6 and 10 in a data container in order to print them after the root is printed. There are two nodes in the container at this time.

Second, node 6 is retrieved from the container prior to node 10 since nodes 6 and 10 are at the same level and we need to print them from left to right. Nodes 5 and 7 are stored to the container after node 6 is printed. There are three nodes in the container now, which are nodes 10, 5, and 7.

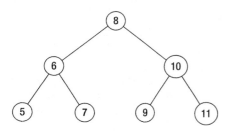

Figure 6-10. *A sample binary tree with three levels*

Third, we retrieve node 10 from the container. Notice that node 10 is stored in the container before nodes 5 and 7 are stored, and it is also retrieved prior to nodes 5 and 7. It is a typical "First In, First Out" order, so the container is essentially a queue. After node 10 is printed, its two children, nodes 9 and 11, are stored in the container, too.

Nodes 5, 7, 9, and 11 do not have children, and they are printed from the head of the queue one by one. The printing process is summarized in Table 6-4.

Table 6-4. *The Process to Print the Binary Tree in Figure 6-10 from Top to Bottom*

Step	Operation	Nodes in the Queue
1	Print Node 8	6, 10
2	Print Node 6	10, 5, 7
3	Print Node 10	5, 7, 9, 11
4	Print Node 5	7, 9, 11
5	Print Node 7	9, 11
6	Print Node 9	11
7	Print Node 11	

Let's summarize the rules needed to print a binary tree from top level to bottom level. Once a node is printed, if it has children, its children nodes are stored in a queue. We continue to print the head of the queue, pop it from the queue, and push its children to the tail of the queue until there are no nodes left in the queue. The sample code in Listing 6-12 is based on the **queue** class in the standard template library (STL) in C++.

Listing 6-12. *C++ Code to Print a Binary Tree Level by Level*

```
void PrintFromTopToBottom(BinaryTreeNode* pRoot) {
    if(pRoot == NULL)
        return;

    std::queue<BinaryTreeNode *> queueTreeNodes;
    queueTreeNodes.push(pRoot);
```

```
    while(queueTreeNodes.size() > 0) {
        BinaryTreeNode *pNode = queueTreeNodes.front();
        queueTreeNodes.pop();

        printf("%d ", pNode->m_nValue);

        if(pNode->m_pLeft)
            queueTreeNodes.push(pNode->m_pLeft);

        if(pNode->m_pRight)
            queueTreeNodes.push(pNode->m_pRight);
    }
}
```

Source Code:

```
057_PrintTreeByLevel.cpp
```

Test Cases:

- Functional Cases (Normal binary trees with multiple levels)

- Boundary Cases (Special binary trees, such a binary tree with only one node, or all nodes in a binary tree only having left/right subtrees)

- Cases for Robustness (The pointer to the tree root is NULL)

■ **Question 58**   How do you print a binary tree by level, in top down order, with each level in a line? Nodes in a level should be printed from left to right.

For example, the result of printing the binary tree in Figure 6-10 is:

8

6 10

5 7 9 11

This problem is quite similar to the preceding one for which a queue is utilized to store nodes to be printed. In order to print each level in a line, it is necessary to define two variables: one for the number of nodes to be printed in the current level, and the other for the number of nodes in the next level. The sample code is shown in Listing 6-13.

Listing 6-13. C++ *Code to Print a Binary Tree Level by Level*

```
void Print(BinaryTreeNode* pRoot) {
    if(pRoot == NULL)
        return;

    std::queue<BinaryTreeNode*> nodes;
    nodes.push(pRoot);
```

```
    int nextLevel = 0;
    int toBePrinted = 1;
    while(!nodes.empty()) {
        BinaryTreeNode* pNode = nodes.front();
        printf("%d ", pNode->m_nValue);

        if(pNode->m_pLeft != NULL) {
            nodes.push(pNode->m_pLeft);
            ++nextLevel;
        }
        if(pNode->m_pRight != NULL) {
            nodes.push(pNode->m_pRight);
            ++nextLevel;
        }

        nodes.pop();
        --toBePrinted;
        if(toBePrinted == 0) {
            printf("\n");
            toBePrinted = nextLevel;
            nextLevel = 0;
        }
    }
}
```

In the code above, the variable `toBePrinted` is the node count to be printed in the current level, and `nextLevel` is the node count on the next level. If a node has children nodes, its children are pushed into the queue, and `nextLevel` is increased by the number of children. When a node is printed, `toBePrinted` is decreased by one. When `toBePrinted` becomes zero, all nodes on the current level have been printed, and it moves on to print nodes on the next level.

Source Code:

 058_PrintTreeALevelInALine.cpp

Test Cases:

- Functional Cases (Normal binary trees with multiple levels)

- Boundary Cases (Special binary trees, such as a binary tree with only one node, all nodes in a binary tree that only have left/right subtrees)

- Cases for Robustness (The pointer to the tree root is NULL)

___

■ **Question 59**   How do you print a binary tree by level in zigzag order, each level in a line? That is to say, nodes on the first level are printed from left to right, nodes on the second level are printed from right to left, nodes on the third level are printed from left to right again, and so on.

For example, the result from printing the binary tree in Figure 6-11 is:

```
1
3 2
4 5 6 7
15 14 13 12 11 10 9 8
```

The process of printing a binary tree in zigzag order is a bit tricky. If a candidate cannot find a solution in a short time, it is a good practice to try some examples to analyze the process step-by-step. Let's take the sample tree with four levels in Figure 6-11 as an example.

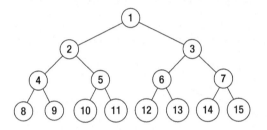

Figure 6-11. *A binary tree with four levels*

When the root node on the first level is printed, its left child (node 2) and right child (node 3) are stored into a data container. Node 3 is pushed into the data container after node 2, but node 3 should be printed before node 2 in zigzag order. Therefore, it sounds like the data container is a stack.

It continues to print nodes on the second level. Since node 3 is printed before node 2, children nodes of node 3 are stored into a data container prior to children nodes of node 2. According to the zigzag rule, children nodes of node 2 (node 4 and node 5) are printed before children nodes of node 3 (node 6 and node 7). Therefore, the data container used to store nodes in the third level is also a stack.

Table 6-5. *The First Seven Steps to Print the Binary Tree in Figure 6-11 in Zigzag Order. The Rightmost Numbers in Stack1 and Stack2 Are on the Top of Stacks.*

Step	Operation	Nodes in the Stack1	Nodes in the Stack2
1	Print Node 1	2, 3	
2	Print Node 3	2	7, 6
3	Print Node 2		7, 6, 5, 4
4	Print Node 4	8, 9	7, 6, 5
5	Print Node 5	8, 9, 10, 11	7, 7
6	Print Node 6	8, 9, 10, 11, 12, 13	7
7	Print Node 7	8, 9, 10, 11, 12, 13, 14, 15	

Additionally, since node 4 (the left child of node 2) should be printed before node 5 (the right child of node 2), the right children nodes in the third level should be pushed into the stack before their left sibling nodes. The stack for the third level is different from the stack for the second level, where the left child node (node 2) is pushed before its right sibling node (node 3).

After nodes in the second level are printed, it moves on to print nodes in the third node. The first node to be printed is node 4, and its children nodes (node 8 and node 9) at the fourth level are stored in a stack. Since node 9 should be printed prior to node 8, the left child is pushed before the right child again on the fourth level. The pushing order is different from the preceding level.

Therefore, two different stacks are needed to print a binary tree in zigzag order. The first stack is for nodes in the first and third levels, where left children nodes are pushed before right children nodes. The second stack is for nodes in the second and fourth level, where right children nodes are pushed before left children nodes.

Table 6-5 summarizes the first seven steps to print nodes. The next step to print nodes on the fourth level are quite simple because they are leaf nodes and do not have children. Nodes remaining in the first stack are popped and printed one by one.

It is time to develop code now that we have clear ideas about the process to print nodes in zigzag order. The sample code is shown in Listing 6-14.

Listing 6-14. C++ Code to Print a Binary Tree in Zigzag Order

```cpp
void Print(BinaryTreeNode* pRoot) {
    if(pRoot == NULL)
        return;

    std::stack<BinaryTreeNode*> levels[2];
    int current = 0;
    int next = 1;

    levels[current].push(pRoot);
    while(!levels[0].empty() || !levels[1].empty()) {
        BinaryTreeNode* pNode = levels[current].top();
        levels[current].pop();

        printf("%d ", pNode->m_nValue);

        if(current == 0) {
            if(pNode->m_pLeft != NULL)
                levels[next].push(pNode->m_pLeft);
            if(pNode->m_pRight != NULL)
                levels[next].push(pNode->m_pRight);
        }
        else {
            if(pNode->m_pRight != NULL)
                levels[next].push(pNode->m_pRight);
            if(pNode->m_pLeft != NULL)
                levels[next].push(pNode->m_pLeft);
        }

        if(levels[current].empty()) {
            printf("\n");
```

```
            current = 1 - current;
            next = 1 - next;
        }
    }
}
```

Two stacks, `levels[0]` and `levels[1]`, are used in the code above. When it prints nodes in one stack, it stores children nodes in the other stack. After all nodes in a level are printed, it interchanges the two stacks and moves on to print the next level.

Source Code:

`059_PrintTreeZigzag.cpp`

Test Cases:

- Functional Cases (Normal binary trees with multiple levels)

- Boundary Cases (Special binary trees, such as a binary tree with only one node, all nodes in a binary tree only have left/right subtrees)

- Cases for Robustness (The pointer to the tree root is `NULL`)

Paths in Binary Trees

■ **Question 60**   Given a binary tree and an integer value, please print all paths where the sum of node values equals the given integer. All nodes from the root node to a leaf node compose a path.

For example, given the binary tree in Figure 6-12, there are two paths with sum 22, of which one contains two nodes with values 10 and 12, and the other contains three nodes with values 10, 5, and 7.

Since paths always start from a root node, it might be easy to solve this problem with a traversal algorithm beginning from the root node in a binary tree. There are three common traversal orders, which are pre-order, in-order, and post-order. The solution first visits the root node with the pre-order traversal algorithm.

It visits node 5 after visiting the root node (10) of the binary tree in Figure 6-12 with the pre-order traversal. Since a binary tree node usually does not have a pointer to its parent, it is unknown what nodes have been visited when it reaches node 5 if the visited nodes on a path are not saved. Therefore, the current node is inserted into a path when it is reached during the traversal. The path contains two nodes with values 10 and 5 when it is visiting node 5. Then node 4 is inserted into the path, too, when it is reached. It arrives at a leaf node, and the sum of the three nodes in the path is 19. Since it is not the same as the target sum 22, the current path is not a qualified one.

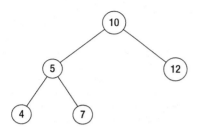

Figure 6-12. *A binary tree with two paths in which the sum of nodes is 22. One is the path through nodes 10, 5, and 7, and the other is the path through nodes 10 and 12.*

It continues to traverse other nodes. It has to return back to node 5, and then node 7 is visited. Notice that node 4 is no longer in the path from node 10 to node 7, so it should be removed from the path. When node 7 is visited, it is inserted into the path, which contains three nodes now. Since the sum of the value of these three nodes is 22, a qualified path has been found.

Last, the solution is going to visit node 12. It has to return back to node 5 and then back to node 10 before it visits node 12. When it returns back from a child node to its parent node, the child node is removed from the path. When it arrives at node 12 eventually, the path contains two nodes, one is node 10 and the other is node 12. Since the sum of the values of these two nodes is 22, the path is qualified, too. Table 6-6 summarizes this whole process.

Let's summarize some rules from the step-by-step analysis. When a node is visited with the pre-order traversal algorithm, it is inserted into the path, and the sum is increased by its value. When the node is a leaf and the sum is the same as specified, the path is qualified and it is printed. It continues to visit children nodes if the current node is not a leaf. After it finishes traversing a path to a leaf node, a recursive function will return back to its parent node automatically, so it has to remove the current node from the path before the function returns in order to make sure the nodes in the path correspond to the path from root node to its parent node.

The data structure to save paths should be a stack because paths should be consistent to the recursion status, and recursion is essentially pushing and popping in a call stack.

Table 6-6. *The Process to Traverse the Binary Tree in Figure 6-12 and Save the Sum of Node Values on Paths*

Step	Operation	A Leaf?	Path	Sum on Path
1	Visit Node 10	No	Node 10	10
2	Visit Node 5	No	Node 10, Node 5	15
3	Visit Node 4	Yes	Node 10, Node 5, Node 4	19
4	Return to Node 5		Node 10, Node 5	15
5	Visit Node 7	Yes	Node 10, Node 5, Node 7	22
6	Return to Node 5		Node 10, Node 5	15
7	Return to Node 10		Node 10	10
8	Visit Node 12	Yes	Node 10, Node 12	22

Listing 6-15 contains some sample code for this problem.

Listing 6-15. *C++ Code to Get Paths with a Specified Sum*

```cpp
void FindPath(BinaryTreeNode* pRoot, int expectedSum) {
    if(pRoot == NULL)
        return;

    std::vector<int> path;
    int currentSum = 0;
    FindPath(pRoot, expectedSum, path, currentSum);
}

void FindPath(BinaryTreeNode* pRoot, int expectedSum, std::vector<int>& path, int currentSum)
{
    currentSum += pRoot->m_nValue;
    path.push_back(pRoot->m_nValue);

    // Print the path is the current node is a leaf
    // and the sum of all nodes value is same as expectedSum
    bool isLeaf = pRoot->m_pLeft == NULL && pRoot->m_pRight == NULL;
    if(currentSum == expectedSum && isLeaf) {
        printf("A path is found: ");
        std::vector<int>::iterator iter = path.begin();
        for(; iter != path.end(); ++ iter)
            printf("%d\t", *iter);

        printf("\n");
    }

    // If it is not a leaf, continue visition its children
    if(pRoot->m_pLeft != NULL)
        FindPath(pRoot->m_pLeft, expectedSum, path, currentSum);
    if(pRoot->m_pRight != NULL)
        FindPath(pRoot->m_pRight, expectedSum, path, currentSum);

    // Before returning back to its parent, remove it from path,
    path.pop_back();
}
```

In this code, it saves the path into a **vector** in the standard template library (STL). It uses the function **push_back** to insert a node and **pop_back** to remove a node to assure that it follows the "First in, Last out" rule in the path. The reason it does not utilize a **stack** in STL is that it can only get an element at the top of a stack, but it needs to get all nodes when it prints a path. Therefore, it simulates a stack with a **vector** rather than to utilize a **stack** directly.

Source Code:

    060_PathInTree.cpp

Test Cases:

- Functional Cases (There are one or more paths with the specified sum; there are no paths with the specified sum)

- Boundary Cases (Special binary trees, such as a binary tree with only one node, or all nodes in a binary tree only have left/right subtrees)

- Cases for Robustness (The pointer to the tree root is NULL)

Divide and Conquer

The divide-and-conquer approach is an important algorithm design paradigm to analyze and solve complicated problems. A divide-and-conquer algorithm works by recursively breaking down a problem into two or more similar subproblems until the subproblems become simple enough to be solved directly. The solutions to the subproblems are then combined to compose a solution to the original problem.

Take the problem to convert a binary search tree to a sorted double-linked list as an example. The problem is to convert a binary search tree; it can be divided into two subproblems to convert the left and right subtrees. After two subtrees are converted to two sorted double-linked lists, they are connected to the root node and the original tree is converted. More details are available in the section *Binary Search Trees and Double-linked Lists*.

The divide-and-conquer algorithm also works when it reduces a problem to only one subproblem. For example, if the problem is to permute characters in a string, it can be divided into a subproblem to permute all characters excluding the first one. Please refer to the section *Permutation and Combination* for more details about this problem.

Traversal Sequences and Binary Trees

■ **Question 61**   Please build a binary tree with a pre-order traversal sequence and an in-order traversal sequence. All elements in these two given sequences are unique.

For example, if the input pre-order traversal sequence is {1, 2, 4, 7, 3, 5, 6, 8} and in-order traversal order is {4, 7, 2, 1, 5, 3, 8, 6}, the built tree is shown in Figure 6-13.

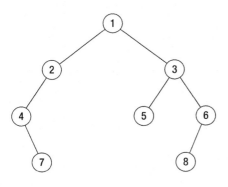

Figure 6-13. *The binary tree built from pre-order traversal sequence {1, 2, 4, 7, 3, 5, 6, 8} and in-order traversal sequence {4, 7, 2, 1, 5, 3, 8, 6}*

The root value is the first number in the pre-order traversal sequence of a binary tree, but it is in the middle of the in-order traversal sequence. Therefore, we have to scan the in-order traversal sequence to get the root value. As shown in Figure 6-14, the first number in the pre-order traversal sequence (number 1) is the root value. The location of root value is found if the whole in-order traversal sequence is scanned.

In the in-order traversal sequence, all numbers at the left side of the root value are for nodes in the left subtree, and all numbers at the right side of the root value correspond to nodes in the right subtree. According to the in-order traversal sequence in Figure 6-14, we find that there are three nodes in the left subtree and four in the right subtree. Therefore, the next three numbers behind the root value in the pre-order traversal sequence are for the left subtree, and the following four are for the right subtree.

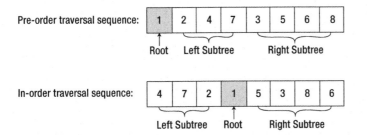

Figure 6-14. *Find the root node, the nodes in the left subtree, and the nodes in the right subtree in the pre-order traversal sequence and in-order traversal sequence.*

After the pre-order and in-order traversal sequences for both left and right subtrees are identified, subtrees can be built with recursion, similar to the process of building the whole tree. The sample code is shown in Listing 6-16 based on the divide-and-conquer approach.

Listing 6-16. *C++ Code to Build Binary Trees from Traversal Sequences*

```
BinaryTreeNode* Construct(int* preorder, int* inorder, int length) {
    if(preorder == NULL || inorder == NULL || length <= 0)
        return NULL;
```

```
        return ConstructCore(preorder, preorder + length - 1,
            inorder, inorder + length - 1);
}

BinaryTreeNode* ConstructCore(int* startPreorder, int* endPreorder, int* startInorder, int*
endInorder) {

    // The first number in the pre-order traversal sequence is the root value
    int rootValue = startPreorder[0];
    BinaryTreeNode* root = new BinaryTreeNode();
    root->m_nValue = rootValue;
    root->m_pLeft = root->m_pRight = NULL;

    if(startPreorder == endPreorder) {
        if(startInorder == endInorder
            && *startPreorder == *startInorder)
            return root;
        else
            throw std::exception("Invalid input.");
    }

    // Get the root value in the in-order traversal sequence
    int* rootInorder = startInorder;
    while(rootInorder <= endInorder && *rootInorder != rootValue)
        ++ rootInorder;

    if(rootInorder == endInorder && *rootInorder != rootValue)
        throw std::exception("Invalid input.");

    int leftLength = rootInorder - startInorder;
    int* leftPreorderEnd = startPreorder + leftLength;
    if(leftLength > 0) {
        // Build left subtree
        root->m_pLeft = ConstructCore(startPreorder + 1,
            leftPreorderEnd, startInorder, rootInorder - 1);
    }
    if(leftLength < endPreorder - startPreorder) {
        // Build rigth subtree
        root->m_pRight = ConstructCore(leftPreorderEnd + 1,
            endPreorder, rootInorder + 1, endInorder);
    }

    return root;
}
```

In the function ConstructCore, first the root value is gotten in the pre-order traversal sequence, and then it is located in the in-order traversal sequence. After the subsequence for the left and right subtrees are partitioned in the pre-order and in-order traversal sequences, the function ConstructCore is called recursively to build the left and right subtrees.

Source Code:

    061_ConstructBinaryTree.cpp

Test Cases:

- Functional Cases (Sequences for normal binary trees, including some full binary trees; no binary trees can be built from the given sequences)

- Boundary Cases (Special binary trees, such as a binary tree with only one node, or all nodes in a binary tree only have left/right subtrees)

- Cases for Robustness (The pointers to one or two arrays are NULL)

■ **Question 62**   How do you serialize and deserialize binary trees?

As discussed before, a binary tree can be built from a pre-order traversal sequence and an in-order traversal sequence. Inspired by this conclusion, if a binary is serialized to two number arrays for the pre-order and in-order traversal sequences, it can be rebuilt from these two arrays during deserialization.

   This solution works, but has two disadvantages. One disadvantage is that there should not be any duplicated numbers in the array; otherwise, it causes problems during deserialization. The other disadvantage is that it has to read all numbers in the two traversal sequences before deserialization begins, so it has to wait for a long time to start deserialization if data comes from a stream. Let's explore other alternatives.

   If serialization of a binary tree starts from the root node, the corresponding deserialization can start once the root value is received. Therefore, the pre-order traversal algorithm is applied to serialize a binary tree, which visits the root node first. When a NULL pointer is reached during traversal, it is serialized as a special character (such as a '$'). Additionally, node values should be separated by another character (such as a comma ','). According to these serialization rules, the binary tree in Figure 6-15 is serialized as a sequence "1,2,4,$,$,$,3,5,$,$,6,$,$". (See Listing 6-17.)

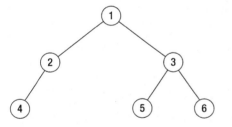

Figure 6-15. A binary tree whose serialization sequence is "1,2,4,$,$,$,3,5,$,$,6,$,$"

Listing 6-17. C++ Code to Serialize Binary Trees

```
void Serialize(BinaryTreeNode* pRoot, ostream& stream) {
    if(pRoot == NULL) {
        stream << "$,";
        return;
    }

    stream << pRoot->m_nValue << ',';
```

```
        Serialize(pRoot->m_pLeft, stream);
        Serialize(pRoot->m_pRight, stream);
}
```

Let's move on to analyze how to deserialize a binary tree. Take the serialization sequence "1,2,4,$,$,$,3,5,$,$,6,$,$" as an example. It first reads a number 1 from the stream, which is the root value of a binary tree. Another number 2 is read. Since the binary tree is serialized with the pre-order traversal algorithm, the number 2 is taken as the left child of the root node. Similarly, the next number, 4, is deserialized as the left child of the node with value 2. The following data read from the stream are two '$'s, which means that the node with value 4 is a leaf and does not have children nodes. It returns back to the parent node, the node with value 2, and continues to deserialize its right child. The right child of the node with value 2 is NULL because the next character read from the stream is also a '$'.

It returns back to the root node to deserialize the right subtree. A number 3 is read, so the right child of the root node contains value 3. The following data from the stream is another number 5, which is taken as the left child value of the node with value 3. The following two '$'s indicate that the node with value 5 is a leaf node. It continues to deserialize the right child of the node with value 3, which is another leaf node with value 6 because the next data from the stream is "6,$,$". It stops deserialization because all children of all non-leaf nodes have been constructed.

Listing 6-18 is the sample code used to deserialize a binary tree in C++.

Listing 6-18. *C++ Code to Deserialize Binary Trees*

```
void Deserialize(BinaryTreeNode** pRoot, istream& stream) {
    int number;
    if(ReadStream(stream, &number)) {
        *pRoot = new BinaryTreeNode();
        (*pRoot)->m_nValue = number;
        (*pRoot)->m_pLeft = NULL;
        (*pRoot)->m_pRight = NULL;

        Deserialize(&((*pRoot)->m_pLeft), stream);
        Deserialize(&((*pRoot)->m_pRight), stream);
    }
}
```

The function ReadStream in this code reads a token (a number or a `$') from a stream at every step. When a token received from the stream is a number, it returns true.

Source Code:

    062_SerializeBinaryTree.cpp

Test Cases:

- Functional Cases (Normal binary trees, including some full binary trees)

- Boundary Cases (Special binary trees, such as a binary tree with only one node, or all nodes in a binary tree only have left/right subtrees)

- Cases for Robustness (The pointer to the root node of a binary tree is NULL)

▪ **Question 63**   Please check whether it is possible for an array to be the post-order traversal sequence of a binary search tree. All numbers in the input array are unique.

For example, the array {5, 7, 6, 9, 11, 10, 8} is the post-order traversal sequence of the binary search tree in Figure 6-16. However, there is not a binary search tree whose post-order traversal sequence is {7, 4, 6, 5}.

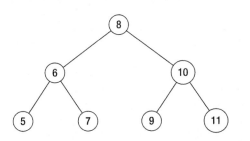

Figure 6-16. *A binary search tree built from a post-order traversal sequence {5, 7, 6, 9, 11, 10, 8}*

The last number in a post-order traversal sequence is the value of the root node. Other numbers in the sequence can be partitioned into two parts. The first numbers at the left side in the array, which are less than the value of the root node, are values of nodes in the left subtree; the following numbers, which are greater than the value of the root node, are values of nodes in the right subtree.

Take the input {5, 7, 6, 9, 11, 10, 8} as an example. The last number 8 in this sequence is the root value. The first three numbers (5, 7, and 6), which are less than 8, are values of nodes in the left subtree. The following three numbers (9, 11, and 10), which are greater than 8, are values of nodes in the right subtree.

The solution continues to construct the left subtree and right subtree according to the two sub-arrays with the same strategy. In the subsequence {5, 7, 6}, the last number 6 is the root value of the left subtree. The number 5 is the value of the left child since it is less than 6, and 7 is the value of the right child since it is greater than 6. Meanwhile, the last number 10 in the subsequence {9, 11, 10} is the root value of the right subtree. The number 9 is the value of the left child, and 11 is the value of right child accordingly.

Let's analyze another array {7, 4, 6, 5}. The last number 5 is the value of the root node. Since the first number 7 is greater than 5, there are no nodes in the left subtree, and the numbers 7, 4, 6 should be values of nodes in the right subtree. However, notice that the number 4, a value in the right subtree, is less than the root value 5. It violates the definition of binary search trees. Therefore, there are no binary search trees with the post-order traversal sequence {7, 4, 6, 5}.

It is not difficult to write code after we have examined this strategy. Some sample code is shown in Listing 6-19.

Listing 6-19. C++ *Code to Verify a Post-Order Traversal Sequence*

```cpp
bool VerifySquenceOfBST(int sequence[], int length) {
    if(sequence == NULL || length <= 0)
        return false;

    int root = sequence[length - 1];
```

```
    // nodes in left sub-tree are less than root node
    int i = 0;
    for(; i < length - 1; ++ i) {
        if(sequence[i] > root)
            break;
    }

    // nodes in right sub-tree are greater than root node
    int j = i;
    for(; j < length - 1; ++ j) {
        if(sequence[j] < root)
            return false;
    }

    // Is left sub-tree a binary search tree?
    bool left = true;
    if(i > 0)
        left = VerifySquenceOfBST(sequence, i);

    // Is right sub-tree a binary search tree?
    bool right = true;
    if(i < length - 1)
        right = VerifySquenceOfBST(sequence + i, length - i - 1);

    return (left && right);
}
```

Source Code:

063_SequenceOfBST.cpp

Test Cases:

- Functional Cases (Post-order traversal sequences correspond to binary search trees, including full binary search trees; post-order traversal sequences do not correspond to any binary search trees)

- Boundary Cases (Special post-order traversal sequences where elements are increasingly or decreasingly sorted; there is only one element in the sequence)

- Cases for Robustness (The pointer to the array of traversal sequence is NULL)

Binary Search Trees and Double-Linked Lists

■ **Question 64**   How do you convert a binary search tree into a sorted double-linked list without creating any new nodes? It is only allowed that you can reconnect links between existing nodes.

For example, after reconnecting links in the binary search tree in Figure 6-17(a), it gets a sorted double-linked list in Figure 6-17(b).

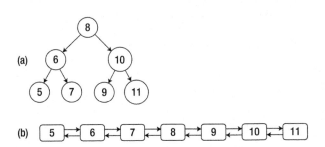

Figure 6-17. A binary search tree and its converted sorted double-linked list

Every node in a binary search tree has two links to its children nodes (some links might be NULL pointers). Every node in a double-linked list also has two links, one to the preceding node and the other to the next node. Additionally, the binary search tree is also a data structure for sorting, so a binary search tree can be converted to a sorted double-linked list in theory. The link to the left child in a binary search tree is connected to the preceding node in the converted double-linked list, and the link to the right child is connected to the next node.

Based on Divide and Conquer

If a binary search tree is scanned with the in-order traversal algorithm, nodes are traversed in increasing order of values. When the root node of the sample tree is visited, the tree can be viewed in three parts: the root value with value 8, the left subtree rooted at the node with value 6, and the right subtree rooted at the node with value 10. According to the sorting requirement, the root node with value 8 should be linked to the node in the left subtree with the maximal value (the node with value 7), as well as the node in the right subtree with the minimum value (the node with value 9), as shown in Figure 6-18.

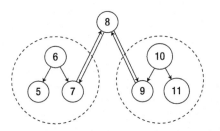

Figure 6-18. Divide a binary tree into three parts: root node, left subtree, and right subtree. After the left subtree and right subtree are converted to double-linked lists, they are connected to the root node and the whole binary search tree is converted to a sorted double-linked list.

Since the tree is scanned with the in-order traversal algorithm, the left subtree is converted when the root node is visited, and the last node in the converted double-linked list has the maximum value so far (node 7). The root node is connected to the list then, and it becomes the new last node in the list. We continue to convert the right subtree and connect the root node to the node with the minimum value in the right subtree (node 9). How do you convert the left and right subtrees? The process should be similar to the process to convert the whole tree, so it can be solved with recursion, as shown in Listing 6-20.

Listing 6-20. *C++ Code to Convert a BSTree to a Double-Linked List (Version 1)*

```
BinaryTreeNode* Convert(BinaryTreeNode* pRootOfTree) {
    BinaryTreeNode *pLastNodeInList = NULL;
    ConvertNode(pRootOfTree, &pLastNodeInList);

    // pLastNodeInList points to the last node in the doule-linked list,
    // but we are going to return the head node.
    BinaryTreeNode *pHeadOfList = pLastNodeInList;
    while(pHeadOfList != NULL && pHeadOfList->m_pLeft != NULL)
        pHeadOfList = pHeadOfList->m_pLeft;

    return pHeadOfList;
}

void ConvertNode(BinaryTreeNode* pNode, BinaryTreeNode** pLastNodeInList) {
    if(pNode == NULL)
        return;

    BinaryTreeNode *pCurrent = pNode;

    if (pCurrent->m_pLeft != NULL)
        ConvertNode(pCurrent->m_pLeft, pLastNodeInList);

    pCurrent->m_pLeft = *pLastNodeInList;
    if(*pLastNodeInList != NULL)
        (*pLastNodeInList)->m_pRight = pCurrent;

    *pLastNodeInList = pCurrent;

    if (pCurrent->m_pRight != NULL)
        ConvertNode(pCurrent->m_pRight, pLastNodeInList);
}
```

In this code, pLastNodeInList always points to the last node with the maximal value in the converted double-linked list. When the root node with value 8 is visited, the left subtree has been converted and pLastNodeInList points to the node with 7. The root node is linked to the list, and then pLastNodeInList points the root node with value 8. It takes pLastNodeInList as a parameter to continue converting the right subtree, and pLastNodeInList is connected to the node with value 9.

Based on Node Rotations

Node rotations are fundamental operations to maintain self-balancing binary trees, such as red-black trees. Let's borrow the ideas of node rotations to convert a binary search tree to a sorted double-linked list.

The conversion process begins from the root node. If the root node of a binary search tree has a left child, a right rotation occurs. As shown in Figure 6-19(b), the tree is rotated clockwise at the root node, 8. After the right rotation, node 6 (the left child of the original root node) becomes the new root, and node 7 (the right child of node 6) becomes the left child of node 8. Other links in the tree remain unchanged.

The tree is rotated clockwise at the new root node because it still has a left child. The left child node becomes the new root with a right rotation (Figure 6-19(c)). Since the new root, node 5, does not have a left child, no more rotations at the root are needed now. It traverses the tree along links to right children until the first node with a left child is found, that is, the node with value 8.

It rotates clockwise at node 8 (Figure 6-19(d)). Node 7, the left child of node 8, becomes the parent of node 8, and it is also linked to a right child of node 6, which is the original parent of node 8.

It continues to traverse on the tree along links to right children, and another node with left child (node 10) is found. The operation to rotate at node 10 is similar to the preceding steps, as shown in (Figure 6-19 (e)).

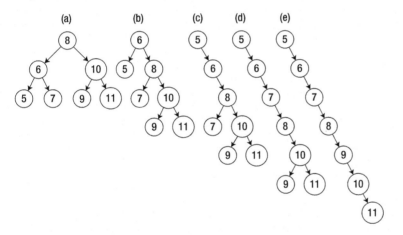

Figure 6-19. *The rotation process to convert a binary search tree to a sorted list. (a) The original binary search tree. (b) The tree with a right rotation at node 8. (c) The tree with a right rotation at node 6. (d) The tree with a right rotation at node 8. (e) The tree becomes a list with a right rotation at node 10.*

As shown in Figure 6-19(e), all nodes in the tree are linked as a single-linked list. Each child node is linked as a right child of its parent and links to left children are NULL pointers. In order to get a double-linked list, the last step is to link the parent node in the tree as the preceding node in the list.

The whole process to convert a binary search tree to a double-linked list can be implemented with C++, as shown in Listing 6-21.

Listing 6-21. *C++ Code to Convert a BSTree to a Double-Linked List (Version 2)*

```
BinaryTreeNode* Convert_solution2(BinaryTreeNode* pRoot) {
    BinaryTreeNode* pNode = pRoot;
```

```
    BinaryTreeNode* pHead = NULL;
    BinaryTreeNode* pParent = NULL;

    while(pNode != NULL) {
        while(pNode->m_pLeft != NULL) {
            // right rotation
            BinaryTreeNode* pLeft = pNode->m_pLeft;
            pNode->m_pLeft = pLeft->m_pRight;
            pLeft->m_pRight = pNode;
            pNode = pLeft;

            if(pParent != NULL)
                pParent->m_pRight = pNode;
        }

        if(pHead == NULL)
            pHead = pNode;

        pParent = pNode;
        pNode = pNode->m_pRight;
    }

    // build double-linked list
    BinaryTreeNode* pNode1 = pHead;
    if(pNode1 != NULL {
        BinaryTreeNode* pNode2 = pNode1->m_pRight;
        while(pNode2 != NULL) {
            pNode2->m_pLeft = pNode1;

            pNode1 = pNode2;
            pNode2 = pNode2->m_pRight;
        }
    }

    return pHead;
}
```

Source Code:

```
064_ConvertBinarySearchTree.cpp
```

Test Cases:

- Functional Cases (Normal binary search trees, including full binary search trees)

- Boundary Cases (Special binary search trees, such as a tree with only one node, or all nodes in a binary search tree only have left/right subtrees)

- Cases for Robustness (The pointer to the root node of a binary search tree is NULL)

Permutation and Combination

Question 65   Please print all permutations of a given string. For example, print "abc", "acb", "bac", "bca", "cab", and "cba" when given the input string "abc".

For many candidates, it is not a simple problem to get all permutations of a set of characters. In order to solve such a problem, candidates might try to divide it into simple subproblems. An input string is partitioned into two parts. The first part only contains the first characters, and the second part contains others. As shown in Figure 6-20, a string is divided into two parts with different background colors.

This solution gets permutations of a given string with two steps. The first step is to swap the first character with the following characters one by one. The second step is to get permutations of the string excluding the first character. Take the sample string "abc" as an example. It gets permutations of "bc" when the first character is 'a'. It then swaps the first character with 'b', gets permutations of "ac", and finally gets permutation of "ba" after swapping the first character with 'c'.

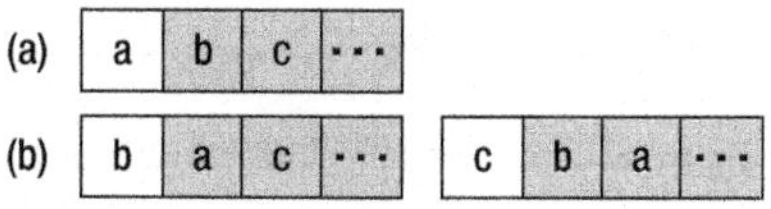

Figure 6-20. *The process to get permutations of a string. (a) A string is divided into two parts of which the first part only contains the first character, and the second part contains others (with gray background). (b) All characters in the second part are swapped with the first character one by one.*

The process to get permutations of a string excluding the first character is similar to the process to get permutations of a whole string. Therefore, it can be solved recursively, as shown in Listing 6-22.

Listing 6-22. *C Code to Get Permutations of a String*

```c
void Permutation(char* pStr) {
    if(pStr == NULL)
        return;

    PermutationCore(pStr, pStr);
}

void PermutationCore(char* pStr, char* pBegin) {
    char *pCh = NULL;
    char temp;

    if(*pBegin == '\0') {
        printf("%s\n", pStr);
    }
    else {
        for(pCh = pBegin; *pCh != '\0'; ++ pCh) {
            temp = *pCh;
```

```
            *pCh = *pBegin;
            *pBegin = temp;

            PermutationCore(pStr, pBegin + 1);

            temp = *pCh;
            *pCh = *pBegin;
            *pBegin = temp;
        }
    }
}
```

Source Code:

    065_StringPermutation.c

Test Cases:

- Functional Cases (The input string contains one or more characters)
- Cases for Robustness (The string is empty; the pointer to the string is NULL)

■ **Question 66**   How many distinct ways are available to place eight queens on a chessboard, where there are no two queens that can attack each other? That is to say, there are no two queens located at the same row, same column, or same diagonal.

For example, a solution in Figure 6-21 places eight queens on an 8×8 chessboard where any queen cannot attack another.

An array columnIndex[8] is defined, of which the ith number stands for the column index of the queen at the ith row. The eight numbers in the array are initialized as numbers 0, 1, 2, 3, 4, 5, 6, 7, and then we try to get all permutations of the array. Since the array is initialized with eight different numbers, any two queens are in different columns. It is only necessary to check whether there are two queens on the same diagonal.

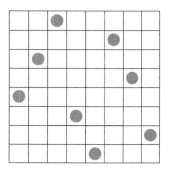

Figure 6-21. Place eight queens (denoted as dots) on a chessboard where no two queens attack each other

Therefore, the eight-queen puzzle can be solved with the code in Listing 6-23.

Listing 6-23. *C Code for the Eight Queens Puzzle*

```c
int EightQueen() {
    int columnIndex[8] = {0, 1, 2, 3, 4, 5, 6, 7};
    int count = 0;
    Permutation(columnIndex, 8, 0, &count);

    return count;
}

void Permutation(int columnIndex[], int length, int index, int* count) {
    int i, temp;

    if(index == length) {
        if(Check(columnIndex, length) != 0) {
            (*count)++;
        }
    }
    else {
        for(i = index; i < length; ++ i) {
            temp = columnIndex[i];
            columnIndex[i] = columnIndex[index];
            columnIndex[index] = temp;

            Permutation(columnIndex, length, index + 1, count);

            temp = columnIndex[index];
            columnIndex[index] = columnIndex[i];
            columnIndex[i] = temp;
        }
    }
}

/* If there are two queens on the same diagonal, it returns 0,
   otherwise it returns 1. */
int Check(int columnIndex[], int length) {
    int i, j;

    for(i = 0; i < length; ++ i) {
        for(j = i + 1; j < length; ++ j) {
            if((i - j == columnIndex[i] - columnIndex[j])
                || (j - i == columnIndex[i] - columnIndex[j]))
            return 0;
        }
    }

    return 1;
}
```

Source Code:

    066_EightQueens.c

■ **Question 67**   There are *n* arrays. A permutation is generated when an element is selected from each array. How do you generate all permutations of *n* arrays?

For example, permutations for the 3 arrays {1, 2}, {3, 4}, {5, 6} are: {1, 3, 5}, {1, 3, 6}, {1, 4, 5}, {1, 4, 6}, {2, 3, 5}, {2, 3, 6}, {2, 4, 5}, and {2, 4, 6}.

Similar to finding permutations of a string, it divides the *n* input arrays into two parts: the first array and the remaining *n*-1 arrays. After an element is selected from the first array, it continues to find permutations of the remaining arrays. The process needed to find permutations of the next *n*-1 arrays is identical to the process to find permutations of all *n* arrays, so it can be solved recursively, as shown in Listing 6-24.

Listing 6-24. Java Code to Permute Arrays

```java
void permute(ArrayList<int[]> arrays) {
    Stack<Integer> permutation = new Stack<Integer>();
    permuteCore(arrays, permutation);
}

void permuteCore(ArrayList<int[]> arrays, Stack<Integer> permutation) {
    if(permutation.size() == arrays.size()) {
        System.out.println(permutation);
        return;
    }

    int[] array = arrays.get(permutation.size());
    for(int i = 0; i < array.length; ++i) {
        permutation.push(array[i]);
        permuteCore(arrays, permutation);
        permutation.pop();
    }
}
```

Source Code:

    067_ArrayPermutation.java

Test Cases:

- Functional Cases (Some normal arrays)

- Boundary Cases (There is only one array; there is only one number in each array)

■ **Question 68**   Please generate all combinations of a given string. For example, combinations of a given string "abc" are "a", "b", "c", "ab", "ac", "bc", and "abc".

Based on Divide and Conquer

Suppose the length of a given string is n and we are going to find one of its combinations with m characters. All characters are divided into two parts: the first character and the other n-1 characters. There are two choices for the first characters. The first choice is to insert the first character in the combination, and it continues to select m-1 characters from the remaining n-1 characters in the string. The other choice is to ignore the first character and select m characters from the next n-1 characters. Therefore, combinations of a given string can be generated recursively, as shown in Listing 6-25.

Listing 6-25. Java Code for String Combinations (Version 1)

```java
void combination(String str) {
    Stack<Character> result = new Stack<Character>();
    for(int i = 1; i <= str.length(); ++ i) {
        combination(str, 0, i, result);
    }
}

void combination(String str, int index, int number, Stack<Character> result) {
    if(number == 0) {
        System.out.println(result);
        return;
    }

    if(index == str.length())
        return;

    // select the character str[index]
    result.push(str.charAt(index));
    combination(str, index + 1, number - 1, result);
    result.pop();

    // ignore the character str[index]
    combination(str, index + 1, number, result);
}
```

Since a combination may contain one characters, two characters, …, or n characters for a given string with length n, there is a loop in the method combination(String str).

Based on Bit Operations

Some characters are selected that compose a combination. A set of bits is utilized, where each bit stands for a character in the string. If the ith character is selected for a combination, the ith bit is true; otherwise, it is false. For instance, three bits are used for combinations of the string "abc". If the first two characters 'a' and 'b' are selected to compose a combination "ab", the corresponding bits are {1, 1, 0}. Similarly, bits corresponding to another combination "ac" are {1, 0, 1}. We are able to get all combinations of a string with length n if we can get all possible combinations of n bits.

A number is composed of a set of bits. All possible combinations of n bits correspond to numbers from 1 to 2^n-1. Therefore, each number in the range between 1 and 2^n-1 corresponds to a combination of a string with length n. For example, the number 6 is composed of bits {1, 1, 0}, so the first and second characters are selected in the string "abc" to generate the combination "ab". Similarly, the number 5 with bits {1, 0, 1} corresponds to the combination "ac".

A new solution is found that generates combinations with n characters based on a set of bits corresponding to numbers from 1 to 2^n-1. The sample code is shown in Listing 6-26.

Listing 6-26. *Java Code for String Combinations (Version 2)*

```java
void combination_solution2(String str) {
    BitSet bits = new BitSet(str.length());
    while(increment(bits, str.length()))
        print(str, bits);
}

boolean increment(BitSet bits, int length) {
    int index = length - 1;

    while(index >= 0 && bits.get(index)) {
        bits.clear(index);
        --index;
    }

    if(index < 0)
        return false;

    bits.set(index);
    return true;
}

void print(String str, BitSet bits) {
    for(int i = 0; i < str.length(); ++i) {
        if(bits.get(i))
            System.out.print(str.charAt(i));
    }

    System.out.println();
}
```

The method increment increases a number represented in a set of bits. The algorithm clears 1 bits from the rightmost bit until a 0 bit is found. It then sets the rightmost 0 bit to 1. For example, in order to increase the number 5 with bits {1, 0, 1}, it clears 1 bits from the right side and sets the rightmost 0 bit to 1. The bits become {1, 1, 0} for the number 6, which is the result of increasing 5 by 1.

Source Code:

    068_StringCombination.java

Test Cases:

- Functional Cases (Some normal strings)

- Boundary Cases (An empty string)

Summary

It is impossible to avoid difficult problems during interviewers. Figures, examples, and the divide-and-conquer approach are three strategies to analyze and solve complicated coding problems.

Figures are helpful tools to visualize difficult problems, especially when the problems are related to data structures such as lists, binary trees, and 2D arrays.

Examples are quite useful to solve problems about abstract algorithms. It is much easier to uncover hidden rules if candidates analyze the step-by-step process with some sample inputs.

The divide-and-conquer approach is an effective strategy to solve complex problems. It divides them into subproblems, solves subproblems recursively, and combines solutions of subproblems into a solution of the original problem.

CHAPTER 7

■ ■ ■

Optimization

Interviewers usually expect efficient solutions that solve problems within the resource constraints, so it is important for candidates to improve code performance from the perspectives of both time and space consumption. This chapter illustrates strategies to optimize programs by selecting appropriate data structures and algorithms, as well as by making trade-off decisions to balance time and space efficiencies.

Time Efficiency

No one likes to wait for a delayed response from a software application, so companies spend a lot of resources on performance optimization before software releases. That is why many interviewers pay so much attention to time efficiency in candidates' code. Besides coding skills, interviewers also examine candidates' passion on performance tuning.

Programming habits greatly impact performance because there are many details that could affect execution efficiency. For instance, C/C++ programmers should get into the habit of passing instances of complex types with references or pointers in argument lists, especially when a parameter is a container such as `vector` with lots of elements. A copy-by-value parameter costs an unnecessary copy, and it should be avoided as much as possible. Take strings in C# as another example. It is not a good practice to utilize the '+' operator repeatedly to concatenate strings because a temp instance of string is returned for each '+' operation, which wastes both time and space. A better choice is to utilize the method `StringBuilder.Append` to concatenate strings.

Recursive and iterative implementations of an algorithm may differ significantly from the perspective of performance. When a complex problem is divided into manageable subproblems and subproblems are solved recursively, it is important to check whether there are overlaps among subproblems. The complexity may grow exponentially if subproblems overlap each other. In order to solve this kind of problem, we can analyze them with recursion but implement iterative code with arrays or matrices to cache resolutions of subproblems. Dynamic programming algorithms are usually applied with these two steps.

Performance optimization requires deep understanding of data structures and algorithms. The costs to insert, delete, and search elements in various data containers are quite different. It is important to choose appropriate data structures to solve coding problems during interviews. For example, arrays, lists, and binary trees are not as efficient as heaps to get the median from a stream. Additionally, it costs $O(n)$ time to search from n numbers sequentially. If the numbers are sorted (or partially sorted), we may try the binary search algorithm, which reduces the time complexity to $O(\log n)$. We can improve the efficiency to $O(1)$ if a hash table is built in advance.

It is important to demonstrate passion for performance optimization during interviews. Often interviewers ask for more efficient solutions after candidates have already proposed several solutions. In such difficult times, candidates should show a positive attitude and try their best to solve problems from various perspectives. Sometimes interviewers may not expect candidates to find a perfect solution in only 30 or 40 minutes. What they are looking for is the attitude and passion to try new solutions and pursue perfection. Usually, they believe candidates who give up easily are not qualified to be outstanding engineers.

Median in a Stream

▪ **Question 69**   How do you find the median from a stream of numbers? The median of a set of numbers is the middle one when they are arranged in order. If the count of numbers is even, the median is defined as the average value of the two numbers in the middle.

Since numbers come from a stream, the count of numbers is dynamic and increases over time. If a data container is defined for the numbers from a stream, new numbers will be inserted into the container when they are deserialized. Let's find an appropriate data structure for such a data container.

An array is the simplest choice. If the array is not sorted, the median can be found based on the **partition** method, which is discussed in the section *Search and Sort* for the quicksort algorithm. It costs $O(1)$ time to add a number into an unsorted array and $O(n)$ time to get the median. More details about this solution are available in the section *Majorities in Arrays* to get the majority element from an array.

We can also keep the array sorted while adding new numbers. Even though it only costs $O(\log n)$ time to find the right position with the binary search algorithm, it costs $O(n)$ time to insert a number into a sorted array because $O(n)$ numbers will be moved if there are n numbers in the array. It is very efficient to get the median since it only takes $O(1)$ time to access a number in an array with an index.

A sorted list is another choice. It takes $O(n)$ time to find the appropriate position to insert a new number. Additionally, the time to get the median can be optimized to $O(1)$ if we define two pointers that point to the central one or two elements.

A better choice is a binary search tree because it only costs $O(\log n)$ on average to insert a new node. However, the time complexity is $O(n)$ for the worst cases when the binary search tree is extremely unbalanced and becomes similar to a sorted list. To get the median number from a binary search tree, auxiliary data to record the number of nodes in subtrees are necessary for each node. It also requires $O(\log n)$ time to get the median node on average, but $O(n)$ time for the worst cases.

We may utilize a balanced binary search tree, AVL, to avoid the worst cases for normal binary search trees. Usually, the balance factor of a node in AVL trees is the height difference between its right subtree and left subtree. We may modify the balance factor a little bit here: we define the balance factor as the count difference of nodes between the right subtree and left subtree. It costs $O(\log n)$ time to insert a new node into an AVL, and $O(1)$ time to get the median for all cases.

An AVL is efficient, but unfortunately it is not implemented in libraries of the most common programming languages. It is also very difficult for candidates to implement the left/right rotation of AVL trees in dozens of minutes during interviews. Let's look for better solutions.

As shown in Figure 7-1, if all numbers are sorted, the numbers that are related to the median are indexed by P_1 and P_2. If the count of numbers is odd, P_1 and P_2 point to the same central number. If the count is even, P_1 and P_2 point to two numbers in the middle.

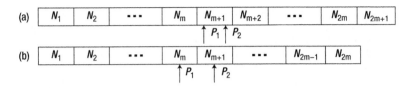

Figure 7-1. *Elements in an array are divided into two parts by one or two numbers in the center. (a) The count of elements is odd. (b) The count of elements is even.*

Median can be calculated with the numbers pointed to by P_1 and P_2. Note that the sequence of numbers is divided into two parts. The numbers in the first half are less in value than the numbers in the second half. Moreover, the number indexed by P_1 is the greatest number in the first half, and the number indexed by P_2 is the least one in the second half.

If numbers are divided into two parts and all numbers in the first half are less than the numbers in the second half, we can get the median with the greatest number of the first part and the least number of the second part, even if numbers in the first and second half are not sorted. How do you get the greatest number efficiently? Utilizing a max heap. A min heap is also an efficient way to get the least number.

Therefore, numbers in the first half are inserted into a max heap, and numbers in the second half are inserted into a min heap. It costs O(log$n$) time to insert a number into a heap. Since the median can be gotten or calculated with the root of a min heap and a max heap, it only takes O(1) time.

The comparisons of the solutions above with an array (sorted or unsorted), a sorted list, a binary search tree, an AVL tree, as well as a min heap and a max heap, are summarized in Table 7-1.

Let's consider the implementation details with heaps. All numbers should be evenly divided into two parts, so the count difference of numbers in the min heap and max heap should be 1 at most. To achieve such a division, a new number is inserted into the min heap if the count of existing numbers is even; otherwise, it is inserted into the max heap.

We also should make sure that the numbers in the max heap are less than the numbers in the min heap. Suppose that the count of existing numbers is even; a new number will be inserted into the min heap. If the new number is less than some numbers in the max heap, it violates our rule that all numbers in the min heap should be greater than numbers in the max heap.

Table 7-1. *Time Efficiency Comparisons of Solutions with a Sorted Array, a Sorted List, a Binary Search Tree, an AVL Tree, as well as a Min Heap and a Max Heap*

Type of Data Container	Time to Insert	Time to Get Median
Unsorted Array	O(1)	O(n)
Sorted Array	O(n)	O(1)
Sorted List	O(n)	O(1)
Binary Search Tree	O(log n) on average, O(n) for the worst case	O(log n) on average, O(n) for the worst case
AVL	O(log$n$)	O(1)
Max and Min Heap	O(log$n$)	O(1)

In such a case, we can insert the new number into the max heap first, then pop the greatest number from the max heap, and finally push it into the min heap. Since the number pushed into the min heap is the former greatest number in the max heap, all numbers in the min heap are still greater than numbers in the max heap even with the newly moved number.

The situation is similar when the count of existing numbers is odd and the new number to be inserted is greater than some numbers in the min heap. Please analyze the insertion process carefully by yourself.

The code in Listing 7-1 is sample code in C++. Even though there are no types for heaps in STL, we can build heaps with vectors utilizing the functions push_heap and pop_heap. Comparison functors less and **greater** are employed for max heaps and min heaps respectively.

Listing 7-1. *C++ Code to Get the Median from a Stream*

```cpp
template<typename T> class DynamicArray {
public:
    void Insert(T num) {
        if(((minHeap.size() + maxHeap.size()) & 1) == 0) {
            if(maxHeap.size() > 0 && num < maxHeap[0]) {
                maxHeap.push_back(num);
                push_heap(maxHeap.begin(), maxHeap.end(), less<T>());

                num = maxHeap[0];

                pop_heap(maxHeap.begin(), maxHeap.end(), less<T>());
                maxHeap.pop_back();
            }

            minHeap.push_back(num);
            push_heap(minHeap.begin(), minHeap.end(), greater<T>());
        }
        else {
            if(minHeap.size() > 0 && minHeap[0] < num) {
                minHeap.push_back(num);
                push_heap(minHeap.begin(), minHeap.end(), greater<T>());

                num = minHeap[0];

                pop_heap(minHeap.begin(), minHeap.end(), greater<T>());
                minHeap.pop_back();
            }

            maxHeap.push_back(num);
            push_heap(maxHeap.begin(), maxHeap.end(), less<T>());
        }
    }

    int GetMedian() {
        int size = minHeap.size() + maxHeap.size();
        if(size == 0)
            throw exception("No numbers are available");

        T median = 0;
        if(size & 1 == 1)
```

```
                median = minHeap[0];
        else
                median = (minHeap[0] + maxHeap[0]) / 2;

        return median;
    }
private:
    vector<T> minHeap;
    vector<T> maxHeap;
};
```

In the code above, the function `Insert` is used to insert a new number deserialized from a stream into the heaps, and `GetMedian` is used to get the median of all existing numbers.

Source Code:

    069_MedianStream.cpp

Test Cases:

- Functional Test Cases (Get the median of a stream with an even/odd number of numbers)

- Boundary Test Cases (Get the median of a stream with only one or two numbers; get the median of a stream with duplicated numbers)

Minimum k Numbers

■ **Question 70**   Please find the smallest k numbers (in value) out of n numbers. For example, if given an array with eight numbers {4, 5, 1, 6, 2, 7, 3, 8}, please return the least four numbers 1, 2, 3, and 4.

The naive solution is to sort the n input numbers increasingly and to have the least k numbers be the first k numbers. Since it needs to sort, its time complexity is O($n\log n$). Interviewers will probably ask to explore more efficient solutions.

O($n\log k$) Time Efficiency

We want to create a container that will contain the least k numbers out of n input numbers. A data container with capacity k is first created to store the k numbers and then numbers are read out of the n input numbers one by one, compared, and entered into k if they meeting the following criteria:

- If the container has less than k numbers, the number read in the current round (denoted as *num*) is inserted into the container directly.

- If it contains k numbers already, *num* cannot be inserted directly any more. An existing number in the container should be replaced with *num* in such a case. We find the maximum number out of the existing k numbers in the container and compare that with *num*. If *num* is less than the maximum number, the maximum number is replaced with *num*. Otherwise *num* is discarded since there have been k numbers in the container that are all less than *num* and *num* cannot be one of the least k numbers.

Three steps may be required when a number is read and the container is full. The first step is to find the maximum number; in the second, the maximum number may be deleted; and third, the new number may be inserted. The second and third steps are optional and depend on the comparison between *num* in the current round and the maximum number in the container.

We have different choices for the data container. If the data container is implemented as a binary search tree, it costs $O(\log k)$ time for these three steps on average, but costs $O(k)$ time in the worst cases. Therefore, the overall time complexity is $O(n \log k)$ for n input numbers on average and $O(nk)$ in the worst cases.

Since we need to get the maximum number out of k numbers, a maximum heap might be a good choice. In a maximum heap, its root is always greater than its children, so it costs $O(1)$ time to find the maximum number. However, it takes $O(\log k)$ time to insert and delete a number. In Java, the default implementation of type `PriorityQueue` is for minimum heaps. A new comparator has to be defined because a maximum heap is needed here, and `ReversedComparator` shown in Listing 7-2 is such an example.

Listing 7-2. *Java Code to Get Minimum k Numbers (Version 1)*

```
void getLeastNumbers_1(int[] input, int[] output) {
    ReversedComparator comparator = new ReversedComparator();
    PriorityQueue<Integer> maxQueue = null;
    maxQueue = new PriorityQueue<Integer>(1, comparator);

    getLeastNumbers(input, maxQueue, output.length);

    Iterator<Integer> iter = maxQueue.iterator();
    for(int i = 0; i < output.length; ++i) {
        output[i] = iter.next();
    }
}

void getLeastNumbers(int[] input, PriorityQueue<Integer> output, int k) {
    output.clear();

    for(int i = 0; i < input.length; ++i) {
        if(output.size() < k)
            output.add(new Integer(input[i]));
        else {
            Integer max = output.peek();
            Integer number = new Integer(input[i]);
            if(output.comparator().compare(number, max) > 0) {
                output.poll();
                output.add(number);
            }
        }
    }
}
```

```
        }
    }
}

class ReversedComparator implements Comparator<Integer> {
    public int compare(Integer int1, Integer int2) {
        int num1 = int1.intValue();
        int num2 = int2.intValue();

        if(num1 < num2)
            return 1;
        else if (num1 == num2)
            return 0;
        else
            return -1;
    }
}
```

O(*n*) Time Efficiency

We can also utilize the method `partition` in quicksort to solve this problem, assuming that n input numbers are contained in an array. If it takes the kth number as a pivot to partition the input array, all numbers less than the kth number should be at the left side and other greater ones should be at the right side. The k numbers at the left side are the least k numbers after the partition. We can develop the code in Listing 7-3 according to this solution.

Listing 7-3. *Java Code to Get Minimum k Numbers (Version 2)*

```
void getLeastNumbers_2(int[] input, int[] output) {
    int start = 0;
    int end = input.length - 1;
    int k = output.length;
    int index = partition(input, start, end);
    while(index != k - 1) {
        if(index > k - 1) {
            end = index - 1;
            index = partition(input, start, end);
        }
        else {
            start = index + 1;
            index = partition(input, start, end);
        }
    }

    for(int i = 0; i < k; ++i)
        output[i] = input[i];
}
```

Comparison between the Two Solutions

The second solution, based on the method `partition,` costs only O(*n*) time, so it is more efficient than the first one. However, it has two obvious limitations. One limitation is that it needs to load all input numbers into an array, and the other is that we have to reorder the input numbers.

Even though the first solution takes more time, it has some advantages. Reordering the input numbers (`input` in the previous code) is not required. We read a number from data at each round, and all write operations are taken in the container `maxQueue`. It does not require loading all input numbers into memory at one time, so it is suitable for huge-sized data sets. If an interviewer asks us get the least *k* numbers from a huge-size input, obviously we cannot load all data with huge size into limited memory at one time. We can read a number from auxiliary space (such as disks) at each round with the first solution and determine whether it should be inserted into the container `maxQueue`. It works once memory can accommodate `maxQueue`, so the first option is especially suitable for scenarios where *n* is huge and *k* is small.

The comparison of these two solutions can be summarized in Table 7-2.

Table 7-2. Pros and Cons of Two Solutions

Criteria	First Solution	Second Solution
Time complexity	O($n\log k$)	O(n)
Reorder input numbers?	No	Yes
Suitable for huge-size data?	Yes	No

Since each solution has its own pros and cons, candidates should ask interviewers for more detailed requirements to choose the most suitable solution, including the input data size and whether it is allowed to reorder the input numbers.

Source Code:

    070_KLeastNumbers.java

Test Cases:

- Functional Test Cases (An input array with/without duplicated numbers)
- Boundary Test Cases (The input *k* is 1, or the length of the input array)

Intersection of Sorted Arrays

■ **Question 71**   Please implement a function that finds the intersection of two sorted arrays. Assume numbers in each array are unique.

For example, if the two sorted arrays as input are {1, 4, 7, 10, 13} and {1, 3, 5, 7, 9}, the output is an intersection array with numbers {1, 7}.

An intuitive solution for this problem is to check whether every number in the first array (denoted as *array1*) is in the second array (denoted as *array2*). If the length of *array1* is *m*, and the length of *array2* is *n*, its overall time complexity is O(*mn*) based on linear search. We have two better solutions.

With O(*m+n*) Time

Note that the two input arrays are sorted. Supposing that a number *number1* in *array1* equals a number *number2* in *array2*, the numbers after *number1* in *array1* should be greater than the numbers before *number2* in *array2*. Therefore, it is not necessary to compare the numbers after *number1* in *array1* with numbers before *number2* in *array2*. This improves efficiency since many comparisons are eliminated.

The sample code for this solution is shown in Listing 7-4.

Listing 7-4. *C++ Code for Intersection of Arrays (Version 1)*

```cpp
void GetIntersection_solution1(const vector<int>& array1,
                      const vector<int>& array2,
                      vector<int>& intersection) {
    vector<int>::const_iterator iter1 = array1.begin();
    vector<int>::const_iterator iter2 = array2.begin();

    intersection.clear();

    while(iter1 != array1.end() && iter2 != array2.end()) {
        if(*iter1 == *iter2) {
            intersection.push_back(*iter1);
            ++ iter1;
            ++ iter2;
        }
        else if(*iter1 < *iter2)
            ++ iter1;
        else
            ++ iter2;
    }
}
```

Since it only requires scanning two arrays once, its time complexity is O(*m+n*).

With O(*n*log*m*) Time

As we know, a binary search algorithm requires O(log*m*) time to find a number in an array with length *m*. Therefore, if we search each number of an array with length *n* from another array with length *m*, its overall time complexity is O(*n*log*m*). If *m* is much greater than *n*, O(*n*log*m*) is actually less than O(*m+n*).

Therefore, we can implement a new and better solution based on binary search in such a situation, as shown in Listing 7-5.

Listing 7-5. *C++ Code for Intersection of Arrays (Version 2)*

```
/* === Supposing that array2 is much longer than array1 === */
void GetIntersection_solution2(const vector<int>& array1,
                      const vector<int>& array2,
                      vector<int>& intersection) {
    intersection.clear();

    vector<int>::const_iterator iter1 = array1.begin();
    while(iter1 != array1.end()) {
        if(binary_search(array2.begin(), array2.end(), *iter1))
            intersection.push_back(*iter1);
    }
}
```

There are some implementation details worthy of attention. The parameters **array1** and **array2** are passed as references. If they were passed by values, it would cost O($m+n$) time to copy them.

Source Code:

071_ArrayIntersection.cpp

Test Cases:

- Functional Test Cases (Two arbitrary arrays with/without intersected numbers)
- Boundary Test Cases (Two arrays are identical to each other; one or two arrays are empty; the intersecting numbers are the first/last number of the input arrays)

Greatest Sum of Sub-Arrays

Question 72   Given an integer array containing positive and negative numbers, how do you get the maximum sum of its sub-arrays? Continuous numbers form a sub-array of an array.

For example, if the input array is {1, -2, 3, 10, -4, 7, 2, -5}, the sub-array with the maximum sum is {3, 10, -4, 7, 2} whose sum 18.

During interviews, many candidates can solve this problem by enumerating all sub-arrays and calculating their sums. An array with n elements has $n(n+1)/2$ sub-arrays. It costs O(n^2) time (at least) to calculate their sums. Usually, the intuitive and brute-force solution is not the most efficient one. It is highly possible for interviewers to ask for better solutions.

Analyzing Numbers in the Array One by One

Let's accumulate each number in the sample array from beginning to end. Our solution initializes *sum* as 0. In the first step, it adds the first number 1, and *sum* becomes 1. And then if it adds the second number -2, *sum* becomes -1. At the third step, it adds the third number 3. Notice that the previous *sum* is less than 0, so the new *sum* will be 2 and it is less than the third number 3 itself. Therefore, the previous accumulated *sum* -1 should be discarded.

The key point here is that when the *sum* becomes a negative number or zero, adding this *sum* to the following array element will not be greater than the element itself, so the new sub-array will start from the next element.

It continues accumulating from the next number with *sum* 3. When it adds the fourth number 10, *sum* becomes 13, and it decreases to 9 when it adds the fifth number -4. Notice that the *sum* with -4 is less than the previous *sum* 13 because of the negative number -4. It saves the previous *sum* 13 since it might be the max sum of sub-arrays.

At the sixth step, it adds the sixth number 7 and *sum* becomes 16. Now *sum* is greater than the previous max sum of sub-arrays, so the max sum is updated to 16. It is similar when it adds the seventh number 2. The max sum of sub-arrays is updated to 18. Lastly it adds -5 and *sum* becomes 13. Since it is less than the previous max sum of sub-arrays, the final max sum of sub-arrays remains 18, and the sub-array is {3, 10, -4, 7, 2} accordingly. The whole process is summarized in Table 7-3.

Table 7-3. *TheProcess to Calculate the Maximum Sum of All Sub-Arrays in the Array {1, -2, 3, 10, -4, 7, 2, -5}*

Step	Operation	Accumulated Sum	Maximum Sum
1	Add 1	1	1
2	Add -2	-1	1
3	Discard sum -1, add 3	3	3
4	Add 10	13	13
5	Add -4	9	13
6	Add 7	16	16
7	Add 2	18	18
8	Add -5	13	18

The code in Listing 7-6 is the sample code according to the step-by-step analysis just discussed.

Listing 7-6. *Java Code to Get Maximum Sum of Sub-Arrays*

```java
int getGreatestSumOfSubArray(int[] numbers) {
    int curSum = 0;
    int greatestSum = Integer.MIN_VALUE;
    for(int i = 0; i < numbers.length; ++i) {
        if(curSum <= 0)
            curSum = numbers[i];
        else
```

```
            curSum += numbers[i];

        if(curSum > greatestSum)
            greatestSum = curSum;
    }

    return greatestSum;
}
```

Dynamic Programming

If a candidate is familiar with dynamic programming, he or she might analyze this problem in a new way. If a function $f(i)$ stands for the maximum sum of a sub-array ending with the ith number, the required output is $max[f(i)]$. The function $f(i)$ can be calculated with the following recursive equation:

$$f(i) = \begin{cases} number\,[i] & i = 0 \text{ or } f(i-1) \leq 0 \\ f(i-1) + number\,[i] & i \neq 0 \text{ and } f(i-1) > 0 \end{cases}$$

If the sum of the sub-array ending with the $(i\text{-}1)^{th}$ number is negative or zero, the sum of the sub-array ending with the ith number should be the ith number itself (for example, the third step in Table 7-3). Otherwise, it gets the sum of the sub-array ending with the ith number by adding the ith number and the sum of the sub-array ending with the $(i\text{-}1)^{th}$ number.

Even though it analyzes the problem recursively, it is usually implemented based on iteration. The iterative code according to the equation above should be the same as the code of the first solution. The variable curSum is the $f(i)$ in the equation, and greatestSum is $max[f(i)]$. Therefore, these two solutions are essentially identical to each other.

Source Code:

072_GreatestSumOfSubarrays.java

Test Cases:

- Functional Test Cases (An array with positive numbers, negative numbers, or zeros; all numbers in the input array are positive/negative/zero)

- Boundary Test Cases (There is only one number in the input array)

Digit 1 Appears in Sequence from 1 to n

■ **Question 73**   How many times does the digit 1 occur in the integers from 1 to n ?

For example, if n is 12, there are four numbers from 1 to 12 containing the digit 1, which are 1, 10, 11, and 12, and the digit 1 occurs five times.

Straightforward but Inefficient

The intuitive way to solve this problem is to get a count of digit 1 in each number. The least important digit in a decimal number can be calculated with the modulo operator (%). If the number is greater than 10 with two digits at least, it is divided by 10 and another modulo operation is applied to calculate the last digit again. The process is repeated until the number is less than 10, which can be implemented as the function NumberOf1 in Listing 7-7.

Listing 7-7. C Code to Get the Number of 1 in Consecutive Integers (Version 1)

```c
int NumberOf1Between1AndN_Solution1(unsigned int n) {
    int number = 0;
    unsigned int i;

    for(i = 0; i <= n; ++ i)
        number += NumberOf1(i);

    return number;
}

int NumberOf1(unsigned int n) {
    int number = 0;
    while(n) {
        if(n % 10 == 1)
            number ++;

        n = n / 10;
    }

    return number;
}
```

It takes a modulo operation and a division on each number to get the count of all 1 digits. A number m has $O(\log m)$ digits, so it costs $O(n \log n)$ time to count all 1 digits in numbers from 1 to n. Let's explore more efficient solutions.

Based on Divide and Conquer

We may have a try to analyze how the 1 digit occurs in numbers. Let's take a somewhat large n as an example, such as 21345. Numbers from 1 to 21345 are divided into two ranges. The first one contains numbers from 1 to 1345 (the number excluding the first digit of 21345), and the other contains numbers from 1346 to 21345.

We first count the 1 digit in the range from 1346 to 21345. Let's focus on the most significant digit in numbers with five digits. The 1 digit occurs 10000 (10^4) times in the 10000 numbers from 10000 to 19999 in the first digit.

It should be noticed that there are cases where the 1 digit occurs less than 10000 times in numbers with five digits. For example, when the most significant digit of the input n is 1, such as 12345, the digit 1 occurs in the most significant digit 2346 times in numbers from 10000 to 12345 in the first digit.

Let's move on to focus on digits except the most significant one. The 1 digit occurs for 2000 times in the last four digits of numbers from 1346 to 21345. Numbers from 1346 to 21345 are divided into two ranges, 10000 numbers in each range: from 1346 to 11345, and from 11346 to 21345. The last four digits in numbers in these two ranges can be viewed as digit permutations. One of the digits is 1, and the other three digits can be any digit from 0 to 9. According to the principle of permutation, the 1 digit occurs 2000 (2×10^3) times.

How do you get the count of the 1 digit in numbers from 1 to 1345? It can be gotten with recursion. The reason we divide numbers from 1 to 21345 into two ranges (from 1 to 1345 and from 1346 to 21345) is that we get 1345 when the first digit is removed from the number 21345. Similarly, numbers from 1 to 1345 are divided into two ranges: from 1 to 345 and from 346 to 1345. It is a typical divide-and-conquer strategy, and it can be implemented as shown in Listing 7-8. A number is converted into a string for coding simplicity.

Listing 7-8. *C Code to Get the Number of 1 in Consecutive Integers (Version 2)*

```c
int NumberOf1Between1AndN_Solution2(int n) {
    char strN[50];

    if(n <= 0)
        return 0;

    sprintf(strN, "%d", n);
    return NumberOf1InString(strN);
}

int NumberOf1InString(const char* strN) {
    int first, length;
    int numOtherDigits, numRecursive, numFirstDigit;

    if(!strN || *strN < '0' || *strN > '9' || *strN == '\0')
        return 0;

    first = *strN - '0';
    length = (unsigned int)(strlen(strN));

    if(length == 1 && first == 0)
        return 0;

    if(length == 1 && first > 0)
        return 1;

    // If strN is 21345, numFirstDigit is the number of digit 1
    // in the most signification digit in numbers from 10000 to 19999
    numFirstDigit = 0;
    if(first > 1)
        numFirstDigit = PowerBase10(length - 1);
    else if(first == 1)
        numFirstDigit = atoi(strN + 1) + 1;

    // numOtherDigits is the number of digit 1 in digits except
    // the most significant digit in numbers from 01346 to 21345
```

```
    numOtherDigits = first * (length - 1) * PowerBase10(length - 2);

    // numRecursive is the number of digit 1 in numbers from 1 to 1345
    numRecursive = NumberOf1InString(strN + 1);

    return numFirstDigit + numOtherDigits + numRecursive;
}
int PowerBase10(unsigned int n) {
    int i, result = 1;
    for(i = 0; i < n; ++ i)
        result *= 10;

    return result;
}
```

A digit is removed at each step, so the recursion depth is the same as the count of digits in the input integer n. An integer n has $O(\log n)$ digits, so the time complexity is $O(\log n)$, and it is more efficient than the preceding solution.

Source Code:

073_NumberOf1.c

Test Cases:

- Functional Test Cases (Input 5, 10, 55, 99, ...)

- Boundary Test Cases (Input 0, and 1)

- Performance Test Cases (Input some large numbers, such as 10000, 21235)

Concatenate an Array to Get a Minimum Number

▪ **Question 74**   Big numbers can be formed if numbers in an array are concatenated together. How do you print the minimum concatenated number of a given array?

For example, if the input array is {3, 32, 321}, there are six concatenated numbers and the minimum one is 321323.

An intuitive solution for this problem is to get all permutations of the given array at first and then concatenate each permutation together. The minimum concatenated number is selected after all concatenated permutations are compared. We have discussed permutation in the section *Permutations and Combinations*.

As we know, there are $n!$ permutations for an array with n element, so this intuitive solution costs $O(n!)$ time. Let's explore more efficient solutions.

It is essential to find a sort rule to reorder elements in an array in order to get the minimum concatenated number. We have to compare numbers in order to sort an array. That is to say, when given two numbers *m* and *n*, it is necessary to find a rule to compare them and place one of them before the other.

Numbers *mn* and *nm* are concatenated from two numbers *m* and *n*. (In this section, a number *mn* stands for a concatenated number of *m* and *n*, rather than m×n.) If *mn* < *nm*, the output is *mn*, in which *m* is placed ahead of *n*. A new operator ∨ is defined. When *m* is placed ahead of *n*, it is denoted as *m∨n*. Similarly, it is denoted as *m∧n* when *m* is placed behind *n*. In such a case, *mn* > *nm* and the output is *nm*. When *mn* = *nm*, it does not matter which number is placed ahead of the other. It is denoted *m≡n* for this case.

In the analysis above, we have found a new way to compare two numbers *m* and *n* according to their concatenated numbers *mn* and *nm*. Therefore, the array can be reordered with a new comparator `NumericComparator`, as shown in Listing 7-9.

Listing 7-9. *Java Code to Reorder an Array to Get Minimum Concatenated Number*

```
void PrintMinNumber(int numbers[]) {
    String strNumbers[] = new String[numbers.length];
    for(int i = 0; i < numbers.length; ++i) {
        strNumbers[i] = String.valueOf(numbers[i]);
    }

    Arrays.sort(strNumbers, new NumericComparator());

    for(int i = 0; i < numbers.length; ++i)
        System.out.print(strNumbers[i]);
    System.out.print("\n");
}

class NumericComparator implements Comparator<String>{
    public int compare(String num1, String num2) {
        String str1 = num1 + num2;
        String str2 = num2 + num1;
        return str1.compareTo(str2);
    }
}
```

In the code above, it converts integers to strings to concatenate numbers. The reason for the conversion is to avoid overflow problems. When two numbers *m* and *n* are in the range for integers, their concatenated numbers *mn* and *nm* may be beyond the range. Numbers *mn* and *nm* can be compared lexicographically in their converted strings because they have the same number of digits.

If there are *n* elements in the input array, the program sorts the array with method `Arrays.sort` in $O(n\log n)$ time. Therefore, it is much more efficient than the intuitive solution with $O(n!)$ time complexity.

A new rule to compare two numbers is defined in the solution above. Is the comparison rule valid? A valid comparison rule is reflective, symmetric and transitive. Let's prove it:

- Reflexivity. It is obvious that *aa=aa*, so *a≡a*.

- Symmetry. If *a∨b*, *ab*<ba. Therefore, *ba>ab*, and b∧a.

- Transitivity. If $a \vee b$, ab<ba. Supposing that there are l and m digits in decimal numbers a and b. Therefore, $ab=a\times10^m+b$, and $ba=b\times10^l+a$.

  $ab<ba \rightarrow a\times10^m+b<b\times10^l+a \rightarrow a\times10^m-a<b\times10^l-b) \rightarrow a\times(10^m-1)<b\times(10^l-1) \rightarrow a/(10^l-1)<b/(10^m-1)$

  If $b \vee c$, bc<cb. Supposing that there are n digits in the decimal number c, it can be proven that $b/(10^m-1)<c/(10^n-1)$ with similar steps as above.

  Because $a/(10^l-1)<b/(10^m-1)$ and $b/(10^m-1)<c/(10^n-1)$, $a/(10^l-1)<c/(10^n-1) \rightarrow a\times(10^n-1)<c\times(10^l-1) \rightarrow a\times10^n+c<c\times10^l+a \rightarrow ac<ca \rightarrow a \vee c$

We have demonstrated that our rule to compare two numbers fulfills the requirements of reflexivity, symmetry, and transitivity, so it is a valid comparison rule.

Let's move on to prove that the number concatenated from the array sorted with our comparison rule is a minimum. We are going to prove it by contradiction.

Supposing that n numbers in an array are sorted, and the concatenated number is $A_1A_2A_3...A_n$. If the concatenated number was not the minimum, there were two numbers x and y ($0<x<y\leq n$) at least. When x and y are swapped, $A_1A_2...A_y...A_x...A_n < A_1A_2...A_x...A_y...A_n$. Additionally, since n numbers are sorted with the comparison rule above, $A_x \vee A_{x+1} \vee A_{x+2}...A_{y-2} \vee A_{y-1} \vee A_y$.

Because $A_{y-1} \vee A_y$, $A_{y-1}A_y<A_yA_{y-1}$. If A_{y-1} and A_y are swapped in $A_1A_2...A_{y-1}A_y...A_n$, $A_1A_2...A_{y-1}A_y...A_n<A_1A_2...A_yA_{y-1}...A_n$. If numbers ahead of A_y are swapped with A_y, $A_1A_2...A_x...A_{y-1}A_y...A_n<A_1A_2...A_x...A_yA_{y-1}...A_n<A_1A_2...A_x...A_yA_{y-2}A_{y-1}...A_n< ... <A_1A_2...A_yA_x...A_{y-2}A_{y-1}...A_n$.

Similarly, $A_xA_{x+1}<A_{x+1}A_x$ because $A_x \vee A_{x+1}$. If numbers A_x and A_{x+1} are swapped in $A_1A_2...A_yA_xA_{x+1}...A_{y-2}A_{y-1}...A_n$, $A_1A_2...A_yA_xA_{x+1}...A_{y-2}A_{y-1}...A_n<A_1A_2...A_yA_{x+1}A_x...A_{y-2}A_{y-1}...A_n$. When numbers behind A_x are swapped with A_x, $A_1A_2...A_yA_xA_{x+1}...A_{y-2}A_{y-1}...A_n<A_1A_2...A_yA_{x+1}A_x...A_{y-2}A_{y-1}...A_n< ... <A_1A_2...A_yA_{x+1}A_{x+2}...A_{y-2}A_{y-1}A_x...A_n$.

Therefore, $A_1A_2...A_x...A_y...A_n<A_1A_2...A_y...A_x...A_n$, and it is contradicted to our assumption $A_1A_2...A_y...A_x...A_n<A_1A_2...A_x...A_y...A_n$. Our initial assumption must be false, and our algorithm is correct.

Source Code:

`074_SortArrayForMinNumber.java`

Test Cases:

- Functional Test Cases (Input an array with a few numbers)

- Boundary Test Cases (Input an array with only a number; numbers in an input array have duplicated digits)

- Performance Test Cases (The size of an input array is somewhat big, such as 50)

Space-Time Trade-Off

In many situations, time and space performance cannot be improved at the same time and a choice has to be made between time efficiency and space efficiency. The space-time trade-off is a situation where the memory consumption can be reduced at the cost of slower program execution or, conversely, the execution time can be reduced at the price of more memory consumption.

In the last couple of decades, the RAM space and hard drive space have been getting cheaper at a much faster rate than other computer components, including CPUs. Therefore, it is more often preferred to sacrifice some space for time-efficiency optimization.

There are many strategies to reduce execution time at the cost of more memory use, and the most common one is to utilize lookup tables in order to avoid recalculations. A table (an array or a 2D matrix for most cases) is utilized that reduces execution time but increases the amount of memory needed.

As discussed in the section *Dynamic Programming and Greedy Algorithms*, arrays or 2D matrices are utilized for many dynamic programming algorithms to avoid recalculations on overlapping subproblems. Similarly, ugly numbers already found are stored to get next ugly numbers. Ugly numbers are discussed in detail in the following section.

It costs $O(n)$ time to sequentially search a character in a string with length n. If a hash table with ASCII values as keys is utilized, it only costs $O(1)$ time to get a character. It accelerates character searches with little more memory consumption because there are only 256 ANSI characters in total. Many coding problems in the interview can be solved with this strategy, as discussed in the section *Hash Tables for Characters*.

Ugly Numbers

■ **Question 75**   If a number only has factors 2, 3, and 5, it is an *ugly number*. For example, 6 and 10 are two ugly numbers, but 14 is not because it has a factor of 7. Usually 1 is considered to be the first ugly number. What is the arbitrary k^{th} ugly number?

Check Every Number One by One

According to the definition of ugly numbers, they have factors 2, 3, and 5. If a number has a factor 2, it is divided by 2 continuously. If it has a factor 3, it is divided by 3 continuously. Similarly, it is divided by 5 continuously if it has a factor 5. If the number becomes 1 finally after divisions, it is an ugly number, as shown in Listing 7-10.

Listing 7-10. C# Code to Check an Ugly Number

```
bool IsUgly(int number) {
    while (number % 2 == 0)
        number /= 2;
    while (number % 3 == 0)
        number /= 3;
    while (number % 5 == 0)
        number /= 5;

    return (number == 1) ? true : false;
}
```

The % operator is used to check whether a number n has a factor m. If n has a factor m, the result of $n\%m$ is 0.

Numbers are verified one by one with the method `IsUgly`, as shown in Listing 7-11.

Listing 7-11. C# Code to Check an Ugly Number (Version 1)

```csharp
int GetUglyNumber_Solution1(int index) {
    if (index <= 0)
        return 0;

    int number = 0;
    int uglyFound = 0;
    while (uglyFound < index) {
        ++number;

        if (IsUgly(number)) {
            ++uglyFound;
        }
    }

    return number;
}
```

The solution in this code looks straightforward, but it is not efficient because it wastes time on non-ugly numbers. Let's try to find a more efficient solution.

Store Found Ugly Numbers into an Array

The new solution only spends time on ugly numbers. According to the definition of ugly numbers, the solution gets a bigger ugly number if it multiplies an ugly number with 2, 3, or 5. An array is created to store found ugly numbers. Any elements in the array except the first one are the multiplication results of an ugly number on the left side by 2, 3, or 5. The first element in the array is initialized as 1.

The key to this solution is how to keep the array sorted. Suppose that there are already some ugly numbers in the array and the greatest one is M. Let's analyze how to get the next ugly number.

The next ugly number should be the multiplication result of an existing ugly number by 2, 3, or 5. First, it multiplies all existing numbers by 2. Some multiplication results may be less than or equal to M, and they should be already in the array, so they are discarded. There may be several multiplication results greater than M, but only the first one is important and others will be recalculated later. The first multiplication result by 2 greater than M is defined as M_2.

Similarly, it also multiplies all existing ugly number by 3 and 5 and defines the first numbers greater than M as M_3 and M_5 respectively. The next ugly number is the minimum one among M_2, M_3, and M_5.

Is it necessary to multiple all existing ugly numbers by 2, 3, and 5? Actually, it is not. Since the existing ugly numbers are sorted, there is a special ugly number T_2 in the array. The multiplication results of numbers before T_2 by 2 are less than M. It stores the index of T_2 and updates the index when a new ugly number is found. Similarly, there are also T_3 and T_5 for factors 3 and 5. In each round, it starts from T_2, T_3, and T_5 to find the next ugly number.

Listing 7-12 shows the sample code of this solution.

Listing 7-12. C# Code to Check an Ugly Number (Version 2)

```csharp
int GetUglyNumber_Solution2(int index) {
    if (index <= 0)
```

```
        return 0;

    int[] uglyNums = new int[index];
    uglyNums[0] = 1;
    int nextUglyIndex = 1;

    int index2 = 0;
    int index3 = 0;
    int index5 = 0;

    while (nextUglyIndex < index) {
        int min = Math.Min(uglyNums[index2] * 2, uglyNums[index3] * 3);
        min = Math.Min(min, uglyNums[index5] * 5);

        uglyNums[nextUglyIndex] = min;

        while (uglyNums[index2] * 2 <= uglyNums[nextUglyIndex])
            ++index2;
        while (uglyNums[index3] * 3 <= uglyNums[nextUglyIndex])
            ++index3;
        while (uglyNums[index5] * 5 <= uglyNums[nextUglyIndex])
            ++index5;

        ++nextUglyIndex;
    }

    int ugly = uglyNums[nextUglyIndex - 1];
    return ugly;
}
```

In this code, the local variables `index2`, `index3` and `index5` are the corresponding indexes of T_2, T_3, and T_5.

The second solution is more efficient from the perspective of execution time because it only takes time on ugly numbers. However, it consumes more memory than the first solution because it creates an array to store known ugly numbers. If it tries to find the 1500th ugly number, it creates an array for 1500 integers and the size is 6KB. This amount of memory is not a big problem in most scenarios. In general, it sacrifices a little space for much better time efficiency.

Source Code:

075_UglyNumbers.cs

Test Cases:

- Functional Test Cases (Input 2, 3, 4, 5, 6, …)

- Boundary Test Cases (Input 0 and 1)

- Performance Test Cases (Input a large index, such as 1500)

Hash Tables for Characters

■ **Question 76**   Implement a function to find the first character in a string that only appears once. For example, the output is the character 'l' when the input is "google".

Our naive solution for this problem involves scanning the input string from its beginning to end. The current scanned character is compared with every one behind it. If there is no duplication after it, it is a character appearing once. Since it compares each character with $O(n)$ ones behind it, the overall time complexity is $O(n^2)$ if there are n characters in a string.

In order to get the number of occurrences for each character in a string, a data container is needed. We need to get and update the occurrence number of each character in a string, so the data container is used to assign an occurrence number to a character. Hash tables fulfill this kind of requirement, in which keys are characters and values are their occurrence numbers in a string.

It is necessary to scan strings twice. When a character is visited, we increase the corresponding occurrence number in the hash table during the first scanning. In the second round of scanning, whenever a character is visited, we also check its occurrence number in the hash table. The first character with occurrence number 1 is the required output.

Hash tables are complex, and they are not implemented in the C++ standard template library. Therefore, we have to implement one by ourselves.

Characters have eight bits, so there are only 256 variances. We can create an array with 256 numbers, in which indexes are ASCII values of all characters and numbers are their occurrence numbers in a string. That is to say, we have a hash table whose size is 256, with ASCII values of characters as keys.

It is time for coding after the solution is clear. Listing 7-13 demonstrates some sample code.

Listing 7-13. *C++ Code for First Character Appearing Once in a String*

```
char FirstNotRepeatingChar(char* pString) {
    if(pString == NULL)
        return '\0';

    const int tableSize = 256;
    unsigned int hashTable[tableSize];
    for(unsigned int i = 0; i<tableSize; ++ i)
        hashTable[i] = 0;

    char* pHashKey = pString;
    while(*(pHashKey) != '\0')
        hashTable[*(pHashKey++)] ++;

    pHashKey = pString;
    while(*pHashKey != '\0') {
        if(hashTable[*pHashKey] == 1)
            return *pHashKey;

        pHashKey++;
    }
```

```
        return '\0';
}
```

In this code, it costs O(1) time to increase the occurrence number for each character. The time complexity for the first scanning is O(*n*) if the length of string is *n*. It takes O(1) time to get the occurrence number for each character, so it costs O(*n*) time for the second scanning. Therefore, the overall time it costs is O(*n*).

In the meantime, an array with 256 numbers is created, whose size is 1K. Since the size of the array is constant no matter how long the input string, the space complexity of this algorithm is O(1).

Source Code:

076_FirstNotRepeatingChar.cpp

Test Cases:

- Functional Test Cases (One or more or no characters in a string appear only once)

- Boundary Test Cases (There is only one character in a string; the string is empty)

- Robust Test Cases (The pointer of the input string is NULL)

■ **Question 77** Implement a function to find the first character in a stream that only appears once at any time while reading the stream.

For example, when the first two characters "go" are read from a stream, the first character which appears once is the character 'g'. When the first six characters "google" are read, the first character appearing only once is 'l'.

Characters are read one by one from a stream. A container is needed to store the indexes of characters in the stream. The first time the character is inserted into the container, its index is stored. If the character has been inserted into the container before, it appears multiple times in the stream and it can be ignored, so its index is updated to a special value (a negative value).

In order to improve performance, it is necessary to check whether a character has been inserted before in O(1) time. Inspired by the solution of the preceding problem, the container is a hash table, which can be implemented as an array. The index of each element in the array is the ASCII value of a character, and the corresponding value is the index of the character in the stream. Listing 7-14 contains sample code.

Listing 7-14. C++ Code for First Character Appearing Once in a Stream

```
class CharStatistics {
public:
    CharStatistics() : index (0) {
        for(int i = 0; i < 256; ++i)
            occurrence[i] = -1;
    }
```

```cpp
    void Insert(char ch) {
        if(occurrence[ch] == -1)
            occurrence[ch] = index;
        else if(occurrence[ch] >= 0)
            occurrence[ch] = -2;

        index++;
    }

    char FirstAppearingOnce() {
        char ch = '\0';
        int minIndex = numeric_limits<int>::max();
        for(int i = 0; i < 256; ++i) {
            if(occurrence[i] >= 0 && occurrence[i] < minIndex) {
                ch = (char)i;
                minIndex = occurrence[i];
            }
        }

        return ch;
    }

private:
    int occurrence[256];

    int index;
};
```

In this code, an element in the array occurrence[i] is for the character with ASCII value i. Every element in the array is initialized to -1. When the character with ASCII value i is read from the stream and inserted into the hash table for the first time, occurrence[i] is updated as the index of the character in the stream. If the character has been inserted before (the value of occurrence[i] is greater than or equal to 0), occurrence[i] is updated to -2.

If we are going to get the first character that appears only once in the deserialized stream so far, it is only necessary to scan the array occurrence to get the minimum index, which is greater than or equal to 0, as implemented in the function FirstAppearingOnce.

Source Code:

077_FirstCharAppearingOnce.cpp

Test Cases:

- Functional Test Cases (Input an arbitrary stream of characters)

- Boundary Test Cases (There is only one character in the input stream; all characters in the input stream are unique/duplicated)

■ **Question 78**   Given two strings, how do you delete characters contained in the second string from the first string? For example, if all characters in the string "aeiou" are deleted from the string "We are students.", the result is "W r stdnts.".

Suppose that we are going to delete from a string s_1 the characters that are contained in another string s_2. Characters in s_1 are scanned one after another. When a character is visited, we have to check whether it is in s_2. If we search in s_2 sequentially, it costs $O(m)$ time when the length of s_2 is m. Therefore, the overall time complexity is $O(mn)$ if the length of s_1 is n.

Inspired by the solution of the preceding problems, a hash table built from s_2 can be utilized to improve efficiency. The hash table is implemented as an array with length 256. The ith element is for the character with ASCII value i. If the character with ASCII value i is contained in s_2, the ith element is set as 1; otherwise, it is set as 0. This solution can be implemented with the code shown in Listing 7-15.

Listing 7-15. C Code to Delete Characters Contained in Another String

```c
void DeleteCharacters(char* pString, char* pCharsToBeDeleted) {
    int hashTable[256];
    const char* pTemp = pCharsToBeDeleted;
    char* pSlow = pString;
    char* pFast = pString;

    if(pString == NULL || pCharsToBeDeleted == NULL)
        return;

    memset(hashTable, 0, sizeof(hashTable));
    while (*pTemp != '\0') {
        hashTable[*pTemp] = 1;
        ++ pTemp;
    }

    while (*pFast != '\0') {
        if(hashTable[*pFast] != 1) {
            *pSlow = *pFast;
            ++ pSlow;
        }
        ++pFast;
    }

    *pSlow = '\0';
}
```

It only costs $O(1)$ time to check whether a character is in s_2 or not with a hash table, so the overall time complexity is $O(n)$ if the length of s_1 is n.

Source Code:

   078_DelelteCharacters.c

Test Cases:

- Functional Test Cases (Some or all characters of s_1 are contained in s_2; no characters of s_1 are contained in s_2)

- Boundary Test Cases (s_1 and/or s_2 are empty)

- Robust Test Cases (The pointers to s_1 and/or s_2 are NULL)

■ **Question 79**   Please implement a function to delete all duplicated characters in a string and keep only the first occurrence of each character left. For example, if the input is string "google", the result after deletion is "gole".

All characters in a string are scanned. When a character is visited, we have to know whether it appeared in the string before. It costs $O(n)$ time to search sequentially in a string with length n. A hash table can be utilized to facilitate character search. Values corresponding to all characters (keys) in the hash table are initialized as 0. When a character is visited for the first time, its corresponding value in the hash table is updated to 1. When the value of a character is already 1, it indicates that the character is duplicated and should be deleted. It costs only $O(1)$ time to check whether a character is duplicated with such a hash table.

The sample code is shown in Listing 7-16.

Listing 7-16. *C Code to Delete Duplicated Characters in a String*

```c
void DeletedDuplication(char* pString) {
    int hashTable[256];
    char* pSlow = pString;
    char* pFast = pString;

    if(pString == NULL)
        return;

    memset(hashTable, 0, sizeof(hashTable));

    while (*pFast != '\0') {
        *pSlow = *pFast;

        if(hashTable[*pFast] == 0) {
            ++ pSlow;
            hashTable[*pFast] = 1;
        }

        ++pFast;
    }

    *pSlow = '\0';
}
```

Source Code:

079_DelelteDuplicatedCharacters.c

Test Cases:

- Functional Test Cases (All/Some/No characters in the input string are duplicated)
- Boundary Test Cases (The input string is empty)
- Robust Test Cases (The pointer to the input string is NULL)

■ **Question 80**   If two English words have the same characters and the occurrence number of each character is also identical respectively, they are anagrams. The only difference between a pair of anagrams is the order of characters. For example, "silent" and "listen", "evil" and "live" are two pairs of anagrams.

Please implement a function to verify whether two words are a pair of anagrams.

Two strings of a pair of anagrams have the same set of characters. The only difference in them is the order of characters. Therefore, they will become the same string if they are sorted. For example, both "silent" and "listen" become "eilnst" after they are sorted. It costs $O(n\log n)$ time to sort a string with n characters. Let's explore more efficient solutions.

A data container is used to store the occurrence number of each character. Each record in the container is composed of a character and its occurrence number. To solve this problem, it scans all characters in a string one by one. It checks the existence of the scanned character in the container. If the character already exists, its occurrence number increases; otherwise, a new record about the scanned character is inserted, with occurrence number as 1. There are two requirements of the data container: (1) each record maps a character to an integer number, and (2) each record can be accessed and updated efficiently. A hash table fulfills these requirements.

In order to solve the preceding problems in C/C++, a hash table is implemented as an array in which the index of an element is the key and the element is the value. If the problem is solved in Java, the solution might be simpler because there is a type `HashMap` for hash tables. The code in Listing 7-17 is based on `HashMap` in Java.

Listing 7-17. *Java Code for Anagrams*

```java
boolean areAnagrams(String str1, String str2) {
    if(str1.length() != str2.length())
        return false;

    Map<Character, Integer> times = new HashMap<Character, Integer>();
    for(int i = 0; i < str1.length(); ++i) {
        Character ch = str1.charAt(i);
        if(times.containsKey(ch))
            times.put(ch, times.get(ch) + 1);
        else
            times.put(ch, 1);
    }
```

```
for(int i = 0; i < str2.length(); ++i) {
    Character ch = str2.charAt(i);
    if(!times.containsKey(ch))
        return false;

    if(times.get(ch) == 0)
        return false;

    times.put(ch, times.get(ch) - 1);
}

return true;
}
```

In this code, it increases the occurrence numbers when it scans the string str1 and decreases the occurrence numbers when it scans the string str2. If two strings compose a pair of anagrams, all occurrence numbers in the hash map times should be 0 eventually.

It scans both strings str1 and str2 once. When a character is scanned, it accesses a record in the hash table and updates it. Both operations cost O(1) time. Therefore, it costs O(n) time if the length of strings is n. It allocates some auxiliary space to accommodate the hash map. If strings only contain ASCII characters, there are 256 characters at most, so there are 256 records in the hash map at most. Therefore, the space efficiency is O(1).

Source Code:

080_Anagram.java

Test Cases:

- Functional Test Cases (Pairs of strings are/are not anagrams)

Reversed Pairs in Array

■ **Question 81**   If an element at the left side is greater than another element at the right side, they form a *reversed pair* in an array. How do you get a count of reversed pairs?

For example, there are five reversed pairs in the array {7, 5, 6, 4}, which are (7, 5), (7, 6), (7, 4), (5, 4), and (6, 4).

The brute-force solution is to find the number of reversed pairs while scanning the array. A scanned number is compared with all numbers behind it. If the number behind is less than the currently visited number, a reversed pair is found. Since it compares a number with O(n) numbers in an array with size n, the time complexity is O(n^2). Let's try to improve the performance.

Since it costs too much time to compare a number with all numbers on its right side, it may improve efficiency if every two adjacent numbers are compared. Let's take the array {7, 5, 6, 4} as an example, as shown in Figure 7-2.

The new solution splits the whole array into two sub-arrays of size 2 (Figure 7-2(a)) and continues to split the sub-arrays till the size of sub-arrays is 1 (Figure 7-2(b)). Then it merges the adjacent sub-arrays and gets number of reversed pairs in them. The number in the sub-array {5} is less than the number in the sub-array {7}, so these two numbers compose a reversed pair. Similarly, numbers in the sub-arrays {4} and {6} also compose a reversed pair. After the number of reversed pairs is found between every two adjacent sub-arrays with size 1, they are merged to form a set of sub-arrays with size 2 (Figure 7-2(c)). Sub-arrays are sorted when they are merged in order to avoid counting the reversed pairs again inside the merged arrays.

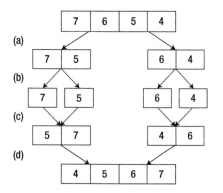

Figure 7-2. *The process to get the number of reversed pairs in the array {7, 5, 6, 4}. (a) Split the array with size 4 into two arrays with size 2. (b) Split each array with size 2 into two arrays with size 1. (c) Merge every two adjacent arrays with size 1, sort them, and get the number of reversed pairs. (d) Merge arrays with size 2, merge them, and get the number of reversed pairs.*

Let's continue to count the number of reversed pairs between sub-arrays with size 2. Figure 7-3 illustrates the detailed process of Figure 7-2(d).

Two pointers (P_1 and P_2) are initialized to the end of two sub-arrays. If the number referenced by P_1 is greater than the number referenced by P_2, there are some reversed pairs in such cases. As shown in Figure 7-3(a) and Figure 7-3(c), the number of reversed pairs is the same as the number of remaining numbers in the second sub-array. There are no reversed pairs if the number referenced by P_1 is less than or equal to the number referenced by P_2 (Figure 7-3(b)). Another pointer P_3 is initialized to the end of the merged array. The greater number of the two referenced by P_1 and P_2 is copied to the location referenced by P_3 in order to keep numbers in the merged array sorted. It moves these three pointers backward and continues to compare, count, and copy until one sub-array is empty. Then the remaining numbers in the other sub-array are copied to the merged array.

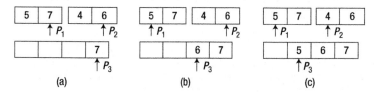

Figure 7-3. *Merge sub-arrays in Figure 7-2(d). The last step, to copy the last remaining number 4 in the second sub-array, is omitted. (a) There are two reversed pairs because the number pointed to by P_1 is greater than the number pointed to by P_2, and P_2 points to the second number and there are two numbers*

in the second sorted sub-array less than the number pointed to by P_1. *Copy the number pointed to by* P_1 *to the merged array and move* P_1 *and* P_3 *backward. (b) There are no reversed pairs because the number pointed to by* P_1 *is less than the number pointed to by* P_2. *Copy the number pointed to by* P_2 *to the merged array and move* P_2 *and* P_3 *backward. (c) There is a reversed pair because the number pointed to by* P_1 *is greater than the number pointed to by* P_2, *and* P_2 *points to the first number in the second sub-array. Copy the number pointed to by* P_1 *to the merged array and move* P_1 *and* P_3 *backward.*

The process to count reversed pairs may be summarized as follows: It recursively splits an array into two sub-arrays. It counts reversed pairs inside a sub-array and then counts reversed pairs between two adjacent sub-arrays while merging them. Therefore, the solution can be implemented based on the merge sort algorithm, as shown in Listing 7-18.

Listing 7-18. *Java Code to Count Reversed Pairs*

```java
int countReversedPairs(int[] numbers) {
    int[] buffer = new int[numbers.length];
    return countReversedPairs(numbers, buffer, 0, numbers.length - 1);
}

int countReversedPairs(int[] numbers, int[] buffer, int start, int end) {
    if(start >= end)
        return 0;

    int middle = start + (end - start) / 2;

    int left = countReversedPairs(numbers, buffer, start, middle);
    int right = countReversedPairs(numbers, buffer, middle + 1, end);
    int between = merge(numbers, buffer, start, middle, end);

    return left + right + between;
}

int merge(int[] numbers, int[] buffer, int start, int middle, int end) {
    int i = middle; // the end of the first sub-array
    int j = end;    // the end of the second sub-array
    int k = end;    // the end of the merged array
    int count = 0;
    while(i >= start && j >= middle + 1) {
        if(numbers[i] > numbers[j]) {
            buffer[k--] = numbers[i--];
            count += (j - middle);
        }
        else {
            buffer[k--] = numbers[j--];
        }
    }

    while(i >= start) {
        buffer[k--] = numbers[i--];
    }
```

```
    while(j >= middle + 1) {
        buffer[k--] = numbers[j--];
    }

    // copy elements from buffer[] to numbers[]
    for(i = start; i <= end; ++i) {
        numbers[i] = buffer[i];
    }

    return count;
}
```

As we know, the time complexity for the merge sort algorithm is $O(n\log n)$, so it is better than the brute-force solution that costs $O(n^2)$ time. The second solution allocates more memory with a buffer size n, so there is a trade-off between time and space efficiency.

Source Code:

081_ReversePairs.java

Test Cases:

- Functional Test Cases (Input a unsorted array; input an increasingly/decreasingly sorted array; some numbers in the array are duplicated)

- Boundary Test Cases (Input an array with one or two numbers)

First Intersection Node in Two Lists

■ **Question 82**   Please find the first common node of two single-linked lists if they intersect with each other.

When asked this question in interviews, many candidates' intuition is the brute-force solution. It scans all nodes on one list. When a node is visited, it scans the other list to check whether the other list contains the node. The first node contained in both lists is the first common node. If the length of one list is m and the other is n, this solution costs $O(mn)$ time to find the first common node on the two lists. The brute-force solution is not the best one. Let's explore alternatives.

The structure of two lists with common nodes looks like a rotated 'Y'. As shown in Figure 7-4, all nodes following the first common node in two lists are identical. There are no branches after the first common node in two lists because each node has only one link to the next node in a singly linked list.

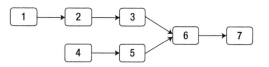

Figure 7-4. Two lists intersecting at node 6

If two lists have common nodes, the common nodes appear in their tails. Therefore, we can compare nodes beginning from the tails of the two lists. If two nodes on two lists are identical, we continue to compare preceding nodes backward. There are only links to next nodes, and the tail node is the last one to be visited in a singly linked list. The last node is the first one to be compared. Does it sound like "Last In, First Out"? Let's have a try with stacks.

Nodes in two lists are pushed into two stacks when they are traversed. When all nodes are visited, the tail nodes are on the top of these two stacks. It continues to pop two nodes on the top of stacks and compares them until they are different. The last two identical nodes are the first common nodes in two singly linked lists.

The solution above utilizes two stacks. If the lengths of two lists are m and n, both time complexity and space complexity are $O(m+n)$. Compared with the brute-force solution, it improves time efficiency with more consumption of space.

Two stacks are utilized because we would like to reach the tail nodes at the same time. The time to reach tail nodes on the two lists with different length is different when two lists are traversed from the head nodes.

There is a better solution to the problem caused by length difference, with two traversals. It traverses two lists and gets their lengths, as well as the length difference. During the second traversal, it advances on the longer list for d steps if the length difference is d, and then traverses the two lists together. The first identical nodes on lists are the first common nodes.

Let's take the lists in Figure 7-4 as an example. The new solution first finds that the lengths of the two lists are 5 and 4, and the longer list has one more node than the shorter one. It moves on the longer list for one step to reach the node 2, and then traverses the two lists until it arrives at the first common node, node 6.

Similar to the previous solution, this solution also costs $O(m+n)$ time. However, it does not need auxiliary stacks.

It is time to write code after the solution is accepted by interviewers, as shown in Listing 7-19.

Listing 7-19. *C++ Code to Get the First Common Node in Two Lists*

```cpp
ListNode* FindFirstCommonNode(ListNode *pHead1, ListNode *pHead2) {
    // Get length of two lists
    unsigned int nLength1 = GetListLength(pHead1);
    unsigned int nLength2 = GetListLength(pHead2);
    int nLengthDif = nLength1 - nLength2;

    ListNode* pListHeadLong = pHead1;
    ListNode* pListHeadShort = pHead2;
    if(nLength2 > nLength1) {
        pListHeadLong = pHead2;
        pListHeadShort = pHead1;
        nLengthDif = nLength2 - nLength1;
    }

    // Move d steps on the longer list if the length difference is d
    for(int i = 0; i < nLengthDif; ++ i)
        pListHeadLong = pListHeadLong->m_pNext;

    // Traverse two lists
    while((pListHeadLong != NULL) &&
        (pListHeadShort != NULL) &&
        (pListHeadLong != pListHeadShort)) {
```

```
        pListHeadLong = pListHeadLong->m_pNext;
        pListHeadShort = pListHeadShort->m_pNext;
    }

    ListNode* pFisrtCommonNode = pListHeadLong;

    return pFisrtCommonNode;
}

unsigned int GetListLength(ListNode* pHead) {
    unsigned int nLength = 0;
    ListNode* pNode = pHead;
    while(pNode != NULL) {
        ++ nLength;
        pNode = pNode->m_pNext;
    }

    return nLength;
}
```

Source Code:

```
082_FirstCommonNodesInLists.cpp
```

Test Cases:

- Functional Test Cases (Two lists have intersection nodes, the first of which is a head/tail node or inside a list; two lists do not have intersection nodes)

- Robustness Test Cases (The pointers to head nodes of one or two lists are NULL)

Summary

There are requirements for time complexity and space complexity for most coding interview problems, and usually interviewers pay more attention to time complexity. However, candidates can always ask interviewers about their requirements when in doubt.

The first strategy to improve time efficiency is to use appropriate data structures. Different types of data structures are suitable for different scenarios. Candidates should consider the pros and cons for each type of data structures and make the most appropriate choice.

The second strategy is to apply appropriate algorithms. For example, the binary search algorithm accelerates searches in a sorted array, and dynamic programming algorithms make it simpler to find the optimized solutions (minimum or maximum values) for many problems. Sometimes mathematical proofs are necessary to demonstrate the correctness of algorithms.

In many cases, we have to sacrifice memory to improve time efficiency. A lookup table (an array or a 2D matrix in most cases) can be utilized to avoid recalculations, and a hash table usually facilitates character searches in a string.

CHAPTER 8

■ ■ ■

Skills for Interviews

Interviews are chances for candidates to demonstrate their communication skills. Sometimes interviewers ask coding questions with new concepts to verify candidates' learning skills. Candidates might solve new interview problems with skills that reapply solutions to classic problems or solve problems abstracted from daily life and work with mathematical modeling skills. Divergent thinking skills are necessary for candidates when conventional solutions are disallowed by interviewers. All of these skills are discussed in detail with several sample coding interview questions in this chapter.

Communication and Learning Skills

Communications Skills

Good communication skills are essential for career success. Engineers have to communicate with developers, testers, and project managers during their daily work, so communication greatly impacts productivity. That is why interviewers like to evaluate candidates' communication skills, which include the following types:

- *Verbal Communication.* If a candidate is able to express his or her project experience and solutions to coding interview problems clearly, confidently, and concisely, he or she demonstrates effective spoken communication skills. Note that communication is not talkativeness with empty words. Candidates should be honest and sincere during interviews.

- *Nonverbal Communication.* Body language means a lot during communications. It is a good practice for a candidate to face his or her interviewer with open, attentive, upright posture and maintain good eye contact (look at the interviewer a lot, but don't stare all the time), smile, and nod from time to time.

- *Listening and asking questions actively.* When candidates are asked a question, they should reflect on the question and state in their own words what they understand the question to be. Sometimes interviewers do not provide enough information about their questions, and they wait for candidates to ask for more clarification. The process of asking for clarification and eliminating misunderstanding is a good indicator of a candidate's communication skills.

■ **Tip**   An interview is a bidirectional communication. Interviewers ask candidates questions and candidates can also ask interviewers questions. The ability to ask questions to get more information and eliminate misunderstanding is a demonstration of effective communication skills.

Learning Skills

Technology has been changing at a fast pace for decades. Software engineers have to have strong learning skills or they will not be able to keep up with technology progress. Outstanding engineers will only stay sharp if they have strong learning ability and aspirations to continuously learn about and evaluate new technologies. Therefore, interviewers in IT companies pay a lot of attention to candidates' learning abilities.

There are two strategies available for interviewers to examine candidates' learning skills. The first one is to ask candidates what books they have recently read or what they learned from their most recent project. If an engineer is eager to learn new things at all times, he or she has learning skills that might be an advantage over other candidates, that is, from the interviewer's perspective.

The other strategy is to ask questions about some new concepts and examine whether a candidate can absorb them in a short period of time. There are many new concepts about coding interview questions covered in this book, such as rotation of arrays, mirrored images of a binary trees, ugly numbers, and reversed pairs in an array. A candidate demonstrates his or her learning skills if he can master new concepts in a few minutes and then solve the problems.

Knowledge Migration Skill

One of the learning skills that is tested is the ability to apply knowledge to new domains in order to learn new things and solve unprecedented problems. Usually, new technology is developed based on old one technology. Take learning programming languages as an example. If we understand the object-oriented mechanisms of C++, it is not difficult for us to learn Java and other object-oriented programming languages. Similarly, if we master the garbage collection mechanism of Java, it is easy to learn other managed languages such as C#.

Since the ability to migrate knowledge is important for software engineers, many IT companies pay attention to it when interviewing candidates. Interviewers like to ask coding questions that are actually variants of classic algorithms. Interviewers expect candidates to find the similarities between the problem and the classic algorithms, and solve the problem accordingly. For example, usually the binary search algorithm is used to find a number in a sorted array. How do you count an element in a sorted array (Question 83)? If we can find the first and last occurrence of the element in the sorted array with the binary search algorithm, we can get the count of the element.

Many candidates try lots of exercises during interview preparation. However, they cannot anticipate all coding interview problems, and it is unavoidable for them to meet new ones during interviews. Therefore, it is more important for them to summarize the characteristics of a solution when they solve a problem and try to reapply the solution when a similar problem is met. For example, in order to solve the problem to reverse the order of words in a sentence, all characters in the sentence are reversed and then characters in each word are reversed. The idea of reversing characters multiple times can be reapplied to rotate a string. Please refer to the section *Reversing Words and Rotating Strings* for more details.

As you have already seen, similar coding interview problems are grouped in a section in this book. Readers may analyze the similarities among a group of problems in order to improve the ability to draw inferences about other cases from a known instance.

Time of Occurrences in a Sorted Array

■ **Question 83**   Please implement a function to find how many times a number occurs in a sorted array. For instance, the output is 4 when the inputs are an array {1, 2, 3, 3, 3, 3, 4, 5} and the number 3 because 3 occurs 4 times in the given array.

In a sorted array, it is natural to utilize the binary search algorithm. In order to count the occurrences of the number 3 in the given sample array, we can find any number with value 3 using the binary search and then scan its two sides sequentially to get the first 3 and the last 3. The target number may occur $O(n)$ times in an array with size n, so the time complexity is still $O(n)$ and it is not better than the linear search. It looks like the binary search algorithm does not help much here. Let's utilize the binary search algorithm thoroughly.

Assume the target value is k. Most of the time in the solution above is spent locating the first and last k. Let's explore more efficient solutions to locate the first and last k.

A better solution always compares the number m in the middle with the target k. If m is greater than k, k can only appear in the first half of the array, and the second half can be ignored in the next round of search. Similarly, k can only appear in the second half when m is less than k, and the first half can be ignored in the next round of search.

How do you continue searching when m equals k? If the number prior to the middle one is not k, the middle number is the first k. If the number before the middle number is also k, the first k should be in the first half of the array, and the second half can be ignored in the next round of search.

It is easy to implement code to find the first k based on recursion, as shown in Listing 8-1.

Listing 8-1. Java Code to Get the First k *in a Sorted Array*

```
int getFirst(int[] numbers, int start, int end, int k) {
    if(start > end)
        return -1;

    int middle = start + (end - start) / 2;
    if(numbers[middle] == k) {
        if((middle > 0 && numbers[middle - 1] != k)
                || (middle == 0))
            return middle;

        end = middle - 1;
    }
    else if(numbers[middle] > k){
        end = middle - 1;
    }
    else {
```

```
            start = middle + 1;
        }

    return getFirst(numbers, start, end, k);
}
```

The method `getFirst` returns -1 if there is not a *k* in the array; otherwise, it returns the index of the first *k*.

It finds the last *k* utilizing a similar process. If the middle number *m* is greater than *k*, *k* can occur only in the first half of the array. If *m* is less than *k*, *k* can occur only in the second half. When *m* equals *k*, it checks whether the number next to the middle one is also *k*. If it is not, the number in the middle is the last *k*; otherwise, the last *k* occurs in the second half of the array.

The recursive code to get the last *k* is shown in Listing 8-2.

Listing 8-2. *Java Code to Get the Last* k *in a Sorted Array*

```
int getLast(int[] numbers, int start, int end, int k) {
    if(start > end)
        return -1;

    int middle = start + (end - start) / 2;
    if(numbers[middle] == k) {
        if((middle < numbers.length - 1 && numbers[middle + 1] != k)
                || (middle == numbers.length - 1))
            return middle;

        start = middle + 1;
    }
    else if(numbers[middle] > k){
        end = middle - 1;
    }
    else {
        start = middle + 1;
    }

    return getLast(numbers, start, end, k);
}
```

Similar to `getFirst`, the method `getLast` returns -1 when there is not a *k* in the array; otherwise, it returns the index of the last *k*.

When the first *k* and last *k* are found, it gets the occurrence numbers of *k* based on their indexes, as shown in Listing 8-3.

Listing 8-3. *Java Code to Count* k *in a Sorted Array*

```
int countOccurrence(int[] numbers, int k) {
    int first = getFirst(numbers, 0, numbers.length - 1, k);
    int last = getLast(numbers, 0, numbers.length - 1, k);

    int occurrence = 0;
    if(first > -1 && last > -1)
```

```
        occurrence = last - first + 1;

    return occurrence;
}
```

It utilizes the binary search algorithm to get the first and last k, which costs O($\log n$) time, so the overall time complexity of the method **countOccurrence** is O($\log n$).

Source Code:

083_Occurrence.java

Test Cases:

- Functional Test Cases (A sorted array with/without the target value; the target value occurs once or multiple times in a sorted array)

- Boundary Test Cases (The target value is at the beginning/end of the sorted array; all numbers in the array are duplicated; there is only one number in the array)

Application of Binary Tree Traversals

▦ **Question 84**   How do you get the kth node in a binary search tree in an incremental order of values? For example, the third node in the binary search tree in Figure 8-1 is node 4.

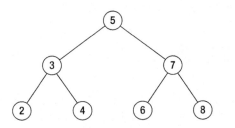

Figure 8-1. *A sample binary search tree with seven nodes, where the third node has value 4*

If a binary search tree is scanned with the in-order traversal algorithm, the traversal sequence is increasingly sorted. For example, the in-order traversal sequence of the binary tree in Figure 8-1 is {2, 3, 4, 5, 6, 7, 8}. Therefore, we can count the visited nodes during traversal and get the kth node with the code in Listing 8-4.

Listing 8-4. *C++ Code to Get the* kth *Node in a Binary Search Tree*

```
BinaryTreeNode* KthNode(BinaryTreeNode* pRoot, unsigned int k) {
    if(pRoot == NULL || k == 0)
        return NULL;
```

```
        return KthNodeCore(pRoot, k);
}

BinaryTreeNode* KthNodeCore(BinaryTreeNode* pRoot, unsigned int& k) {
    BinaryTreeNode* target = NULL;

    if(pRoot->pLeft != NULL)
        target = KthNodeCore(pRoot->pLeft, k);

    if(target == NULL) {
        if(k == 1)
            target = pRoot;

        k--;
    }

    if(target == NULL && pRoot->pRight != NULL)
        target = KthNodeCore(pRoot->pRight, k);

    return target;
}
```

Source Code:

```
084_KthNodeInBST.cpp
```

Test Cases:

- Normal Test Cases (Get the kth node out of a normal binary search tree)

- Boundary Test Cases (The input k is 0, 1, or the number of nodes in the binary tree)

- Robustness Test Cases (The pointer to the root node is NULL; special binary search trees, including those whose nodes only have right subtrees or left subtrees)

■ **Question 85**   How do you get the depth of a binary tree? Nodes from the root to a leaf form a path. Depth of a binary tree is the maximum length of all paths.

For example, the depth of the binary tree in Figure 8-2 is 4, with the longest path through nodes 1, 2, 5, and 7.

We have discussed how to store nodes of a path in a stack while traversing a binary tree in the section *Paths in Binary Trees*. The depth of a binary tree is the length of the longest path. This solution works, but it is not the most concise one.

The depth of a binary tree can be gotten in another way. If a binary tree has only one node, its depth is 1. If the root node of a binary tree has only a left subtree, its depth is the depth of the left subtree plus 1. Similarly, its depth is the depth of the right subtree plus 1 if the root node has only a right subtree.

What is the depth if the root node has both left subtree and right subtree? It is the greater value of the depth of the left and right subtrees plus 1.

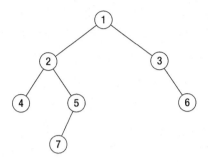

Figure 8-2. A binary tree with depth 4

For example, the root node of the binary tree in Figure 8-2 has both left and right subtrees. The depth of the left subtree rooted at node 2 is 3, and the depth of the right subtree rooted at node 3 is 2, so the depth of the whole binary tree is 4; 1 plus the greater value of 3 and 2.

It is easy to implement this solution recursively, with little modification on the post-order traversal algorithm, as shown in Listing 8-5.

Listing 8-5. C++ Code to Get a Depth of a Binary Tree

```
int TreeDepth(BinaryTreeNode* pRoot) {
    if(pRoot == NULL)
        return 0;

    int nLeft = TreeDepth(pRoot->m_pLeft);
    int nRight = TreeDepth(pRoot->m_pRight);

    return (nLeft > nRight) ? (nLeft + 1) : (nRight + 1);
}
```

Source Code:

085_TreeDepth.cpp

Test Cases:

- Normal Test Cases (A normal binary tree with one level or multiple levels)
- Robustness Test Cases (The pointer to the root node is NULL; special binary search trees, including those whose nodes only have right subtrees or left subtrees)

■ **Question 86**   How do you verify whether a binary tree is balanced? If the depth difference between a left subtree and right subtree of any node in a binary tree is not greater than 1, it is balanced. For instance, the binary tree in Figure 8-2 is balanced.

Visiting Nodes for Multiple Times

According to the definition of balanced binary trees, this problem can be solved by getting the depth difference between the left and right subtrees of every node. When a node is visited, the function Depth is invoked to get the depth of its left and right subtrees. If the depth different is 1 at most for all nodes in a binary tree, it is balanced. This solution can be implemented based on the TreeDepth discussed in the preceding problem, as shown in Listing 8-6.

Listing 8-6. C++ Code to Verify Balanced Binary Trees (Version 1)

```
bool IsBalanced_Solution1(BinaryTreeNode* pRoot) {
    if(pRoot == NULL)
        return true;

    int left = TreeDepth(pRoot->m_pLeft);
    int right = TreeDepth(pRoot->m_pRight);
    int diff = left - right;
    if(diff > 1 || diff < -1)
        return false;

    return IsBalanced_Solution1(pRoot->m_pLeft)
        && IsBalanced_Solution1(pRoot->m_pRight);
}
```

This solution looks concise, but it is inefficient because it visits some nodes for multiple times. Take the binary tree in Figure 8-2 as an example. When the function TreeDepth takes the node 2 as a parameter, it visits nodes 4, 5, and 7. When it verifies whether the binary tree rooted at node 2 is balanced, it visits nodes 4, 5, and 7 again. Obviously, we could improve performance if nodes are visited only once.

Visiting Every Node Only Once

If a binary tree is scanned with the post-order algorithm, its left and right subtrees are traversed before the root node. If we record the depth of the currently visited node (the depth of a node is the maximum length of paths from the node to its leaf nodes), we can verify whether the subtree rooted at the currently visited node is balanced. If any subtree is unbalanced, the whole tree is unbalanced.

This new solution can be implemented as shown in Listing 8-7.

Listing 8-7. C++ Code to Verify Balanced Binary Trees (Version 2)

```
bool IsBalanced_Solution2(BinaryTreeNode* pRoot) {
    int depth = 0;
    return IsBalanced(pRoot, &depth);
}

bool IsBalanced(BinaryTreeNode* pRoot, int* pDepth) {
    if(pRoot == NULL) {
        *pDepth = 0;
        return true;
    }
```

```
int left, right;
if(IsBalanced(pRoot->m_pLeft, &left)
    && IsBalanced(pRoot->m_pRight, &right)) {
    int diff = left - right;
    if(diff <= 1 && diff >= -1) {
        *pDepth = 1 + (left > right ? left : right);
        return true;
    }
}

return false;
}
```

After verifying left and right subtrees of a node, the solution verifies the subtree rooted at the current visited node and passes the depth to verify its parent node. When the recursive process returns to the root node finally, the whole binary tree is verified.

Source Code:

086_BalancedBinaryTree.cpp

Test Cases:

- Normal Test Cases (A normal binary tree is or is not balanced)

- Robustness Test Cases (The pointer to the root node is NULL; special binary search trees, including those whose nodes only have right subtrees or left subtrees; there is only one node in a binary tree)

Sum in Sequences

■ **Question 87**   Given an increasingly sorted array and a number s, is there a pair of two numbers in the array whose sum is s?

For example, if the inputs are an array {1, 2, 4, 7, 11, 15} and the number 15, there are two numbers, 4 and 11, whose sum is 15.

Let's first have a try selecting two numbers (n_1 and n_2) from the input array. If their sum equals to s, it is lucky because two required numbers have been found. If the sum is less than s, it replaces n_1 with its next number because the array is increasingly sorted and the next number of n_1 should be greater than n_1. If the sum is greater than s, the number n_2 can be replaced with its preceding number in the sorted array, which should be less than n_2.

Take the array {1, 2, 4, 7, 11, 15} and the number 15 as an example. At the first step, n_1 is the first number (also the least one) 1 and n_2 is the last number (also the greatest one) 15. It moves n_2 backward to the number 11 because their sum 16 is greater than 15.

At the second step, the two numbers are 1 and 11, and their sum, 12, is less than 15. Therefore, it moves the n_1 forward and n_1 becomes 2.

The two numbers are 2 and 11 at the third step. Since their sum, 13, is less than 15, it moves n_1 forward again.

Now the two numbers are 4 and 11 and their sum is 15, which is the expected sum.

The process is summarized in Table 8-1.

Table 8-1. *The Process to Find a Pair of Numbers Whose Sum Is 15 out of the Array {1, 2, 4, 7, 11, 15}*

Step	n_1	n_2	$n_1 + n_2$	Comparing $n_1 + n_2$ with s	Operation
1	1	15	16	Greater	Select the preceding number of n_2
2	1	11	12	Less	Select the next number of n_1
3	2	11	13	Less	Select the next number of n_1
4	4	11	15	Equal	-

It is not difficult to write code with the detailed analysis above, as shown in Listing 8-8.

Listing 8-8. *Java Code to Get a Pair with a Sum*

```java
boolean hasPairWithSum(int numbers[], int sum) {
    boolean found = false;

    int ahead = numbers.length - 1;
    int behind = 0;

    while(ahead > behind) {
        int curSum = numbers[ahead] + numbers[behind];

        if(curSum == sum) {
            found = true;
            break;
        }
        else if(curSum > sum)
            ahead --;
        else
            behind ++;
    }

    return found;
}
```

In this code, ahead is the index of n_2, and behind is the index of n_1. The time complexity is O(n) for an array with n elements because it only scans the input array once.

Source Code:

087_TwoNumbersWithSum.Java

Test Cases:

- Normal Test Cases (An array with/without a pair of numbers whose sum is the target sum)

- Boundary Test Cases (There is only one element in the array; there are two elements in the array)

■ **Question 88**   Given an array, please check whether it contains three numbers whose sum equals 0.

This problem is also required to find some numbers with a given array and sum, so it is similar to the previous problem. We may get some hints from the solution above.

The solution above is based on an increasingly sorted array, so first, the input array is sorted increasingly, too. Second, the sorted array is scanned from beginning to end. When the ith number with value a_i is scanned, we try to find a pair of numbers whose sum is $-a_i$ in the array excluding the ith number.

Let's modify the method hasPairWithSum above, as demonstrated in Listing 8-9.

Listing 8-9. Java Code to Get a Pair with a Sum Excluding a Number

```java
boolean hasPairWithSum(int numbers[], int sum, int excludeIndex) {
    boolean found = false;

    int ahead = numbers.length - 1;
    int behind = 0;

    while(ahead > behind) {
        if(ahead == excludeIndex)
            ahead--;
        if(behind == excludeIndex)
            behind++;

        int curSum = numbers[ahead] + numbers[behind];

        if(curSum == sum) {
            found = true;
            break;
        }
        else if(curSum > sum)
            ahead --;
        else
            behind ++;
    }
```

```
        return found;
    }
```

It checks whether there are two numbers whose sum is sum in numbers excluding the number with index excludeIndex. It then checks whether there are three numbers in an array with sum 0 with the method in Listing 8-10.

Listing 8-10. *Java Code to Get Three Numbers with Sum 0*

```
boolean hasTripleWithSum0(int numbers[]) {
    boolean found = false;
    if(numbers.length < 3)
        return found;

    Arrays.sort(numbers);

    for(int i = 0; i < numbers.length; ++i) {
        int sum = -numbers[i];
        found = hasPairWithSum(numbers, sum, i);

        if(found)
            break;
    }

    return found;
}
```

It contains two steps in the function hasTripleWithSum0. It costs O($n\log n$) time to sort n numbers in its first step. At the second step, it costs O(n) time for each number to call hasPairWithSum, so it costs O(n^2) time in the for loop. Therefore, its overall time complexity is O(n^2).

Source Code:

088_ThreeNumbersWithSum.Java

Test Cases:

- Normal Test Cases (An array with/without three numbers whose sum is 0)

- Boundary Test Cases (There are only two or three elements in the array)

■ **Question 89**   Given an array, please check whether it contains a subset of numbers (with one number at least) whose sum equals 0.

A subset of an array is a combination of numbers in the array. We have discussed two different algorithms to get combinations of characters in a string in the section *Permutations and Combinations*.

It is a similar process to get combinations of an array. Listing 8-11 shows the sample code based on bit operations to get subsets of an array.

Listing 8-11. Java Code to Get a Subset with Sum 0

```java
boolean hasSubsetWithSum0(int numbers[]) {
    BitSet bits = new BitSet(numbers.length);
    while(increment(bits, numbers.length)) {
        int sum = 0;
        boolean oneBitAtLeast = false;
        for(int i = 0; i < numbers.length; ++i) {
            if(bits.get(i)) {
                if(!oneBitAtLeast)
                    oneBitAtLeast = true;

                sum += numbers[i];
            }
        }

        if(oneBitAtLeast && sum == 0)
            return true;
    }

    return false;
}
```

The method `increment` is the same as the method in the section *Permutations and Combinations* to get combinations of a string.

Source Code:

089_SubsetWithSum.Java

Test Cases:

- An array with one, two, three, four, or more numbers whose sum is 0

- The sum of all numbers in an array is 0

- There is not a subset of numbers whose sum is 0

▨ **Question 90**   Given a positive value *s*, print all sequences with continuous numbers (with two numbers at least) whose sum is *s*.

Take the input *s*=15 as an example. Because 1+2+3+4+5=4+5+6=7+8=15, three continuous sequences should be printed: 1~5, 4~6, and 7~8.

A continuous sequence is specified with two numbers at its two ends. The least number in the sequence is denoted as *small*, and the greatest number is denoted as *big*. At first, *small* is initialized as 1, and *big* is initialized as 2. If the sum of numbers from *small* to *big* is less than the given *s*, *big* is increased to include more numbers; otherwise, *small* is increased to exclude some numbers if the sum of numbers in the sequence is greater than *s*. Since there are two numbers at least in the sequence, the process stops when *small* is $(1 + s)/2$.

Let's take the sum 9 as an example. First, *small* is initialized as 1, and *big* is initialized as 2. The sequence between *small* and *end* is {1, 2}, and the sum of sequence is 3, which is less than 9, so more numbers should be included into the sequence. *big* is increased to 3, and there are three numbers {1, 2, 3} in the sequence. The sum of the sequence is 6, and it is still less than 9, so *big* is increased again. The sum of the sequence {1, 2, 3, 4} is 10, and it is greater than 9, so *small* is increased to exclude a number. The sum of sequence {2, 3, 4} is 9, which is equal to the given sum, so the sequence should be printed.

In order to get other sequences, *big* is increased again. Similarly to the steps above, another sequence {4, 5} with sum 9 can be found. The whole process is summarized in Table 8-2.

Table 8-2. The Process to Find Ccontinuous Sequences with Sum 9

Step	*small*	*big*	Sequence	Sum	Comparison	Next Step
1	1	2	1, 2	3	Less	Increasing *big*
2	1	3	1, 2, 3	6	Less	Increasing *big*
3	1	4	1, 2, 3, 4	10	Greater	Increasing *small*
4	2	4	2, 3, 4	9	Equal	Printing, and Increasing *big*
5	2	5	2, 3, 4, 5	14	Greater	Increasing *small*
6	3	5	3, 4, 5	12	Greater	Increasing *big*
7	4	5	4, 5	9	Equal	Printing

It is time to write code after we have clear ideas about the process. The sample code is found in Listing 8-12.

Listing 8-12. Java Code to Get a Sequence with a Given Sum

```java
void findContinuousSequence(int sum) {
    if(sum < 3)
        return;

    int small = 1;
    int big = 2;
    int middle = (1 + sum) / 2;
    int curSum = small + big;

    while(small < middle) {
        if(curSum == sum)
            printContinuousSequence(small, big);

        while(curSum > sum && small < middle) {
```

```
                curSum -= small;
                ++small;

                if(curSum == sum)
                    printContinuousSequence(small, big);
            }

            ++big;
            curSum += big;
        }
    }

    void printContinuousSequence(int small, int big){
        for(int i = small; i <= big; ++i)
            System.out.print(String.valueOf(i) + " ");
        System.out.println("");
    }
```

There is a detail in the code in Listing 8-12 that is worthy of attention. Usually, it takes $O(n)$ time to calculate the sum of a sequence with n numbers. However, it only costs $O(1)$ time here. Only one number is inserted or removed at each step, so all numbers except one in a sequence are the same compared with the sequence at the preceding step. Therefore, the sum of the sequence can be gotten based on the sum of the preceding sequence with fewer calculations.

Source Code:

   090_ContinousSequenceWithSum.Java

Test Cases:

   • Functional Test Cases (The sum *s* with only one continuous sequence, such as 6; the sum *s* with multiple continuous sequences, such as 9 and 100; the sum *s* without a continuous sequence, such as 4)

   • Boundary Test Cases (The minimum sum 3 with a continuous sequence)

Reversing Words and Rotating Strings

■ **Question 91**   How do you reverse the order of words in a sentence, but keep words themselves unchanged? Words in a sentence are separated by blanks. For instance, the reversed output should be "student. a am I" when the input is "I am a student.".

This is a very popular interview question. It can be solved with two steps. First, we reverse all characters in a sentence. If all characters in the sentence "I am a student." are reversed, they become ".tneduts a ma I". Not only the order of words is reversed, but also the order of characters inside each word is reversed.

Secondly, we reverse characters in every word. We can get "student. a am I" from the example input string with these two steps.

The key of our solution is to implement a function to reverse a string, which is shown as the `Reverse` function in Listing 8-13.

Listing 8-13. *C++ Code to Reverse a Segment in a String*

```cpp
void Reverse(char *pBegin, char *pEnd) {
    if(pBegin == NULL || pEnd == NULL)
        return;

    while(pBegin < pEnd) {
        char temp = *pBegin;
        *pBegin = *pEnd;
        *pEnd = temp;

        pBegin ++, pEnd --;
    }
}
```

Now we can reverse the whole sentence and each word based on this `Reverse` function with the code in Listing 8-14.

Listing 8-14. *C++ Code to Reverse Words in a Sentence*

```cpp
char* ReverseSentence(char *pData) {
    if(pData == NULL)
        return NULL;

    char *pBegin = pData;

    char *pEnd = pData;
    while(*pEnd != '\0')
        pEnd ++;
    pEnd--;

    // Reverse the whole sentence
    Reverse(pBegin, pEnd);

    // Reverse every word in the sentence
    pBegin = pEnd = pData;
    while(*pBegin != '\0') {
        if(*pBegin == ' ') {
            pBegin ++;
            pEnd ++;
        }
        else if(*pEnd == ' ' || *pEnd == '\0') {
            Reverse(pBegin, --pEnd);
            pBegin = ++pEnd;
        }
```

```
    else {
        pEnd ++;
    }
}

return pData;
}
```

Since words are separated by blanks, we can get the beginning position and ending position of each word by scanning blanks. In the second phase to reverse each word in the previous sample code, the pointer `pBegin` points to the first character of a word, and `pEnd` points to the last character.

Source Code:

091_ReverseWordsInSentence.cpp

Test Cases:

- Functional Test Cases (A sentence with multiple words)

- Boundary Test Cases (A sentence with only a word; an empty string; a sentence with only blanks)

- Robustness Test Cases (The pointer to the input string is `NULL`)

▧ **Question 92**   Left rotation of a string is to move some leading characters to its end. Please implement a function to rotate a string to the left.

For example, if the input string is "abcdefg" and a number 2, two characters are rotated and the result is "cdefgab".

It looks difficult to get rules of left rotation on a string. Fortunately, we get some hints from the solution of the previous problem.

If the input string of the preceding problem is "hello world", the reversed result should be "world hello". Note that the result "world hello" can be viewed as a rotated result of "hello world". It becomes "world hello" when we move some leading characters of the string "hello world" to its end. Therefore, this problem is quite similar to the previous problem.

Let's take a string "abcdefg" as another example. We divide it into two parts: the first part contains the two leading characters "ab", and the second part contains all other characters "cdefg". We first reverse these two parts separately, and the whole string becomes "bagfedc". It becomes "cdefgab" if the whole string is reversed, which is the expected result of left rotation of the string "abcdefg" with two characters.

According to the analysis above, we can see that left rotation of a string can be implemented by invoking the `Reverse` function three times to reverse a segment or the whole string. The sample code is shown in Listing 8-15.

Listing 8-15. *C++ Code for Left Rotation in a String*

```cpp
char* LeftRotateString(char* pStr, int n) {
    if(pStr != NULL) {
        int nLength = static_cast<int>(strlen(pStr));
        if(nLength > 0 && n > 0 && n < nLength) {
            char* pFirstStart = pStr;
            char* pFirstEnd = pStr + n - 1;
            char* pSecondStart = pStr + n;
            char* pSecondEnd = pStr + nLength - 1;

            // Reverse the n leading characters
            Reverse(pFirstStart, pFirstEnd);
            // Reverse other characters
            Reverse(pSecondStart, pSecondEnd);
            // Reverse the whole string
            Reverse(pFirstStart, pSecondEnd);
        }
    }

    return pStr;
}
```

Source Code:

092_LeftRotateString.cpp

Test Cases:

- Functional Test Cases (Rotate a string with n characters to the left side for $0/1/2/n$-$1/n/n$+1 characters respectively)

- Robustness Test Cases (The pointer to the input string is NULL)

Maximum in a Queue

■ **Question 93**   Given an array of numbers and a sliding window size, how do you get the maximum numbers in all sliding windows?

For example, if the input array is {2, 3, 4, 2, 6, 2, 5, 1} and the size of the sliding windows is 3, the output of maximums are {4, 4, 6, 6, 6, 5}, as illustrated in Table 8-3.

Table 8-3. *Maximums of All Sliding Windows with Size 3 in an Array {2, 3, 4, 2, 6, 2, 5, 1}. A pair of Brackets Indicates a Sliding Window.*

Sliding Windows in an Array	Maximums in Sliding Windows
[2, 3, 4], 2, 6, 2, 5, 1	4
2, [3, 4, 2], 6, 2, 5, 1	4
2, 3, [4, 2, 6], 2, 5, 1	6
2, 3, 4, [2, 6, 2], 5, 1	6
2, 3, 4, 2, [6, 2, 5], 1	6
2, 3, 4, 2, 6, [2, 5, 1]	5

It is not difficult to get the brute-force solution: scan numbers in every sliding window to get the maximum value. The overall time complexity is $O(nk)$ if the length of array is n and the size of the sliding windows is k.

The naive solution is not the best solution. Let's explore alternatives.

Maximum Value in a Queue

A window can be viewed as a queue. When it slides, a number is pushed into its end and the number at its beginning is popped off. Therefore, the problem is solved if we can get the maximum value of a queue.

There are no straightforward approaches to getting the maximum value of a queue. However, there are solutions to get the maximum value of a stack, which is similar to the solution to "Stack with Min Function." Additionally, a queue can also be implemented with two stacks (details are discussed the section *Build a Queue with Two Stacks*).

If a new type of queue is implemented with two stacks in which a function max is defined to get the maximum value, the maximum value in a queue is the greater number of the two maximum numbers in the two stacks.

This solution works. However, we may not have enough time to write all code to implement data structures for our own queue and stack during interviews. Let's continue exploring a more concise solution.

Saving the Maximum Value into a Queue

Instead of pushing every number inside a sliding window into a queue, we try to only push the candidates of maximum into a double-ended queue. Let's take the array {2, 3, 4, 2, 6, 2, 5, 1} as an example to analyze the solution step-by-step.

The first number in the array is 2, and it is pushed into a queue. The second number is 3, which is greater than the previous number, 2. The number 2 should be popped off because it is less than 3 and it has no chance to be the maximum value. There is only one number left in the queue when 2 is removed and then 3 is inserted. The operations are similar when the next number, 4, is inserted. There is only a number 4 remaining in the queue. Now the sliding window already has three elements and the maximum value is at the beginning of the queue.

Table 8-4. *The Process to Get the Maximum Number in all Sliding Windows with Window Size 3 in the Array {2, 3, 4, 2, 6, 2, 5, 1}. In the Column Indexes in Queue, the Number inside a Pair of Parentheses Is the Number Indexed by the Number before It in the Array.*

Step	Pushed Number	Sliding Window	Indexes in Queue	Maximum
1	2	2	0(2)	N/A
2	3	2, 3	1(3)	N/A
3	4	2, 3, 4	2(4)	4
4	2	3, 4, 2	2(4), 3(2)	4
5	6	4, 2, 6	4(6)	6
6	2	2, 6, 2	4(6), 5(2)	6
7	5	6, 2, 5	4(6), 6(5)	6
8	1	2, 5, 1	6(5), 7(1)	5

We continue to push the fourth number. It is pushed to the end of queue because it is less than the previous number 4 and it might be a maximum number in the future when the previous numbers are popped off. There are two numbers, 4 and 2, in the queue, and 4 is the maximum.

The next number to be pushed is 6. Since it is greater than the existing numbers 4 and 2, these two numbers can be popped off because they have no chance of being the maximum. Now there is only one number in the queue, which is 6, after the current number is pushed. Of course, the maximum is 6.

The next number is 2, which is pushed to the end of the queue because it is less than the previous number 6. There are two numbers in the queue, 6 and 2, and the number 6 at the beginning of the queue is the maximum value.

It is time to push the number 5. Because it is greater than the number 2 at the end of the queue, 2 is popped off and then 5 is pushed. There are two numbers in the queue, 6 and 5, and the number 6 at the beginning of the queue is still the maximum value.

Now, let's push the last number 1. It can be pushed into the queue. Note that the number 6 at the beginning of the queue is beyond the scope of the current sliding window, and it should be popped off. How do we know whether the number at the beginning of the queue is out of the sliding window? Rather than storing numbers in the queue directly, we can store indexes instead. If the distance between the index at the beginning of queue and the index of the current number to be pushed is greater than or equal to the window size, the number corresponding to the index at the beginning of queue is out of the sliding window.

The analysis process above is summarized in Table 8-4. Note that maximum numbers of all sliding windows are always indexed by the beginning of the queue.

We can implement a solution based on this analysis. Some sample code in C++ is shown in Listing 8-16 that utilizes the type deque in the STL.

Listing 8-16. *C++ Code for Maximums in Sliding Windows*

```cpp
vector<int> maxInWindows(const vector<int>& numbers, int windowSize) {
    vector<int> maxInSlidingWindows;
    if(numbers.size() >= windowSize && windowSize >= 1) {
        deque<int> indices;
```

```
        for(int i = 0; i < windowSize; ++i) {
            while(!indices.empty() && numbers[i] >= numbers[indices.back()])
                indices.pop_back();

            indices.push_back(i);
        }

        for(int i = windowSize; i < numbers.size(); ++i) {
            maxInSlidingWindows.push_back(numbers[indices.front()]);

            while(!indices.empty() && numbers[i] >= numbers[indices.back()])
                indices.pop_back();
            if(!indices.empty() && indices.front() <= i - windowSize)
                indices.pop_front();

            indices.push_back(i);
        }
        maxInSlidingWindows.push_back(numbers[indices.front()]);
    }

    return maxInSlidingWindows;
}
```

Source Code:

```
093_MaxInSlidingWindows.cpp
```

Test Cases:

- Functional Test Cases (Various n and k where n is the size of the array and k is the size of sliding windows; various arrays, including increasingly and decreasingly sorted arrays)

- Boundary Test Cases (The size of sliding window k is 1, or the same as the size of the array; the size of sliding window k is less than 1, or greater than the size of the array)

▤ **Question 94**   Define a queue in which we can get its maximum number with a function max. In this stack, the time complexity of max, push_back, and pop_front are all O(1).

As we mentioned before, a sliding window can be viewed as a queue. Therefore, we can implement a new solution to get the maximum value of a queue based on the second solution to get the maximums of sliding windows.

Listing 8-17 shows the sample code.

Listing 8-17. *C++ Code to Get Maximum in Queue*

```cpp
template<typename T> class QueueWithMax {
public:
    QueueWithMax(): currentIndex(0) {
    }

    void push_back(T number) {
        while(!maximums.empty() && number >= maximums.back().number)
            maximums.pop_back();

        InternalData internalData = {number, currentIndex};
        data.push_back(internalData);
        maximums.push_back(internalData);

        ++currentIndex;
    }

    void pop_front() {
        if(maximums.empty())
            throw new exception("queue is empty");

        if(maximums.front().index == data.front().index)
            maximums.pop_front();

        data.pop_front();
    }

    T max() const {
        if(maximums.empty())
            throw new exception("queue is empty");

        return maximums.front().number;
    }
private:
    struct InternalData {
        T number;
        int index;
    };

    deque<InternalData> data;
    deque<InternalData> maximums;
    int currentIndex;
};
```

Since this solution is similar to the second solution to get maximums of sliding windows, we will not analyze the process step-by-step but leave it as an exercise if you are interested.

Source Code:

```
094_QueueWithMax.cpp
```

Test Cases:

- Insert elements into an empty queue and then delete them
- Insert elements into a non-empty stack and then delete them
- Push and pop multiple elements continuously

Mathematical Modeling Skill

The computer is a tool to solve problems in our daily life and work, and the duty of programmers is to abstract mathematical models from real problems and solve them with programming languages. Therefore, the mathematic modeling skill is important for software engineers.

Candidates should select the appropriate data structure to model a problem. The problems in our life and work are various, but there are only a few common data structures. Candidates could make choices according to properties of the problem as well as performance and difficulties of development. For instance, candidates may model a circle with a set of numbers as a looped linked list in order to solve the problem "Last Number in a Circle" (Question 96).

Candidates should also analyze the hidden rules or patterns inside the problem and implement them with appropriate algorithms. For example, the interview problem of "Probabilities of Dice Points" (Question 95) is essentially equivalent to calculate a sequence of $f(n)=f(n-1)+f(n-2)+f(n-3)+f(n-4)+f(n-5)+f(n-6)$. Additionally, in order to find the minimum number of moves to sort a set of cards, we have to find the longest increasing subsequence at first. If candidates are familiar with algorithms, they should be able to find the longest increasing subsequence with dynamic programming.

Probabilities of Dice Points

■ **Question 95**   Given a number n, which stands for n dice, please print probabilities of all possible sums of dice points.

For example, if there are two dice, there are two ways to get three points: (1) one die has one point, and the other has two points; and (2) one die has two points, and the other has one. However, there is only one way to get twelve points, with six points on each die. Therefore, the possibility to get three points is higher than to get twelve points with two dice.

A die is often a rounded cube, with each of its faces showing a different number from 1 to 6. The minimum sum of n dice is n, and the maximum is $6n$. Additionally, points shown by n dice have 6^n permutations.

A function $f(i)$ is defined for the number of situations for dice to show i points. When we get $f(i)(0<n\leq 6n)$, the probability to get i points with n dice is $f(i)/6^n$.

When there is only one die, $f(1)$, $f(2)$, ..., $f(6)$ are initialized to 1. A die is added at each step. If there are $f(i)$ situations to get i points at a certain step, there are $f(i)=f(i-1)+f(i-2)+f(i-3)+f(i-4)+f(i-5)+f(i-6)$ with one more die at the next step. This is a typical recursive equation. However, the complexity grows exponentially if it is solved recursively because there are overlapped calculations. A better choice is based on iteration. More discussions about the efficiency difference between recursion and iteration are available in the section *Fibonacci Sequence*.

The iterative solution can be implemented as shown in Listing 8-18.

Listing 8-18. *C++ Code to Get Probabilities of Dice Points*

```cpp
void PrintProbability(int number) {
    if(number < 1)
        return;

    const int maxValue = 6;
    int* pProbabilities[2];
    pProbabilities[0] = new int[maxValue * number + 1];
    pProbabilities[1] = new int[maxValue * number + 1];
    for(int i = 0; i < maxValue * number + 1; ++i) {
        pProbabilities[0][i] = 0;
        pProbabilities[1][i] = 0;
    }

    int flag = 0;
    for (int i = 1; i <= maxValue; ++i)
        pProbabilities[flag][i] = 1;

    for (int k = 2; k <= number; ++k) {
        for(int i = 0; i < k; ++i)
            pProbabilities[1 - flag][i] = 0;

        for (int i = k; i <= maxValue * k; ++i) {
            pProbabilities[1 - flag][i] = 0;
            for(int j = 1; j <= i && j <= maxValue; ++j)
                pProbabilities[1 - flag][i] += pProbabilities[flag][i - j];
        }

        flag = 1 - flag;
    }

    double total = pow((double)maxValue, number);
    for(int i = number; i <= maxValue * number; ++i) {
        double ratio = (double)pProbabilities[flag][i] / total;
        printf("%d: %e\n", i, ratio);
    }

    delete[] pProbabilities[0];
    delete[] pProbabilities[1];
}
```

Two arrays, `pProbabilities[0]` and `pProbabilities[1]`, are defined in the code above. The ith element in these two arrays stands for the number of situations for dice to show *i* points. These two arrays are swapped (modifying the variable `flag`) for the next step to add one more die.

Source Code:

    `095_DicesProbability.cpp`

Test Cases:

- Normal Test Cases (Probabilities of points for 1, 2, 3, 4 dice)

- Boundary Test Cases (Input 0)

- Performance Test Cases (Somewhat big numbers for the count of dice, such as 11)

Last Number in a Circle

■ **Question 96**   A circle is composed of n numbers, 0, 1, ..., n-1. The mth number is removed every time, counting from the number 0 for the first removal. What is the last number left?

For example, a circle is composed of five numbers 0, 1, 2, 3, and 4 (Figure 8-3). If the third number is removed from the circle repeatedly, four numbers are deleted in the sequence of 2, 0, 4, and 1, and the last number remaining in the circle is 3.

This is the classic Josephus problem, and there are two solutions for it. The first solution is to simulate a circle with a looped list, and the other one is to analyze the pattern of deleted numbers at each step.

Simulating a Circle with a Looped List

Since this problem is about a circle, an intuitive solution is to simulate the circle with a looped list. A loop with n nodes is created first, and then the mth node is deleted from it at each step.

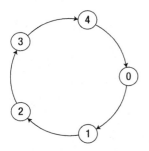

Figure 8-3. *A circle with five numbers*

    The code in Listing 8-19 is based on the type `list` in the C++ standard template library. An instance of `std::list` is not looped. When the iterator reaches the tail node, it returns back to the head node, so the list is traversed in a circled sequence. This solution can be implemented as the code in C++ as shown in Listing 8-19.

Listing 8-19. _C++ Code for the Last Number Remaining in a Circle (Version 1)_

```
int LastRemaining_Solution1(unsigned int n, unsigned int m) {
    if(n < 1 || m < 1)
        return -1;

    list<int> numbers;
    for(unsigned int i = 0; i < n; ++ i)
        numbers.push_back(i);

    list<int>::iterator current = numbers.begin();
    while(numbers.size() > 1) {
        for(int i = 1; i < m; ++ i) {
            current ++;
            if(current == numbers.end())
                current = numbers.begin();
        }

        list<int>::iterator next = ++ current;
        if(next == numbers.end())
            next = numbers.begin();

        -- current;
        numbers.erase(current);
        current = next;
    }

    return *(current);
}
```

This solution has to traverse the circled list many times. It costs O(m) time to delete a node, so its overall complexity is O(mn) on a circle with n nodes originally. Additionally, it consumes O(n) space to create a looped list. Let's explore a more effective solution.

Analyzing the Pattern of Deleted Numbers

A function $f(n,m)$ is defined for the last remaining number in a circle with n numbers from 0 to $n-1$ when the mth number is deleted at every step.

Among the n numbers in the circle, the first deleted number is $(m-1)\%n$. $(m-1)\%n$ is denoted as k for simplicity. When k is deleted, there are $n-1$ numbers (0, 1, ..., k-1, k+1, ..., n-1) left, and it counts from k+1 to delete the next m^{th} number. Therefore, numbers can be reordered as k+1, ..., n-1, 0, 1, ..., k-1 in order to place k+1 as the first number. The pattern of the reordered sequence is different from the original sequence since it does not start from 0. Another function $f(n-1,m)$ is defined for the last remaining number in these n-1 numbers, and $f(n,m)=f(n-1,m)$.

The sequence with n-1 numbers k+1, ..., n-1, 0, 1, ..., k-1 can be projected to a new sequence from 0 to n-2:

k+1 → 0
k+2 → 1

...
n-1 → n-k-2
0   → n-k-1
1   → n-k
...
k-1 → n-2

If the projection is defined as p, $p(x)=(x$-k-1$)\%n$. The reversed projection is $p^{-1}(x)=(x+k+1)\%n$.

Since the projected sequence starts from 0 and has a pattern similar to the original sequence from 0 to n-1, the last number left in the projected sequence with n-1 numbers also follows the function f, and it is $f(n$-1$,m)$.

Therefore, the last number remaining in the sequence before the projection is f(n-1,m)=p^{-1}[f(n-1,m)]=[f(n-1,m)+k+1]$\%n$. Because k=(m-1)$\%n$, $f(n,m)$=f(n-1,m) =[f(n-1),m)+m]$\%n$.

We have found a recursive equation to get the last remaining number from n numbers when the mth number is deleted at each step. If there is only one number in the original circle, it is obvious that the last remaining number is 0. Therefore, $f(n,m)$ is defined as follows:

$$f(n, m) = \begin{cases} 0 & n = 1 \\ (f(n - 1, m) + m)\%n & n > 1 \end{cases}$$

The equation can be implemented easily with both recursion and iteration. The code in Listing 8-20 is based on iteration.

Listing 8-20. *C++ Code for the Last Number Remaining in a Circle (Version 2)*

```cpp
int LastRemaining_Solution2(unsigned int n, unsigned int m) {
    if(n < 1 || m < 1)
        return -1;

    int last = 0;
    for (int i = 2; i <= n; i ++)
        last = (last + m) % i;

    return last;
}
```

Even though this analysis is very complicated, the implementation code looks quite concise. More importantly, it is more efficient because its time complexity is O(n) and space complexity is O(1).

Source Code:

096_LastNumberInCircle.cpp

Test Cases:

- Normal Test Cases (The input m is less than n, such as to delete the 3rd number at each step from a circle with 5 numbers originally; the input m is greater than or equal to n, such as to delete the 6th or 7th number at each step from a circle with 6 numbers originally)

- Boundary Test Cases (The circle is empty)

- Performance Test Cases (The inputs *m* and *n* are somewhat big, such as to delete the 997th number at each step from a circle with 4000 numbers originally)

Minimum Number of Moves to Sort Cards

Question 97   You are required to sort *n* cards numbered from 1 to *n*. You can choose one card and move it to any place you want (insert to any place, not swap). Given a sequence, please implement a function to return the minimum move count to sort these cards.

For example, given a sequence {1, 2, 5, 3, 4, 7, 6}, you can move 5 and insert it between 4 and 7, and the sequence becomes {1, 2, 3, 4, 5, 7, 6}. This is one move. If 7 is moved behind 6, the whole sequence gets sorted. Therefore, it needs two steps at least to sort cards in the sequence of {1, 2, 5, 3, 4, 7, 6}.

In order to sort a sequence with minimum number of moves, we first find the longest increasing subsequence, and then it is only necessary to insert numbers out of the longest increasing subsequence into the appropriate places. For example, one of the longest increasing subsequences of {1, 2, 5, 3, 4, 7, 6} is {1, 2, 3, 4, 6}. If the two numbers 5 and 7 are inserted into right places of {1, 2, 3, 4, 6}, the whole sequence is sorted.

Therefore, if we get the length of the longest increasing subsequence (which is not necessarily to be continuous), it is easy to know the minimum number of moves, as shown in Listing 8-21.

Listing 8-21. Java Code for the Minimum Number of Moves to Sort a Sequence

```
int minMoveCount(int[] seq) {
    return seq.length - longestIncreasingLength(seq);
}
```

It is a classic problem to get the length of the longest increasing subsequence, and there are two solutions available for it.

Based on Dynamic Programming Costing $O(n^2)$ Time

A function $f(i)$ is defined to indicate the maximum length of all subsequences ending with the ith number in the input array (denoted as $A[i]$). We define another function $g(i,j)$, which stands for the maximum length of incremental subsequences ending with $A[i]$, whose preceding number in the incremental subsequence is $A[j]$.

The required output is $max[f(i)]$ where $0 \le i < n$ and *n* is the length of array. We can get $f(i)$ with the following equation:

$$f(i) = max(g(i,j)) \text{ where } g(i,j) = \begin{cases} 1 & A[i] < A[j] \\ f(j) + 1 & A[i] > A[j] \end{cases}, 0 \le j < i$$

Take the sample sequence {1, 2, 5, 3, 4, 7, 6} as an example. The longest increasing subsequence ending with the third element is the subsequence {1, 2, 5} itself, and the length is 3.

Let's move on to analyze the longest increasing subsequence ending with the fourth element. The increasing subsequence may come from the first element and the length of {1, 3} is 2.

Similarly, the increasing subsequence may come from the second element, and the length of {1, 2, 3} is 3. However, the increasing subsequence cannot come from the third element because {1, 2, 5, 3} is not incremental. Therefore, the maximum length of the increasing subsequence ending with the fourth element is 3.

The maximum lengths of increasing subsequences ending with the last three elements are 4, 5, and 5 respectively. Therefore, the maximum length of all increasing subsequences is 5.

Even though this problem is analyzed recursively, it is more efficient to implement a solution iteratively with an array, as demonstrated in Listing 8-22.

Listing 8-22. *Java Code for the Length of Longest Increasing Subsequence (Version 1)*

```java
int longestIncreasingLength(int[] seq){
    int len = seq.length;
    int[] lookup = new int[len];

    for(int i = 0; i < len; ++i) {
        int longestSoFar = 0;
        for(int j= 0; j < i; ++j) {
            if(seq[i] > seq[j] && lookup[j] > longestSoFar)
                longestSoFar = lookup[j];
        }
        lookup[i] = longestSoFar + 1;
    }

    int longestLength = 0;
    for(int i = 0; i < len; ++i) {
        if(lookup[i] > longestLength)
            longestLength = lookup[i];
    }

    return longestLength;
}
```

The ith number in the auxiliary array `lookup` is for $f(i)$ in the equation above.

It has to compare each number with $O(n)$ numbers ahead of it in an array with n numbers, so it costs $O(n^2)$ to get maximum length of all increasing subsequences.

Based on Binary Search Costing O($n$log$n$) Time

An auxiliary array is utilized to store ending elements of the increasing subsequences while we scan the input sequence and analyze its elements one by one. When the first number 1 of the sequence {1, 2, 5, 3, 4, 7, 6} is scanned, the longest increasing subsequence so far only has one element, and we insert the number 1 at the end into the auxiliary array, and the array becomes {1}.

Similarly, when the second and third numbers are scanned, the longest increasing subsequence so far has three elements and the auxiliary array contains {1, 2, 5}.

The next number to be scanned is 3. The longest increasing subsequence so far has three elements, which are {1, 2, 5} or {1, 2, 3}. At this time, the new end number 3 is not added into the auxiliary array directly, but it replaces the last number 5 because it is less than 5 and so the array becomes {1, 2, 3}.

The reason the number 5 was replaced by 3 is that for the step to insert, the number 4 has no effect as the number 5 is the last number in the subsequence {1, 2, 5}, and the next number 4 cannot be appended to the subsequence because 4 is less than 5. However, when the number is replaced with 3, the array still keeps increasing after the number 4 is inserted, and a longer increasing subsequence {1, 2, 3, 4} with four numbers is found.

When a number in the input sequence is scanned, it is compared with the greatest number in the auxiliary array. If the newly scanned number is greater, it is inserted into the array directly. Otherwise, it replaces the least number of those greater than it in the array in order to allow a wider range of values to be added after it. In order to find the greatest number in the array as well as to find the first number greater than a target value efficiently, the array keeps sorted.

When the next number 7 is scanned, it is inserted into the auxiliary array and the array becomes {1, 2, 3, 4, 7}. And then the array becomes {1, 2, 3, 4, 6} after the last number 6 is scanned. The previous end number 7 is replaced because it is greater than 6.

The maximum length of all increasing subsequences of {1, 2, 5, 3, 4, 7, 6} is five because there are five elements in the auxiliary array {1, 2, 3, 4, 6} finally.

It should be noticed that the auxiliary array is not guaranteed to be the longest increasing subsequence. For example, the auxiliary array is {1, 3, 5, 6} after all numbers in the sequence {2, 4, 1, 5, 6, 3} are handled. The auxiliary array is not the longest increasing subsequence, but its length is the same as the longest increasing subsequence, which is {2, 4, 5, 6}.

Because the auxiliary array is sorted, the binary search algorithm is applied to find the first number greater than a target. This solution can be implemented as shown in Listing 8-23.

Listing 8-23. *Java Code for the Length of Longest Increasing Subsequence (Version 2)*

```java
int longestIncreasingLength(int[] seq) {
    int len = seq.length;
    int[] lookup = new int[len];

    lookup[0] = seq[0];
    int longestLength = 1;
    for(int i = 1; i < len; ++i) {
        if(seq[i] > lookup[longestLength - 1]) {
            longestLength++;
            lookup[longestLength - 1] = seq[i];
        }
        else {
            int low = 0;
            int high = longestLength - 1;
            while(low != high) {
                int mid = (low + high) / 2;
                if(lookup[mid] < seq[i]) {
                    low = mid + 1;
                }
                else {
                    high = mid;
                }
            }
```

```
            lookup[low] = seq[i];
        }
    }

    return longestLength;
}
```

As we know, it takes O(log$n$) time to search in a sorted array with n elements, so the overall time complexity is ($n$log$n$).

Source Code:

> 097_MinimalMoves.java

Test Cases:

- Normal Test Cases (An arbitrary array with some numbers)
- Boundary Test Cases (There is only one number in the array; the array is increasingly/decreasingly sorted)

Most Profit from Stock

■ **Question 98**   Stock prices are stored in an array in the order of date. How do you get the most profit from a sequence of stock prices?

For example, the most profit to be gained from the sequence of ordered stock prices {9, 11, 5, 7, 16, 1, 4, 2} is 11, bought when the price was 5 and sold when the price was 16.

The stock profit is the difference in prices in buying and selling stock. Of course, we can sell stock only after we buy it. A pair is composed of a buying price and a selling price. Therefore, the most profit is the maximum difference of all pairs in a sequence of stock prices. This problem is essentially to get the maximum difference for all pairs in an array.

The naive brute-force solution is quite straightforward. We can get the result for each number minus every number on its left side, and then get the maximum difference after comparisons. Since O(n) minus operations are required for each number in an array with n numbers, the overall time complexity is O(n^2). A brute-force solution usually is not the best one. Let's try to reduce the times for these minus operations.

Based Divide and Conquer

An array is divided into two sub-arrays of the same size. The maximum difference of all pairs occurs in one of the three following situations: (1) two numbers in a pair are both in the first sub-array; (2) two numbers in a pair are both in the second sub-array; or (3) the minuend is the maximum number in the second sub-array, and the subtrahend is the minimum number in the first sub-array.

It is not difficult to get the minimum number in the first sub-array and the maximum number in the first sub-array. How about getting the maximum difference of all pairs inside two sub-arrays? They are actually subproblems of the original problem and we can solve them via recursion. Listing 8-24 contains the sample code of this solution.

Listing 8-24. C++ Code to Get Pair with Maximum Difference (Version 1)

```cpp
int MaxDiff_Solution1(int numbers[], unsigned length) {
    if(numbers == NULL && length < 2)
        return 0;

    int max, min;
    return MaxDiffCore(numbers, numbers + length - 1, &max, &min);
}

int MaxDiffCore(int* start, int* end, int* max, int* min) {
    if(end == start) {
        *max = *min = *start;
        return 0x80000000;
    }

    int* middle = start + (end - start) / 2;

    int maxLeft, minLeft;
    int leftDiff = MaxDiffCore(start, middle, &maxLeft, &minLeft);

    int maxRight, minRight;
    int rightDiff = MaxDiffCore(middle + 1, end, &maxRight, &minRight);

    int crossDiff = maxRight - minLeft;

    *max = (maxLeft > maxRight) ? maxLeft : maxRight;
    *min = (minLeft < minRight) ? minLeft : minRight;

    int maxDiff = (leftDiff > rightDiff) ? leftDiff : rightDiff;
    maxDiff = (maxDiff > crossDiff) ? maxDiff : crossDiff;
    return maxDiff;
}
```

With the function `MaxDiffCore`, we get the maximum difference of pairs in the first sub-array (`leftDiff`), and then get the maximum difference of pairs in the second sub-array (`rightDiff`). We continue to calculate the difference between the maximum in the second sub-array and the minimum number in the first sub-array (`crossDiff`). The greatest value of the three differences is the maximum difference of the whole array.

We can get the minimum and maximum numbers, as well as their difference in O(1) time, based on the comparison of minimum and maximum numbers of sub-arrays, so the time complexity of the recursive solution is $T(n)=2T(n/2)+O(1)$. We can demonstrate that its time complexity is $O(n)$ with the Master Theory.

Storing the Minimum Numbers while Scanning

Let's define $diff[i]$ for the difference of a pair whose minuend is the ith number in an array, and the subtrahend corresponding to the maximum $diff[i]$ should be the minimum of all numbers on the left side of the ith number in an array. We can get the minimum numbers on the left side of each ith number in an array while scanning the array once. The code in Listing 8-25 is based on this solution.

Listing 8-25. *C++ Code to Get Pair with Maximum Difference (Version 2)*

```cpp
int MaxDiff_Solution2(int numbers[], unsigned length) {
    if(numbers == NULL && length < 2)
        return 0;

    int min = numbers[0];
    int maxDiff =  numbers[1] - min;

    for(int i = 2; i < length; ++i) {
        if(numbers[i - 1] < min)
            min = numbers[i - 1];

        int currentDiff = numbers[i] - min;
        if(currentDiff > maxDiff)
            maxDiff = currentDiff;
    }

    return maxDiff;
}
```

It is obvious that its time complexity is $O(n)$ since it is only necessary to scan an array with length n once. It is more efficient than the first solution on memory consumption, which requires $O(\log n)$ memory for call stack due to recursion.

Source Code:

    098_MaximalProfitBuyingSellingStock.cpp

Test Cases:

- Normal Test Cases (An arbitrary array with some numbers for stock prices)
- Boundary Test Cases (There is only one number in the array; the array is increasingly/decreasingly sorted)
- Robustness Test Cases (The pointer to the array is NULL)

Divergent Thinking Skills

Divergent thinking is a thought process to generate creative ideas in a short period of time by looking for new opportunities and ways to get things done. Instead of taking obvious steps and walking in a straight line from a problem to the solution, we try to see different aspects of the situation and use unusual points of view.

Interviewers pay a lot of attention to candidates' divergent thinking skills because divergent thinking skills demonstrate creativity and passion to explore new solutions. Sometimes interviewers intentionally disallow candidates from taking the traditional solutions. What they expect is for candidates to think from creative perspectives. For example, some interviewers ask candidates to add, subtract, multiply, and divide without using +, -, ×, and ÷ operations. They expect candidates to jump outside the boundary of arithmetic calculation and find solutions with bit operations.

Divergent thinking skills also demonstrate the breadth and depth of knowledge. Candidates are able to explore solutions from various points of view only when they have deep understanding of various domains. For instance, there is a popular interview problem that requires calculating 1+2+...+n without using loops, multiplication and division, keywords including `if`, `switch`, and `case`, as well as the conditional operator. If a candidate has a broad and deep understanding of C++, he or she could solve it with constructors, virtual functions, function pointers, and template specialization.

Calculating $1+2+...+n$

■ **Question 99**   How do you calculate $1+2+...+n$ without multiplication, division, key words including `for`, `while`, `if`, `else`, `switch`, and `case`, as well as a conditional operator (`A?B:C`)?

As we know, $1+2+...+n=n(n+1)/2$. However, this equation cannot be utilized because multiplication and division are disallowed. $1+2+...+n$ is also usually calculated iteratively or recursively. Since `for` and `while` have been disallowed, loops cannot be utilized. If we are going to calculate recursively, we have to use `if` or the conditional operator to determine when to end the recursion. However, neither are they allowed.

Based on Constructors

The purpose of a loop is to repeat execution n times. Actually, we can repeat execution without `for` and `while` statements. For example, a type is defined first and its constructor will be invoked n times if n instances are created. If the code to accumulate is inserted into the constructor, $1+2+...+n$ is calculated, as shown in Listing 8-26.

Listing 8-26. *C++ Code to Calculate 1+2+...+n (Version 1)*

```cpp
class Temp {
public:
    Temp() { ++ N; Sum += N; }

    static void Reset() { N = 0; Sum = 0; }
    static unsigned int GetSum() { return Sum; }

private:
    static unsigned int N;
    static unsigned int Sum;
};
```

```
unsigned int Temp::N = 0;
unsigned int Temp::Sum = 0;

unsigned int Sum_Solution1(unsigned int n) {
    Temp::Reset();

    Temp *a = new Temp[n];
    delete []a;
    a = NULL;

    return Temp::GetSum();
}
```

Based on Virtual Functions

The difficulty with utilizing recursion without `if` and the conditional operator is that we cannot determine when to stop. If it is difficult to end recursion inside a function, how about defining two functions? The first function takes the calculation, and the second one acts as a terminator. We have to choose one of them at every step during execution. That is to say, the terminator is selected when n becomes 0; otherwise, the first function is selected for all non-zero n. Therefore, we have another solution, as shown in Listing 8-27.

Listing 8-27. C++ Code to Calculate 1+2+…+n (Version 2)

```
class A;
A* Array[2];

class A {
public:
    virtual unsigned int Sum (unsigned int n) {
        return 0;
    }
};

class B: public A {
public:
    virtual unsigned int Sum (unsigned int n) {
        return Array[!!n]->Sum(n-1) + n;
    }
};

int Sum_Solution2(int n) {
    A a;
    B b;
    Array[0] = &a;
    Array[1] = &b;

    int value = Array[1]->Sum(n);

    return value;
}
```

It makes choices based on virtual functions A::Sum and B::Sum in the code above. When n is not zero, the result of !!n is 1 (true), so it invokes B::Sum to accumulate; otherwise, it tells A::Sum to stop when n is zero.

Based on Function Pointers

Virtual functions are not available in C, so the preceding solution does not work for C programmers. Fortunately, we could simulate virtual functions with function pointers, as shown in Listing 8-28.

Listing 8-28. *C Code to Calculate 1+2+...+n (Version 3)*

```
typedef unsigned int (*fun)(unsigned int);

unsigned int Solution3_Teminator(unsigned int n)  {
    return 0;
}

unsigned int Sum_Solution3(unsigned int n) {
    static fun f[2] = {Solution3_Teminator, Sum_Solution3};
    return n + f[!!n](n - 1);
}
```

The function Sum_Solution3 calls itself recursively till n is decreased to 0 because !!0 is 0 (false).

Based on Templates

We could also utilize compilers to calculate with the code in Listing 8-29.

Listing 8-29. *C++ Code to Calculate 1+2+...+n (Version 4)*

```
template <unsigned int n> struct Sum_Solution4 {
    enum Value { N = Sum_Solution4<n - 1>::N + n};
};

template <> struct Sum_Solution4<1> {
    enum Value { N = 1};
};
```

The value of Sum_Solution4<100>::N is the result of 1+2+...+100. When the C++ compiler sees Sum_Solution4<100>, it generates code for the class template Sum_Solution4 with 100 as the template argument. Note that the type Sum_Solution4<100> depends on the type Sum_Solution4<99> because in the code above Sum_Solution4<100>::N=Sum_Solution4<99>::N+100. The compiler generates code for Sum_Solution4<99>, which depends on Sum_Solution4<98>. The recursive process stops at the type Sum_Solution4<1> because it is explicitly defined.

The process to calculate `Sum_Solution4<100>::N` for 1+2+...+100 is in the compiling time, so the input *n* should be a constant value. Additionally, C++ compilers have constraints on the depth of recursive compiling, so *n* cannot be a large value.

Source Code:

   `099_Accumulate.cpp`

Test Cases:

- Normal Test Cases (Input 5 and 10 to calculate 1+2+...+5 and 1+2+...+10)
- Boundary Test Cases (Input 1)

Implementation of +, -, *, and /

▪ **Question 100**   How do you implement a function to add two integers without utilization of arithmetic +, -, *, and / operators?

First of all, let's analyze how we add decimals with three steps. Take 5+17=22 as an example. The first step is to add digits without carries, and we get 12. (The digits of the least significant bits are 5 and 7, and the sum of them is 2 without a carry. The tens digits are 0 and 1, and the sum of them 1.) The second step is for carries. There is a 1 carry for the least significant digits, and the actual value for the carry is 10 (1×10=10 in decimal). The last step is to add the sums of the two steps together, and we get 12+10=22.

What can we calculate without arithmetic operators? It seems that we do not have other choices except bit operations. Bit operations are based on binary numbers. Let's have a try at adding binary numbers with three steps similar to the process above.

The binary representations of 5 and 17 are 101 and 10001 respectively. We get 10100 without carries in the first step. (They are two 1 digits at the least significant digits. In binary 1+1=10, and the sum is 0 without carries.) Carries are recorded in the second step. There is a carry 1 at the least significant digits to add 101 and 10001, and the actual value of the carry is 10 (1×10=10 in binary). When 10100 and 10 are added, the sum is 10110, and it is 22 in decimal. Therefore, binary numbers can also be added in three steps.

Let's move on now to replace the steps with binary operations. The first step is to add digits without carries. The results are 0 when adding 0 and 0, as well as adding 1 and 1. The results are 1 when adding 0 and 1, as well as 1 and 0. Note that these results are the same as bitwise XOR operations. The bitwise XOR results of 0 and 0, as well as 1 and 1, are 0, while the XOR results of 0 and 1, as well as 1 and 0, are 1.

The second step is for carries. There are no carries while adding 0 and 0, 0 and 1, as well as 1 and 0. There is a carry only when 1 and 1 are added. These results are the same as bitwise AND operations. Additionally, we have to shift carries to the left for one bit to get the actual carry value.

The third step is to add results of the first two steps. The adding operations can be replaced with bit operations again. These two steps above are repeated until there are carries.

It is time to write code after we have clear picture of how to simulate addition with bit operation. The sample code is shown in Listing 8-30.

Listing 8-30. Java Code to Add

```java
int add(int num1, int num2) {
    int sum, carry;
    do {
        sum = num1 ^ num2;
        carry = (num1 & num2) << 1;
        num1 = sum;
        num2 = carry;
    } while (num2 != 0);

    return num1;
}
```

Source Code:

    100_103_ArithmeticOperations.java

Test Cases:

- Add positive numbers, negative numbers, and 0

▓ **Question 101**   How do you implement a function for the subtraction operation without utilization of arithmetic +, -, *, and / operators?

Subtraction can be implemented with addition because a-b=a+(-b). Additionally, -b can be gotten with bit operations because -b=~b+1. We have simulated addition with bit operations, so there are no problems in simulating subtraction with bit operations, as shown in Listing 8-31.

Listing 8-31. *Java Code to Subtract*

```java
int subtract(int num1, int num2) {
    num2 = add(~num2, 1);
    return add(num1, num2);
}
```

Source Code:

    100_103_ArithmeticOperations.java

Test Cases:

- Two numbers for subtraction are positive numbers, negative numbers, or 0

▓ **Question 102**   How do you implement a function for the multiplication operation without utilization of arithmetic +, -, *, and / operators?

As we know, $a \times n$ ($n \geq 0$) is the same as $a+a+...+a$ (for n times). Therefore, we could invoke the **add** method above in a loop to implement multiplication. If we are going to multiply a number with n, we have to invoke **add** for n times. Is it possible to reduce the times that are necessary to be invoked?

Let's take $a \times 6$ as an example. The number 6 is 110 in binary, which is 2 (10 in binary) plus 4 (100 in binary), so $a \times 6 = a \times 2 + a \times 4$. Note that $a \times 2$ and $a \times 4$ can be calculated based on left-shift operations, which are $a<<1$ and $a<<2$, respectively.

Therefore, $a \times n$ can be implemented with a left-shift and additions. Since there are $O(\log n)$ 1 bits in the binary representation of n, the new solution invokes the **add** method for $O(\log n)$ times, as implemented in Listing 8-32.

Listing 8-32. *Java Code to Multiply*

```java
int multiply(int num1, int num2) {
    boolean minus = false;
    if ((num1 < 0 && num2 > 0) || (num1 > 0 && num2 < 0))
        minus = true;

    if (num1 < 0)
        num1 = add(~num1, 1);
    if (num2 < 0)
        num2 = add(~num2, 1);

    int result = 0;
    while (num1 > 0) {
        if ((num1 & 0x1) != 0) {
            result = add(result, num2);
        }

        num2 = num2 << 1;
        num1 = num1 >> 1;
    }

    if (minus)
        result = add(~result, 1);

    return result;
}
```

Source Code:

```
100_103_ArithmeticOperations.java
```

Test Cases:

- The two numbers for multiplication are positive numbers, negative numbers, or 0

■ **Question 103**   How do you implement a function to divide an integer by another without utilization of arithmetic +, -, *, and / operators?

For two positive integers, if $a/b=n$, a-b×$n \geq 0$ and a-b× $(n+1)<0$. Therefore, the division can be implemented with the subtract method in a loop. It invokes the method **subtract** for $O(n)$ times when the result is n.

There is a more efficient solution available. If the result of a/b is n, and m bits are 1 in the binary representation of n (the n_1, n_2, ..., n_m bit counting from the right end),

$$n = \sum_{i=1}^{m} 2^{n_t-1},$$

and

$$a - b \times \sum_{i=1}^{m} 2^{n_t-1} \geq 0.$$

Similar to before,

$$b \times 2^{n_t-1}$$

can be implemented with left-shift operation. Therefore, the division can be implemented with the code shown in Listing 8-33.

Listing 8-33. *Java Code to Divide*

```java
int divide(int num1, int num2) {
    if (num2 == 0)
        throw new ArithmeticException("num2 is zero.");

    boolean minus = false;
    if ((num1 < 0 && num2 > 0) || (num1 > 0 && num2 < 0))
        minus = true;

    if (num1 < 0)
        num1 = add(~num1, 1);
    if (num2 < 0)
        num2 = add(~num2, 1);

    int result = 0;
    for (int i = 0; i < 32; i=add(i, 1)) {
        result = result << 1;
        if ((num1 >> (31 - i)) >= num2) {
            num1 = subtract(num1, num2 << (31 - i));
            result = add(result, 1);
        }
    }

    if (minus)
        result = add(~result, 1);

    return result;
}
```

Source Code:

100_103_ArithmeticOperations.java

Test Cases:

- The two numbers for multiplication are positive numbers, negative numbers, or 0

Final/Sealed Classes in C++

■ **Question 104**   Please design a class in C++ that cannot be inherited.

In C# there is a keyword `sealed`, indicating a class that cannot be a parent class of other classes. In Java, there is a similar keyword `final`. There are no such keywords in C++, so we have to implement a mechanism for `sealed` or `final` classes.

Based on Private Constructors

As we know, a constructor of a C++ class invokes the constructor of its parent class, and a destructor invokes its parent class's destructor. If a constructor or destructor is declared as a private function, it cannot be invoked outside the class where it is defined. Therefore, a class whose constructors and destructor are private cannot have children classes. If we are going inherit it, a compiling error is raised.

How do you create and release instances of a class whose constructors and destructor are private? We may utilize public static member functions, as shown in Listing 8-34.

Listing 8-34. C++ Code for Sealed/Final Classes (Version 1)

```
class SealedClass1 {
public:
    static SealedClass1* GetInstance() {
        return new SealedClass1();
    }

    static void DeleteInstance( SealedClass1* pInstance) {
        delete pInstance;
    }

private:
    SealedClass1() {}
    ~SealedClass1() {}
};
```

It is a bit inconvenient to use these classes because there are some differences from normal classes. For example, we can only create instances of a `SealedClass1` on the heap, but we cannot create instances on the stack.

Based on Private Constructors

It is a little bit tricky to define a sealed/final class whose instances can be created on the stack. Listing 8-35 contains the sample code.

Listing 8-35. C++ Code for Sealed/Final Classes (Version 2)

```
template <typename T> class MakeSealed {
    friend T;

private:
    MakeSealed() {}
    ~MakeSealed() {}
};

class SealedClass2 : virtual public MakeSealed<SealedClass2> {
public:
    SealedClass2() {}
    ~SealedClass2() {}
};
```

We can create instances of the class SealedClass2 on both the heap and stack space, so it is more convenient to use than SealedClass1.

Even though the constructor and destructor of MakeSealed<SealedClass2> are defined as private functions, they can be invoked by the class SealedClass2 because SealedClass2 is a friend class of MakeSealed<SealedClass2>.

The compiler raises an error when we are trying to derive a new class from SealedClass2, such as the class Try in Listing 8-36.

Listing 8-36. C++ Code to Derive a Class from SealedClass2

```
class Try2 : public SealedClass2 {
public:
    Try2() {}
    ~Try2() {}
};
```

Since the class SealedClass2 is virtually inherited from MakeSealed<SealedClass2>, the constructor of Try skips SealedClass2 and invokes the constructor of MakeSealed<SealedClass2>. The class Try is not a friend of MakeSealed<SealedClass2>, so it raises a compiling error to invoke the constructor of MakeSealed<SealedClass2> from Try.

Therefore, we cannot inherit children classes from SealedClass2, and it is a sealed/final class.

The source code for SealedClass2 can be compiled smoothly in Visual Studio, but it cannot be compiled in GCC. Currently, the template argument cannot be a friend type in GCC. Therefore, the second type has problems from the perspective of portability.

Source Code:

104_SealedClass.cpp

Array Construction

■ **Question 105** Given an array $A[0, 1, \ldots, n\text{-}1]$, please construct an array $B[0, 1, \ldots, n\text{-}1]$ in which $B[i]=A[0]\times A[1]\times\ldots \times A[i\text{-}1]\times A[i+1]\times\ldots\times A[n\text{-}1]$. No division should be involved to solve this problem.

If there are no limitations to utilize the division operation, $B[i]$ can be calculated by $\prod_{j=0}^{n-1} A[j] / A[i]$. Be careful when $A[i]$ is zero.

It is not allowed to use division here, so we have to explore alternatives. An intuitive solution to calculate $B[i]$ is to multiply $n\text{-}1$ numbers, so the time complexity to construct the array B is $O(n^2)$. There are more efficient solutions available.

$B[i]$ is $A[0]\times A[1]\times\ldots\times A[i\text{-}1]\times A[i+1]\times\ldots\times A[n\text{-}1]$, which is the multiplication result of two sequences $A[0]\times A[1]\times\ldots\times A[i\text{-}1]$ and $A[i+1]\times\ldots\times A[n\text{-}2]\times A[n\text{-}1]$. Therefore, the array B can be visualized as a matrix, as shown in Figure 8-4. The multiplication result of numbers in the ith row is $B[i]$.

Let's define $C[i]=A[0]\times A[1]\times\ldots\times A[i\text{-}1]$ and $D[i]= A[i+1]\times\ldots\times A[n\text{-}2]\times A[n\text{-}1]$, so $B[i]=C[i]\times D[i]$. Note that $C[i]=C[i\text{-}1]\times A[i\text{-}1]$, and $D[i]=D[i+1]\times A[i+1]$. Therefore, $C[i]$ can be calculated in a top down order, and $D[i]$ can be calculated in bottom up order. After $C[i]$ and $D[i]$ are calculated, they are multiplied for $B[i]$.

B_0	1	A_1	A_2	$\cdots$	A_{n-2}	A_{n-1}
B_1	A_0	1	A_2	$\cdots$	A_{n-2}	A_{n-1}
B_2	A_0	A_1	1	$\cdots$	A_{n-2}	A_{n-1}
$\cdots$	A_0	A_1	$\cdots$	1	A_{n-2}	A_{n-1}
B_{n-2}	A_0	A_1	$\cdots$	A_{n-3}	1	A_{n-1}
B_{n-1}	A_0	A_1	$\cdots$	A_{n-3}	A_{n-2}	1

Figure 8-4. The constructed array B is visualized as a matrix.

This solution can be implemented in Java with the code in Listing 8-37.

Listing 8-37. Java Code to Construct an Array

```java
void multiply(double array1[], double array2[]){
    if(array1.length == array2.length && array1.length > 0){
        array2[0] = 1;
        for(int i = 1; i < array1.length; ++i){
            array2[i] = array2[i - 1] * array1[i - 1];
```

```
        }

        int temp = 1;
        for(int i = array1.length - 2; i >= 0; --i){
            temp *= array1[i + 1];
            array2[i] *= temp;
        }
    }
}
```

The time complexity of this solution is O(n) obviously, and it is more efficient than the intuitive solution above.

Source Code:

```
105_ConstuctArray.java
```

Test Cases:

- Normal Test Cases (There are positive numbers, negative numbers, and 0 in the array A)

- Special Test Cases (There are no, only one, or more 0s in the array A)

Summary

Besides programming abilities, it is important for candidates to demonstrate other skills, such as communication skills, knowledge migration skills, mathematical modeling skills, and divergent thinking skills.

Candidates show their communication skills when they describe project experiences and solutions to coding interview problems clearly. Additionally, it is an indication of good communication skills if they ask pertinent questions proactively.

Knowledge migration skills are helpful in solving new problems. When an interview problem is similar to a classic algorithm or other popular problems, candidates may focus on the similarities and try to reapply the classic algorithm or known solutions of other problems.

There are many interesting interview problems abstracted from daily life that require mathematical modeling skills. In order to solve such problems, candidates have to choose appropriate data structures to algorithms according to the hidden model.

Sometimes interviewers disallow candidates from using traditional solutions. In such cases, candidates have to show their divergent thinking skills by solving problems with creative ideas from unusual perspectives.

CHAPTER 9

▪ ▪ ▪

Interview Cases

We have discussed five key factors that determine performance of candidates in the previous chapters:

- Basics of programming languages, data structures, and algorithms
- Approaches to writing code of high quality
- Strategies to solve difficult problems
- Methods to optimize code
- Skills required in interviews

In the following sections, two typical interview cases are discussed. The first case covers common mistakes many candidates make, and the second one discusses behaviors that are received positively by interviewers. We hope candidates make few, or even no mistakes, and are able to showcase their skills during code interviews. We also sincerely hope candidates get their dream offers.

Integer Value from a String

Interviewer: You mentioned in your résumé that you are proficient on C/C++. How many years have you used these two languages?

Candidate: It has been six or seven years since I learned them at my university.

Interviewer: Cool, it sounds like you are a veteran. Let's discuss some C++ problems. (The interviewer hands a piece of paper with the source code from Listing 9-1 to the candidate.) What is the output when this piece of code executes?

Listing 9-1. C++ Code for the Member Initialization Order

```
class A {
private:
    int n1;
    int n2;
public:
    A(): n2(0), n1(n2 + 2) {
    }
```

```
        void Print() {
            std::cout << "n1: " << n1 << ", n2: " << n2 << std::endl;
        }
};

int main(int argc, char* argv[]) {
    A a;
    a.Print();
    return 0;
}
```

Candidate:	(Reads code for a while) n1 is 2, and n2 is 0.
Interviewer:	Why?
Candidate:	In the initialization list of the constructor, n2 is initialized as 0, so the result of n2 is 0. And then n1 is initialized with n2+2, so it is 2.

■ **Note:** This answer is NOT correct. Please refer to the comments at the end of this section for more details.

Interviewer:	Are members initialized according to their order in the initialization list?
Candidate:	(Confused) I am not quite sure.
Interviewer:	No problem. Let's move on to another problem. What is the usage for the function **atoi** in the C library?
Candidate:	It converts a numeric string to an integer. For example, if the input string is "123", it returns 123.
Interviewer:	That's right. Please write a function **StrToInt** to convert a string to an integer. Of course, it is not allowed to call **atoi** or other similar functions in the library. Are there any questions?
Candidate:	(Smiles with confidence) No problem.

The candidate writes down the code in Listing 9-2 on paper in a short period of time.

Listing 9-2. *C++ Code to Convert a String to an Integer (Version 1)*

```
int StrToInt(char* string) {
    int number = 0;
    while(*string != 0) {
        number = number * 10 + *string - '0';
        ++string;
    }

    return number;
}
```

Candidate: I have finished.

Interviewer: Oh, that was quick. (Reads the code quickly) Do you think it is complete? Scrutinize your code.

Candidate: (Reads the code from the beginning) Sorry that I forgot to verify the NULL pointer for the input string.

The candidate adds two lines of code. The revised code is shown in Listing 9-3.

Listing 9-3. *C++ Code to Convert a String to an Integer (Version 2)*

```cpp
int StrToInt(char* string) {
    if(string == NULL)
        return 0;

    int number = 0;
    while(*string != 0) {
        number = number * 10 + *string - '0';
        ++string;
    }

    return number;
}
```

Interviewer: Have you finished? (Reads the code again) Your output is 0 when the input string is NULL. What is the output when the input is a string "0"?

Candidate: It is also 0.

Interviewer: It returns 0 for two different cases. How do you distinguish these cases when its caller gets a 0?

Candidate: (Confused) I do not know.

Interviewer: Similar to the library function atoi, we may distinguish them with a global variable. When the input is invalid, the variable is set to a special value. However, it is not set when the input is "0". When the caller gets a 0 from the function StrToInt, it knows what happens according to the global variable.

Candidate: Oh, I see. (Picks up the pen) Let me rewrite that.

Interviewer: Wait. Are there any other invalid inputs besides the NULL pointer?

Candidate: (Thinking, with sweat on forehead) If a string has some characters beyond the range from '0' to '9', it is invalid.

Interviewer: Are all characters beyond the range from '0' to '9' invalid?

Candidate: The positive sign ('+') and negative sign ('-') should be valid.

Interviewer: Correct. Think carefully before you start to write code.

The candidate thinks for a few minutes, and writes down the code shown in Listing 9-4.

Listing 9-4. C++ Code to Convert a String to an Integer (Version 3)

```
enum Status {kValid = 0, kInvalid};
int g_nStatus = kValid;

int StrToInt(const char* str) {
    g_nStatus = kInvalid;
    int num = 0;

    if(str != NULL) {
        const char* digit = str;
        bool minus = false;

        if(*digit == '+')
            digit ++;
        else if(*digit == '-') {
            digit ++;
            minus = true;
        }

        while(*digit != '\0') {
            if(*digit >= '0' && *digit <= '9') {
                num = num * 10 + (*digit - '0');
                digit++;
            }
            else {
                num = 0;
                break;
            }
        }

        if(*digit == '\0') {
            g_nStatus = kValid;
            if(minus)
                num = 0 - num;
        }
    }

    return num;
}
```

Interviewer: Can you explain your code?

Candidate: I defined a global variable g_Status to mark whether the input is valid. It is initialized to the invalid status and is set to valid only when all characters in the string are converted smoothly. It is possible for a positive or negative sign to appear in the first character, so the first character of the input string is handled specially. Any non-digital character after a positive or negative sign indicates an invalid input string, so the conversion stops immediately.

Interviewer: It sounds good. Is there anything missing?

Candidate: (Thinks for about two minutes) Is it necessary to handle overflow issues?

Interviewer:	Isn't it necessary? It seems that there is no more time left for you to make changes again. I am going to leave the last minutes for you to ask a few questions. Do you have any questions to me?
Candidate:	What is the salary package at your company?
Interviewer:	What is your expectation?
Candidate:	Many of my classmates got a package of more than a hundred thousand dollars per year. I do not want to have less than them.
Interviewer:	The package of the entry level for graduates is determined by our human resources department, so I cannot answer your questions, but I will forward your expectation to the recruiter.
Candidate:	That is OK. Thank you.
Interviewer:	Any more questions?
Candidate:	No.
Interviewer:	Cool. That is the end of this round of interview. Thank you.

The Interviewer's Comments

I was very disappointed when the candidate provided an incorrect answer to the question about the initialization list in a C++ constructor because he mentioned that he was proficient on C++. The initialization list is a commonly used concept in C++. Data members in an initialization list are initialized in the order of the member variable declarations in the class. Since n1 was declared before n2 in the given code, n1 should be initialized before n2. When n1 was initialized with n2+2, n2 had not been initialized yet, and it might be a random value. Therefore, the value of n1 was random after initialization, and then n2 was initialized as 0.

The next question was a coding interview problem to convert a string to an integer. It looked like a simple problem, and the candidate implemented it within less than 10 lines of code at first. However, what I expected was complete and robust code, which should handle cases including a normal numeric string, a NULL pointer, an empty string, a string with non-digital characters, a string with a positive or negative sign, as well as overflow issues. It was not necessary for the candidate to implement a function identical to atoi, but he should define the behavior of his function with various inputs and explain it to me explicitly. The most serious problem for the candidate was that he did not have a habit of considering all possible inputs in advance before writing code, so his code was problematic and incomplete. After I gave him many hints, there still were many bugs left in his code.

Listing 9-5 contains the sample code, which covers more cases than the candidate's code:

Listing 9-5. C++ Code to Convert a String to an Integer (Version 4)

```cpp
enum Status {kValid = 0, kInvalid};
int g_nStatus = kValid;

int StrToInt(const char* str) {
    g_nStatus = kInvalid;
```

```
        long long num = 0;

        if(str != NULL && *str != '\0') {
            bool minus = false;
            if(*str == '+')
                str ++;
            else if(*str == '-') {
                str ++;
                minus = true;
            }

            if(*str != '\0') {
                num = StrToIntCore(str, minus);
            }
        }

        return (int)num;
}

long long StrToIntCore(const char* digit, bool minus) {
        long long num = 0;

        while(*digit != '\0') {
            if(*digit >= '0' && *digit <= '9') {
                int flag = minus ? -1 : 1;
                num = num * 10 + flag * (*digit - '0');

                if((!minus && num > 0x7FFFFFFF)
                    || (minus && num < (signed int)0x80000000)) {
                    num = 0;
                    break;
                }

                digit++;
            }
            else {
                num = 0;
                break;
            }
        }

        if(*digit == '\0') {
            g_nStatus = kValid;
        }

        return num;
}
```

What the candidate cared about was salary during the Q & A phase. Often employees who only care about salary are prone to be job-hoppers. Additionally, his expectation was based on his classmates' salary packages. Did it indicate that he was lacking self-evaluation skills?

To sum up, my opinion was not to hire the candidate because he currently does not have the competence to write complete and robust code.

Source Code:

106_StringToInt.cpp

Test Cases:

- Normal Test Cases (Numeric strings for positive/negative numbers or zero; strings with non-digital characters besides '+' and '-')

- Boundary Test Cases (Strings for the maximal and minimal integers)

- Robustness Test Cases (A NULL point to a string; an empty string)

Lowest Common Parent Node in a Tree

Interviewer:	Are you ready for your interview?
Candidate:	Yeah, I am ready.
Interviewer:	Would you please introduce me to your most recent project?
Candidate:	I finished a Multi-Target project in Civil 3D (software for civil engineering based on AutoCAD) a few weeks ago. The target is the edge of a road. Previously, the road edge could only be a data structure called Alignment in Civil. My task was to support other data structures, such as Polyline in AutoCAD.
Interviewer:	Is it possible to add new data structures for road edges in the future?
Candidate:	It was a requirement to support new data structures during development. A new road edge named Pipeline was added in the second version of the specification. Since my design took scalability into consideration, it was only necessary to add new classes for Pipeline, and little existing code was modified.
Interviewer:	It sounds interesting. How did you do it?

The candidate draws a UML figure to show the hierarchy of several classes. (The figure has been omitted here.)

Candidate:	(Explaining while pointing to the figure) According to the class hierarchy, it was only necessary to add a new class for Pipeline when it was to support a new target type, and it had no impact on other classes.
Interviewer:	(Nods) Yeah, it is cool. OK, let's change topics and try a coding problem. The requirement is to find the lowest common ancestor with two given nodes in a tree.
Candidate:	Is the tree a binary search tree?
Interviewer:	Why do you ask such a question?
Candidate:	If it is binary search tree, there is a solution available.

Interviewer:	OK, let's suppose it is a binary search tree. How do you get the lowest common ancestor?
Candidate:	(A bit excited and speaking quickly) A binary search tree is sorted where value in a parent node is greater than values in the left subtree and less than values in the right subtree. We begin to traverse the tree from the root node and compare the value of the visited node with the values in the two given nodes. If the value of the current visited node is greater than the values of two given nodes, the lowest common ancestor should be in the left subtree, so it moves to the left child node for the next round of comparison. Similarly, it moves to the right child node if the value of the current visited node is less than the values of the two given nodes. The first node whose value is between the values of two given nodes is the lowest common ancestor.
Interviewer:	It seems that you are quite familiar with this problem. Did you see it before?
Candidate:	(Embarrassed) Uh, I happened to see it …
Interviewer:	(Smiles) Let's modify the requirement a little bit. How do you solve it when the tree is a normal tree rather than a binary search tree or a binary tree?
Candidate:	(Thinks for dozens of seconds) Do nodes have links to their parents?
Interviewer:	Why do you need links to parent nodes?

The candidate draws a tree, as shown in Figure 9-1.

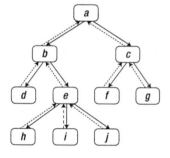

Figure 9-1. *Nodes in a tree have links to parents, which are drawn with dashed arrows.*

Candidate:	(Explaining while pointing to her drawing) If all nodes except the root in a tree have links to their parents, this problem is equivalent to finding the first common node in two intersected lists. A path in the tree can be viewed as a list connected by links to parents, starting from a leaf to the root. For example, if the input two nodes are the nodes *h* and *f*, the node *h* is on the path though $h \to e \to b \to a$, and the node *f* is on the path though $f \to c \to a$. Node *a* is the first common node on these two paths, and it is also the lowest ancestor of the nodes *h* and *f*.
Interviewer:	Where did you see the problem to get the first common node in two lists?
Candidate:	(Smiles with embarrassment) Uh, it was by accident …
Interviewer:	No problem. Let's modify the requirement again. How do you get the lowest ancestor in a normal tree, where every node does not have a link to its parent?

Candidate:	(Disappointed and depressed) OK, give me a few minutes.
Interviewer:	It is only a bit more difficult than the previous two problems, and I believe you can solve it.
Candidate:	(Thinking silently) Let's traverse the tree from the root. When a node is visited, we check whether the two input nodes are in its subtrees. If both nodes are in the subtrees, it moves to the children nodes for the next round. The first node whose subtrees contain two input nodes, but its children nodes do not, is the lowest common ancestor.
Interviewer:	Can you explain your ideas with an example?
Candidate:	(Explaining while drawing Figure 9-2) Let's assume the two given nodes are *d* and *i*. The tree is scanned with the pre-order traversal algorithm. Note that the subtrees of node *a* contain both node *d* and *i*, so we move on to check whether the subtrees of node *b* and *c* contain the given nodes. Since both nodes *d* and *i* are in the subtree of node *b*, we continue to check whether these two nodes are contained in the subtrees of nodes *d* and *e*, which are children of *b*. The subtree rooted at node *d* does not contain node *i*, and the subtree rooted at node *e* does not contain node *d*. Therefore, node *b* is the first node whose subtrees contain two input nodes but its children nodes do not, and it is the lowest ancestor of *d* and *i*.

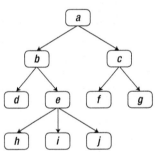

Figure 9-2. *Nodes in a tree do not have links to parents.*

Interviewer:	It seems that your solution visits nodes multiple times. For instance, when you check whether the subtree root at *a* contains node *i*, nodes *h*, *i*, and *j* will be visited. When you check whether the subtree root at *b* contains *i*, nodes *h*, *i*, and *j* will be visited again. Is it possible to visit each node only once?
Candidate:	(Ponders for more than two minutes) Can I use auxiliary space?
Interviewer:	How much space do you want?
Candidate:	I'm going to utilize two lists for two paths from the root node to the two given nodes. The lowest ancestor is equivalent to the last common node on the two paths.
Interviewer:	(Nods) It sounds interesting. Give me more details about your solution.
Candidate:	A path from the root is stored while the tree is traversed. For example, the process to get the path from the root to node *i* can be described as follows. (1) Node *a* is visited, and inserted into the path. Now there is a node *a* in the path. (2) Node *b* is visited and

inserted into the path. The path is $a \rightarrow b$. (3) Node d is visited and inserted into the path. The path is $a \rightarrow b \rightarrow d$ at this time. (4) Since d is a leaf node, we have to return back to node b, and node d is removed from the path. The path becomes $a \rightarrow b$ again. (5) Node e is visited and inserted into the path. The path is $a \rightarrow b \rightarrow e$ now. (6) Node h is visited and inserted into the path, which becomes $a \rightarrow b \rightarrow e \rightarrow h$. (7) Since node h is a leaf, we have to return back to its parent node e. Node h is removed from the path, and the path becomes $a \rightarrow b \rightarrow e$. (8) The target node i is visited and inserted into the path. The path from the root to node i is $a \rightarrow b \rightarrow e \rightarrow i$.

Interviewer: And then?

Candidate: Similarly, the path from the root to node d is $a \rightarrow b \rightarrow d$. The last common nodes on these two paths are node b, and it is also the lowest ancestor of the nodes d and i.

Interviewer: What is the time and space complexity?

Candidate: We have to traverse the tree twice, so it costs $O(n)$ time in a tree with n nodes. Additionally, we utilize two lists to store paths. The length of a path is $O(\log n)$ on average, and it is $O(n)$ for worst cases.

Interviewer: (Nods and smiles) Pretty good. Can you implement your code in C/C++?

Candidate: No problem.

The candidate writes the three functions in Listing 9-6.

Listing 9-6. *C++ Code to Get the Lowest Ancestor of Two Tree Nodes*

```
TreeNode* GetLowestAncestor(TreeNode* pRoot, TreeNode* pNode1, TreeNode* pNode2) {
    if(pRoot == NULL || pNode1 == NULL || pNode2 == NULL)
        return NULL;

    list<TreeNode*> path1;
    GetNodePath(pRoot, pNode1, path1);

    list<TreeNode*> path2;
    GetNodePath(pRoot, pNode2, path2);

    return GetLastCommonNode(path1, path2);
}

bool GetNodePath(TreeNode* pRoot, TreeNode* pNode, list<TreeNode*>& path) {
    if(pRoot == pNode)
        return true;

    path.push_back(pRoot);

    bool found = false;

    vector<TreeNode*>::iterator i = pRoot->m_vChildren.begin();
    while(!found && i < pRoot->m_vChildren.end()) {
        found = GetNodePath(*i, pNode, path);
```

```
        ++i;
    }

    if(!found)
        path.pop_back();

    return found;
}
TreeNode* GetLastCommonNode(const list<TreeNode*>& path1, const list<TreeNode*>& path2) {
    list<TreeNode*>::const_iterator iterator1 = path1.begin();
    list<TreeNode*>::const_iterator iterator2 = path2.begin();

    TreeNode* pLast = NULL;

    while(iterator1 != path1.end() && iterator2 != path2.end()) {
        if(*iterator1 == *iterator2)
            pLast = *iterator1;

        iterator1++;
        iterator2++;
    }

    return pLast;
}
```

Candidate:	The function GetNodePath gets a path from the root node pRoot to the node pNode. The function GetLastCommonNode gets the last common node of two paths path1 and path2. The function GetLowestAncestor calls the function GetNodePath twice in order to get the paths from the root node to the two given nodes respectively, and then calls the function GetLastCommonNode to get the lowest ancestor.
Interviewer:	That is good. I do not have any more questions. Do you have any questions for me?
Candidate:	Would you please introduce me to your project briefly?
Interviewer:	We are developing a UI framework named Winforms on .NET, with which others can develop a UI for desktop applications. Our Winforms framework provides traditional windows controls such as the ListBox and TreeView, as well as new controls such as the TableLayoutPanel for flexible layout.
Interviewer:	Any more questions?
Candidate:	(Thinks for a while) No more.
Interviewer:	OK. That is the end of this interview. Thank you.

The Interviewer's Comments

There are a series of problems about the lowest ancestor of two nodes in a tree and the solutions are quite different with various requirements. I did not provide enough detail about the tree intentionally. I expected the candidate to ask for more clarification.

The candidate performed well during the interview. She asked me whether the tree was a binary search tree and then whether there were links to parents in each node. These questions showed her proactive attitude and strong communication skills.

Once I specified my requirements, she found solutions in a very short period of time. When I told her there was a link to the parent node in each node, she converted the problem to find the first common node in two lists. When I removed the link to the parent, she converted the problem to find the last common node in two paths. She demonstrated her deep understanding of data structures as well as strong competence in problem solving.

Additionally, her code was clean and complete, which indicated that she was a professional programmer.

She showed her interests in joining our team in the Q & A phase. Actually, I am looking forward to working with her. In general, my recommendation is to hire her because of her competence in problem solving, programming, and communication.

Source Code:

`107_LowestAncestorInTrees.cpp`

Test Cases:

- Normal Test Cases (Two nodes in a trees have/do not have common ancestor)
- Robustness Test Cases (The pointer to the root node and/or pointers to two nodes are NULL; special trees like linked lists)

Index

A

Anagrams, 212
Arrays.sort in O($n$log$n$) time, 202

B

Backtracking
    definition, 90
    robot move
        C++ code, 93–4
        source code, 94
        test cases, 94
    string path in matrix
        C++ code, 91–2
        source code, 92
        test cases, 92
Bidirectional communication, 220
Big numbers as strings
    function to add two arbitrary positive
            integers, 120–1, 123
    simulating increment on a string,
            118–9
    simulating permutation, 120
    source code, 120
    test cases, 120
    underestimating complexity, 117
Binary search algorithm
    on a diagonal, 38–40
    Java code, 37
    partially sorted matrix, 40–42
    source code, 38
    test cases, 38
Binary search trees and double-linked lists
    divide and conquer, 175–6
    node rotations, 177–8
Binary trees
    binary search trees and double-linked
            lists
        divide and conquer, 175–6
        node rotations, 177–8
    mirror of, 143–146
    paths, 165–168
    print
        line printing, 161–2
        printing process, 160
        queue class, 160–1
        three levels sample, 159–60
        tree traversal algorithms, 159
        zigzag printing, 162–165
    traversal sequences
        deserialization, 171–2
        disadvantages, 171
        in-order traversal sequence, 168–9
        post-order traversal sequence, 173–4
        pre-order traversal sequence, 168–9
        sample code, 169
        serialization, 171–2
Binary tree traversals
    balanced binary trees, 225–7
    depth of a binary tree, 224–5
    k^{th} node in a binary search, 223–4

Bit operations
  bitwise AND, OR, and XOR, 101
  find missing two numbers
    based on arithmetic calculation,
        107–8
    based on bit operations, 108
    source code, 108
    test cases, 108
  modify a number to another, 105
  number of 1s in binary
    checking rightmost bit with endless
        loop, 102
    left-shift operation on 1, 102–3
    minus one and then bitwise AND,
        103–4
    source code, 104
    test cases, 104
  numbers occurring only once
    Java code, 106
    source code, 107
    test cases, 107
Breadth-first traversal algorithm, 63

C

C, 13
  allocateMemory, 14–5
  macros, 15–6
  palindrome numbers, 16–7
  static variable, 13
C#, 22
  definition, 22
  singleton, 23, 25–27
  static constructor, 22
C++, 17
  assignment operator, 19–21
  classimplementation/member
        function, 19
  execution of, 18–9
  keyword sizeof, 18
Clone complex lists
  boundary cases, 152
  first step cloning, 150
  five nodes, 149

  functional cases, 152
  m_pNext link, 149
  m_pSibling link, 149
  robustness cases, 152
  second step cloning, 150–1
  third step cloning, 151–2
combination(String str) method, 183
Communications skills, 219
ConstructCore function, 170
curSum, 198

D

Data structures
  arrays
    C code, 33
    definition, 33
    hash table, 33
    Java code to get duplicated number,
        34–6
    sorted matrix search (see Binary
        search algorithm)
  linked lists (see Linked lists)
  stack and queue
    definition, 70
    queue with two stacks, 70–2
    stack with two queues, 72–4
  string (see Strings)
  trees (see Trees)
Divergent thinking skills
  array construction, 261–2
  1+2+…+n calculation
    based on constructors, 252–3
    based on function pointers, 254
    based on templates, 254–5
    based on virtual functions, 253–4
  final/sealed classes in C++, 259–60
  +, -, *, and / implementation
    code to add, 255–6
    code to divide, 257–9
    code to multiply, 256–7
    code to subtract, 256
Divide and conquer approach

binary search trees (*see* Binary search trees and double-linked lists)
permutation and combination
bit operations, 183–5
eight queens puzzle, 180–2
n arrays, 182
string, 179–80
string combinations, 183
sorted double-linked list, 168
traversal sequences and binary trees (*see* Binary trees, traversal sequences)
Double-linked lists, 168, 175
divide and conquer, 175–6
node rotations, 177–8
Dynamic programming, 198
Dynamic programming and greedy algorithms
definition, 95
edit distance, 95–7
minimal number of coins for change, 98–9
minimal times of presses on keyboards, 99–100

E

Equality of decimals, 116

F

Fibonacci sequence
efficient O(log*n*) time solution, 78–9
iterative solution with O(*n*) time complexity, 77
recursive and inefficient solution, 76–7
source code, 79
test cases, 80
FirstAppearingOnce, 209

H

HashMap, 212
Hash table
anagrams, 212
delete characters contained in another string, 210
delete duplicated characters in string, 211
index of character in stream, 208
occurrence numbers in string, 207
High-quality code
clearness, 111–2
completeness
big numbers as strings (*see* Big numbers as strings)
delete nodes from a list, 123–7
partition numbers in arrays (*see* Partition numbers in arrays)
power of integers (*see* Power of integer codes)
strategies to handle errors, 113–4
test cases, 112–3
robustness
k^{th} node from end, 132–5
reverse a list, 135–8
substructures in trees, 138–41

I

Increment method, 184
In-order traversal algorithm, 63
Interview cases
integer value from a string
code for member initialization order, 263
code to convert a string to an integer, 264–6
interviewer's comments, 267, 269
source code, 269
test cases, 269
lowest common parent node in a tree

code to get the lowest ancestor, 272–3
interviewer's comments, 273
source code, 274
test cases, 274
tree diagram, 270
tree with no links to parents, 271
Interview process, 1
behavior, 4
avoid complaints, 6
project experience, 4–5
technical skills, 5
on-site interview, 3
phone-interview, 1–3
Q/A time, 11
technical, 7
high quality code, 8–9
problem solving, 10
programming knowledge, 7
soft skills, 11
time and space efficiency, 10–1
Interviews skills
communications skills, 219
divergent thinking skills (*see* Divergent thinking skills)
knowledge migration skills (*see* Knowledge migration skills)
learning skills, 220
mathematical modeling skills (*see* Mathematical modeling skills)

J

Java, 27
data containers, 29–30
final variables, 28–9
keyword final, 28
thread scheduler, 30, 32
Josephus problem, 243

K

Knowledge migration skills

binary tree traversals (*see* Binary tree traversals)
maximums in queue, 239–41
maximums in sliding window, 236–9
reversing words and rotating strings
reversing a segment, 233–5
string left rotation, 235–6
sorted array
boundary test cases, 223
code to count k, 222
code to get first k, 221
code to get last k, 222
functional test cases, 223
source code, 223
sum in sequences
finding continuous sequences with sum s, 231–3
finding number pairs, sum equals s, 227–9
getting a pair with a sum excluding a number, 229–30
getting a subset with sum 0, 230–1

L

Learning skills, 220
Linked lists
loop in list, 59–62
memory allocation, 53
printing lists from tail to head, 54–5
sort lists, 56–9

M

Master theory, 250
Mathematical modeling skills
last number in a circle
deleted numbers pattern, 244–6
looped list circle simulation, 243–4
minimum number of moves to sort cards
binary search costing O($n$log$n$) time, 247–9

dynamic programming costing $O(n^2)$
time, 246–7
most profit from stock
divide and conquer based, 249–50
storing minimum mumbers while
scanning, 251
probabilities of dice points, 241–3
max[f(i)], 198
maxQueue, 194
Median in a stream
binary search algorithm, 188
C++ code, 190
numbers sorting, 188–9
time efficiency comparisons, 189
Minimum *k* numbers
comparison between two solutions, 194
$O(n)$ time efficiency, 193
$O(n\log k)$ time efficiency, 191

N

Nonverbal communication, 219
NumericComparator, 202

O

occurrence[i], 209
Optimization
space-time trade-off
first intersection node in two lists,
216–8
hash tables for characters, 207–13
reversed pairs in array, 213–6
ugly numbers, 204–6
time efficiency
data structures and algorithms, 187
Digit 1 occurrence, 198–201
greatest sum of sub-arrays, 196–8
median in stream, 188–91
minimum *k* numbers, 191–4
sorted arrays intersection, 194–6
StringBuilder.Append, 187
$O(m+n)$ time, 195

$O(n\log m)$ time, 195
$O(n)$ time efficiency, 193
$O(n\log k)$ time efficiency, 191

P

Partition numbers in arrays
move numbers for $O(k)$ times, 131–2
move numbers for $O(n)$ times, 130
scalable solution, 128, 130
workable but not scalable solution,
127–8
Performance optimization. *See*
Optimization
pLastNodeInList, 176
pop_heap, 190
Post-order traversal algorithm, 63
Power of integer codes
complete and efficient solution, 116–7
complete but inefficient solution, 115–6
incomplete solutions, 114–5
source code, 117
test cases, 117
Pre-order traversal algorithm, 63, 144–5
Print binary trees
line printing, 161–2
printing process, 160
queue class, 160–1
three levels sample, 159–60
tree traversal algorithms, 159
zigzag printing, 162–5
Print Matrix, spiral order
java code, 147
printRing method, 147
ring printing code, 148–9
set of rings, 147
Problem solutions
divide and conquer approach (*see*
Divide and conquer approach)
examples
binary tree paths, 165–8
print binary trees (*see* Print binary
trees)

push and pop sequence of stacks, 157–9

stack with min function (*see* Stack with min function)

figures

clone complex lists (*see* Clone complex lists)

mirror of binary trees, 143–6

print matrix, spiral order (*see* Print matrix, spiral order)

Programming languages

C, 13

allocateMemory, 14–5

macros, 15–6

palindrome numbers, 16–7

static variable, 13

C#, 22

definition, 22

singleton, 23–7

static constructor, 22

C++, 17

assignment operator, 19–21

classimplementation/member function, 19

execution of, 18–9

keyword sizeof, 18

Java, 27

data containers, 29–30

final variables, 28–9

keyword final, 28

thread scheduler, 30, 32

push_heap, 190

■ R

ReadStream function, 172

Recursion and iteration

disadvantages, 76

Fibonacci sequence

efficient O(log*n*) time solution, 78–9

iterative solution with O(*n*) time complexity, 77

recursive and inefficient solution, 76–7

source code, 79

test cases, 80

iterative C code, 75

recursive C code, 75

Reversed pair in array

Java code to count, 215–6

merge sub-arrays, 214

process to get the number of, 214

■ S

Search and sort algorithms

binary search

code for turning number in array, 87

Java code to get minimum element, 85–6

minimal element search, 84

source code, 86

test cases, 86

two rotations of sorted array, 85

Java code

of count sort, 83

to partition an array, 81–2

for quicksort, 82

majorities in arrays

definition of majority, 89

partition method, 88–9

source code, 90

test cases, 90

Stack and queue

definition, 70

queue with two stacks, 70–2

stack with two queues, 72–4

Stack with min function

with auxiliary stack, 153–5

without auxiliary stack, 155–6

Strings

in C#, 43–4

in C/C++, 42

in Java, 44–5

replacing blanks

from left to right in O(n^2) time, 45–6

merging sorted arrays, 48–9

from right to left in O(*n*) time, 46, 48

source code, 48
test cases, 48
string matching
    code to scan digits, 52
    code to verify an exponential
        notation, 53
    code to verify numeric strings, 52
    simple regular expression matching,
        50–1
Symmetrical trees, 145–6

T

toBePrinted variable, 162
Trees
    binary search tree verification
        increasing in-order traversal
            sequence, 67–8
        value range of each node, 66–7
        code to get the largest size of subtrees,
            68–70
        next nodes in binary trees, 64–6
        sample binary tree, 63–4
        traversal algorithms, 63

U

Ugly number
    check, 204
    store found numbers into array, 205

V

Verbal communication, 219

CPSIA information can be obtained at www.ICGtesting.com
Printed in the USA
LVOW03s1824141114

413762LV00008B/126/P